'This book is an excellent contemporary account of self-injury and approaches to supporting people who self-injure. The book will be an invaluable resource for anyone working in the field.'

Hilary Lindsay, Director, Self-injury Support, Bristol

'This is an immensely useful text that carefully combines sociological insights with practical advice on responding well to self-injury. The book provides a broad basis through which to develop a deeper understanding of the meanings self-injury has for diverse social groups, before going on to chart the similarly diverse ways that people who hurt themselves can be supported – or support themselves. Grounded in principles of social justice, this is a thoroughly refreshing guide that will be of use to anyone who encounters self-injury in their personal or professional lives.'

Dr Amy Chandler, Chancellor's Fellow in Health, University of Edinburgh.

SAFE WITH SELF-INJURY

A PRACTICAL GUIDE TO UNDERSTANDING, RESPONDING AND HARM-REDUCTION

Kay Inckle

First published 2017

PCCS Books Ltd
Wyastone Business Park
Wyastone Leys
Monmouth
NP25 3SR
contact@pccs-books.co.uk
www.pccs-books.co.uk

Safe with Self-Injury:
a practical guide to understanding, responding and harm-reduction

British Library Cataloguing in Publication data: a catalogue record for this book is
available from the British Library.

ISBN 978 1 910919 16 3

Cover design by Phipps Design
Cover illustration by Mayisha Ahsan – www.maymayworld.com
Typeset in-house by PCCS Books using Minion Pro and Myriad Pro
Printed by Ashford Colour Press, Gosport, UK

CONTENTS

ACKNOWLEDGEMENTS

First and foremost, my heartfelt thanks to all the people who participated in my research and shared their experiences with me. I am deeply grateful for your honesty and your generosity in trusting me with your stories. I hope that this book does justice to all that I learned from you.

Thanks also to the Irish Research Council for the Humanities and Social Science for the two-year post-doctoral fellowship that enabled me to conduct the primary research upon which this book is largely based.

I am also deeply grateful to a number of organisations who have allowed me to reference their work in a variety of ways. Thank you to 42nd Street (Manchester) and Self-injury Support (Bristol) for allowing me to reprint their confidentiality and complaints policies. Many thanks to Depaul for allowing me to reprint the self-injury policy from Tus Nua (Dublin). Thank you also to Conor McCafferty and Noella McConnellogue for enabling me to write a case study of Zest (Derry/Londonderry) and for unfailing warmth and hospitality.

Special thanks are also due to the exemplary and committed learners who attended the course 'Understanding and Responding to Self-Injury: a harm-reduction approach', which ran in Trinity College Dublin from 2009–2012. Your openness, engagement and willingness to be challenged was an inspiration to me, and I will not forget the creativity and the laughter that we shared. I hope this book will be as valuable a resource to you as your participation and engagement were to me.

I am especially grateful to Mayisha Ahsan for the beautiful artwork that I am honoured to use on the cover of this book.

I would also like to give special thanks to Professor Robbie Gilligan and Dr Evelyn Mahon of the School of Social Work and Social Policy, Trinity College Dublin, for the years during which they supported and encouraged my work.

Sincere thanks also to Heather Allen, Catherine Jackson and everyone at PCCS Books for your hard work in seeing this book to fruition.

Finally, my personal thanks to Marín ni Bhríain for the years behind the scenes, and to my dear friends Catherine Lamont, Brid O'Farrell and Orlaith Tunney for your support and confidence in me. Last, but most certainly not least, love and gratitude as always to Princess, my own anam ċara.

Introduction

The last two decades have seen a significant rise in awareness about self-injury as a phenomenon, but there remain many areas of uncertainty. These include questions about the underlying reasons for self-injury, whether or not some groups of people (such as young women) are more likely to hurt themselves, and how best to respond when someone does self-injure. Many myths, stereotypes and stigma about self-injury also remain in common circulation, causing further confusion and impeding helpful responses.

This book provides a comprehensive and in-depth understanding of self-injury, the experiences that may give rise to it, and how to respond helpfully. Its ethos is holistic, rights-based and person-centred, and it is informed by principles of social justice. These principles and values are crucial for challenging stigma and providing effective responses that go beyond simple notions of individual pathology. They highlight that all human experiences, but particularly mental and emotional distress, emerge from external factors as much as internal issues, and that these external factors require significant attention and redress. In practice, this approach combines an embodied understanding of human experience, the therapeutic elements of person-centredness, and the politics and activism of the social model.

This ethos has been one of the underpinning motivations for this book. I have a multi-dimensional perspective on self-injury, as a result of a range of experiences over many years. For example, I have worked with young people in local authority care, adult psychiatric service-users and recipients of social care, many of whom experienced self-injury. I have also conducted academic research with people who hurt themselves, produced academic papers and learning modules and devised training and resources for health and social practitioners. Some of my knowledge about self-injury also emerges from my personal life and relationships, and I have been politically active around both mental health and disability for a number of years. From all of these vantage points, it seemed

1

to me that there was no single, rigorous but accessible text about self-injury that explored the complexities of the experience while remaining practical, holistic and rights-based – and this is what I have attempted to produce.

This book, then, is shaped by years of knowledge that I have gained in a range of contexts, in addition to academic research.[1] The primary research in this book consists of interview-based narratives from individuals who hurt themselves and service-providers from across the UK and Ireland. I used an unstructured and person-centred approach to conducting the research interviews. I wanted people to be able to discuss their experiences on their own terms rather than be shaped by my agenda. I also met and discussed my research with participants before formally interviewing them, as I felt that it was important that they could meet me, ask questions and set boundaries before participating. I audio-recorded each interview and then transcribed it into a written document, anonymising it as I did so. I offered copies of their transcript to each participant, and allowed them time to review and reflect on the content before I made use of it. Participants also chose the name by which they would like to be known. For most this was a pseudonym, but often one that had some personal relevance or meaning to them; others elected to use their real name. All participants were over 18 years of age at the time of the interviews, with ages ranging up to the mid-40s.

The chapter topics and focus of this book reflect the key themes that emerged as I analysed the data and contextualised it within the wider research, policy and practice framework. The participants' voices remain central throughout this book, as their experiences and insights are crucial to an understanding of self-injury and a response to it that is grounded in lived experience.

The service-providers I interviewed largely consisted of those working in the voluntary and community sectors. Practitioners such as psychiatric nurses were unable to formally participate in the research without extensive, and potentially restrictive, oversight from their health authority. However, I did meet and discuss a range of issues with some specialist psychiatric nurses and, while I cannot quote from them directly, these conversations were certainly useful in reinforcing what other participants were able to disclose on the record.[2] I purposively selected to interview service-providers who

---

1. I do not explicitly draw on any experiences from my professional work in this book as I feel to do so would be a violation of the trust, confidentiality and respect that service-users are entitled to expect.

2. The discussions and feedback during training workshops and courses I have conducted over the past number of years also continually reiterate and reinforce the core themes and issues in this book.

had a specialist interest in self-injury as I wanted to explore some of the most contemporary developments in the field, rather than simply report a cross-section of perspectives.

This book also draws on extensive secondary research in the form of a literature search. This involved a number of international academic databases, journal search engines and policy searches, which I conducted over a number of years. It is not possible to provide an overview of all of the existing self-injury literature, as the material reflects a diverse range of disciplines, perspectives and research methods. Here, rather than using up extensive wordage categorising and critiquing the full range of the available material, I have focused on the most relevant and substantive for the purposes of this book.

In public and policy discourse self-injury is usually referred to as self-harm. Throughout this book I use the terms 'self-injury' and 'people who hurt themselves' for technical accuracy and ethical reasons, which are explored in detail in Chapter 1. I also frequently refer to 'helpers', by which I mean someone who is acting in a supportive role to the person who hurts themself. This role might be in a professional capacity (such as a youth worker, therapist, social worker or nurse), or it might be a lay person who wishes to help a friend, partner, family member or colleague. Clearly, there will be some differences in terms of the relationship, role and boundaries that come with these different support capacities, but the principles for responding helpfully remain the same.

This book is intended to be a resource for people who hurt themselves and those who work or share their lives with them. The in-depth analysis of self-injury and its functions, meaning and purpose in someone's life can provide an important insight for a helper who is trying to make sense of why the person they care for is hurting themself. For people who self-injure, it is intended to be a validating account of self-injury that perhaps gives voice to something they have struggled to articulate and that empowers them to challenge misperceptions and bad practice. The chapters on embodied and social interventions and harm-reduction are equally intended as resources for people who hurt themselves and their helpers. This book is also relevant for students undertaking a variety of practice-based studies, including social work, nursing, health and social care, counselling and psychology. It is also useful as an applied text for students in sociology, social policy and social science who are interested in critical approaches to health, illness and health care.

The first chapter sets out the basis for a comprehensive understanding of self-injury. It explores the rates and types of self-injury and its relationship with self-harm and suicide and challenges myths about the 'typical self-injurer'.

Chapter 2 uses the concept of embodiment to explore the complex and often contradictory ways in which self-injury functions as a means of coping with and expressing traumatic feelings and experiences. It draws on cross-cultural and historical evidence to highlight that, rather than being an incomprehensible anomaly, self-injury is deeply connected to what it is to be human. Chapter 3 sets out some of the experiences that may underlie self-injury. It explores the ways in which various forms of invalidation and violation, such as neglect, abuse and institutionalisation, give rise to the intense and ongoing distress that self-injury alleviates. In Chapter 4, the relationship between social and contextual factors and self-injury is highlighted, using the concept of minority stress. Here, the mental health impacts of marginalised social identities and prejudice, discrimination and victimisation are shown to be directly related to self-injury. This chapter underscores why a social model perspective and a social justice ethos is crucial to understanding and responding helpfully to self-injury.

Chapter 5 highlights some of the embodied and social interventions that have been beneficial to people who hurt themselves. These interventions are significant for a number of reasons, including their direct reflection of some of the functions of self-injury, their holistic ethos and user-led origins, and their accessibility. Chapter 6 focuses on another user-led intervention, namely harm-reduction. Once controversial among statutory services, harm-reduction is increasingly recognised as a much more effective and meaningful response to self-injury than attempting to stop it.[3] This chapter outlines the history, ethos and rationale of a harm-reduction approach to self-injury, as well as a step-by-step guide to a harm-reduction response. Chapter 7 takes a similar format, but this time in relation to writing an effective self-injury policy. It includes a policy template that can be applied across a range of services and organisations. The focus on policy writing and implementation is intended not only to be useful to those who work within services, but also to those who use services. An understanding of how policy is developed and implemented can provide a significant insight and resource for challenging poor practice and misunderstandings about self-injury.

Each chapter concludes with a section on 'learning into practice', which is devoted to translating the learning from each topic into practical strategies for responding helpfully. All of these sections are grounded in principles

3. Since 2004, the guidelines of the National Institute for Health and Care Excellence (NICE) have recommended the use of harm-reduction techniques in both short-term (NICE, 2004) and long-term (NICE, 2011) interventions with people who hurt themselves.

that create a guiding ethos, rather than a fixed model or protocol. Principles allow for flexible and person-centred responses, whereas fixed models can be restrictive and oppressive. Each 'learning into practice' section also highlights a key defining feature of self-injury drawn from the content of that chapter. These definitions are intended to be cumulative and to build up into a comprehensive overall definition that can be used as a policy, practice or theoretical resource. The final sections of each chapter also include two brief individual exercises that will help to consolidate and apply the principles and practices.

The epilogue, 'Going the Distance', contextualises the key issues, principles and practices explored throughout the book with a brief case study of Zest, the Derry/Londonderry self-injury and suicide service. Zest, which was founded in 1996, is a community-based service that embodies some of the most pioneering and effective responses to self-injury and has been integrated into the Northern Irish statutory services referral pathway. Finally, there is an appendix of learning exercises at the end of the book, which can be used by groups or individuals to explore some of the key themes and issues in more dynamic or discussion-focused ways.

1

Self-injury essentials: understanding before intervention

This chapter lays the foundation for the book. It sets out the framework for a thorough understanding and meaningful response to self-injury. The chapter:

- distinguishes self-injury from suicide and highlights the breadth of self-injury
- critically explores the evidence for rates of self-injury across the population and analyses the range and types of self-injury
- suggests appropriate terminology to describe the experience of self-injury, especially in the wider context of self-harm
- explores the relationship between gender, age and self-injury.

This multifaceted approach builds a working definition that dismantles the myths, stereotypes and misinformation about self-injury and provides a clear and accurate understanding on which good practice can be established. In contrast, responses that are based on misinformation, fear or prejudice do more harm than good.

Self-injury and suicide

The term self-injury describes actions where the immediate and direct intention and purpose is to cause pain and/or damage to the body. Babiker and Arnold describe self-injury as 'inflicting pain and/or injury to one's own body, but without suicidal intent' (1997: 3). The distinction between suicide and self-injury is crucial. Self-injury is a coping mechanism that is 'the very *reverse* of self-destructiveness. They [people who self-injure] are seeking to preserve themselves. Rather than wishing to destroy themselves, their self-injury helps them to stay "together", to struggle to survive' (1997: 7). Self-injury is a coping mechanism that provides people with a degree of control, relief and self-comforting that is absent in their life situation. Spandler and Warner describe self-injury as 'the expression of, and temporary relief from, overwhelming, unbearable and often conflicting emotions, thoughts or memories, [which] through a self-injurious act they can control and regulate' (2007: ix).

People who hurt themselves also emphasise this distinction between self-injury and suicide. For example, Joseph said:

> To me it's *very obvious,* that just because you're self-harming does not
> mean that you want to commit suicide. You *don't* want to do yourself deep,
> irreversible damage... It's not about suicide. I *never ever, ever* wanted to
> commit suicide.

This is replicated by service-providers who stated that: 'People say they self-injure in order to be able to manage and to carry on,' and that: '[Clients are] very clear about what self-harm meant: it was *not* a suicide attempt, it was in fact a *survival* attempt.'

This clear distinction between self-injury and suicide is also evidenced in research from as far back as 1936, when Karl Menninger published *Man Against Himself.* However, at statutory and policy level, self-injury and suicide are often conflated and self-injury is assumed to be an attempt at suicide, or a first step towards it. This is particularly common when a person has taken an overdose of medication or has cut vulnerable parts of their body, or when terminology such as 'deliberate self-harm' or 'para-suicide' is used (eg. National Suicide Research Foundation, 2010). These two terms correctly refer to repeated failed suicide attempts, but are also often used to describe self-injury, or to conflate self-injury and attempted suicide. Joseph's experience of undergoing a psychological assessment after being hospitalised following an overdose highlights the negative consequences of this approach: it not only added to his distress but also resulted in a missed opportunity to provide support and decreased the likelihood of him seeking help in the future. Joseph said:

> I was embarrassed – because when you swallow tablets they think that
> you're trying to commit suicide, and I *wasn't.* I was doing the swallowing
> of tablets for the same reason that I was cutting myself... I always

associated it in the same way, but to *them* you were trying to commit
suicide. And I wasn't. And I didn't need it defined or looked upon like that,
so I just wanted to get out of there as quickly as possible.

Suicide and self-injury are clearly distinct in terms of intention: self-injury is an
attempt to continue and cope with life by whatever means possible, even if that
is destructive to the body; suicide is about no longer wanting life to continue.
'Self-injury *continues* the discourse of a person's life, whereas a suicide attempt
separates the person from that discourse, removing the individual from their
awareness or from being' (Babiker & Arnold, 1997: 2). Furthermore, people
commonly describe self-injury as the means by which they avert suicidal
thoughts and feelings and preserve their life (Arnold, 1995; Gallup, 2002;
Pembroke, 2007a). As Elaine put it: 'Had I *not* done that [ie. self-injured], I
might not be sat here today.' However, while the underlying intentions between
self-injury and suicide are entirely different, the actual injuries may be very
similar. For example, tying a ligature around the neck, cutting the body where
there are arteries and veins, and taking overdoses of medication or swallowing
harmful substances may all be used as a means of both self-injury and suicide.
Furthermore, the perceived severity of the wound or injury does not indicate
the intention behind it: some people swallow very small amounts of medication
with the intention to die as a result, while others may take large quantities of
toxic substances (which may actually put their life at risk) without death ever
being the intended outcome. Likewise, a severed artery may be seen as a suicide
attempt and apparently more minor cuts regarded as non-suicidal, when the
reverse may be true of their intention. Some people also accidentally end their
life through self-injury, and this is why harm-reduction (Chapter 6) is crucial.
Therefore, while self-injury and suicide have entirely different motivations and
functions, these cannot be simply read off from the type or severity of the injury;
it is the individual's intention behind the act that clarifies this distinction.

To complicate things further, while in most cases individuals are clear
about the purpose of their actions – ie. to continue or to end their life – they
may also disregard their consequences: 'The individual may have complex
and ambivalent, and also confused views of their exact intent' (Babiker &
Arnold, 1997: 6). Mark described periods of 'ambivalence towards suicide, like
I wouldn't care if I was going to live or die, even though I was not *wanting* to
die, but it would have got to that sort of grey area, "Well I don't care".' Moreover,
some people who have a history of self-injury also attempt suicide. 'Individuals
who frequently self-injure may also at some other times harm themselves with

suicidal intent, often using different means' (Babiker & Arnold, 1997: 6). This was true for Amanda: 'I was hospitalised three times and the self-harm had turned to suicide sort of stuff. It was no longer about what I wanted to do to myself, it was about wanting to kill myself.' However, there are two distinctive features to recognise here. The first is that, if someone attempts to die by suicide, they will use a different method of causing harm to themselves than when they self-injure, which reflects the different purpose and intentions of the acts. This is evident in Amanda's distinction between what she 'wanted to do to' herself and 'wanting to kill' herself. Furthermore, as we shall see in Chapter 6 on harm-reduction, individuals who self-injure (even those who are sometimes ambivalent about the potential lethality of their injuries) make efforts to avoid injuries that would put their life at risk. Joseph described how 'people who didn't know what I was doing thought I was trying to commit suicide, but there was *no* way I was going to cut my neck, there was *no* way I was going to cut my wrist'. Likewise, Mark said: 'I cut myself so I bled at times, but I knew there was never any *danger*, I was never going to need medical treatment.'

The next important feature of the distinction between self-injury and suicide is that, while statistics often indicate that people who self-injure may be more vulnerable to suicide (eg. National Suicide Research Foundation, 2010), this is not the same as the self-injury being an attempt at or a step towards suicide in itself. Self-injury is a response to distress and, as such, is already an indication of the level of difficulty an individual is experiencing, in the quite straightforward way that, if hurting one's own body feels *better*, then the situation must be painful indeed. Following on from that, it is equally straightforward that, if the cause of the distress is increasing, or if an individual's situation is deteriorating, or, indeed, if their coping mechanism is removed from them, they may well lose the motivation to cope and become suicidal. People who experience all kinds of distress and related 'harmful' coping mechanisms, including self-injury, eating disorders and addictions, are all more vulnerable to suicide (Conner et al, 2014; Pompili et al, 2004), but this does not make the use of food, drugs and alcohol of itself suicidal, even though all of these acts may also have potentially lethal consequences.

Overall then, while self-injury, suicide and para-suicide are often defined as equivalents or positions along a continuum, they are entirely different in their motivations and functions. Self-injury is the mechanism by which people cope with their circumstances and continue with their life by whatever means possible; suicide is an attempt to escape those circumstances through death. However, the type and severity of the injury does not indicate the underlying intention; only the person who hurts themself knows the intention behind it. Furthermore, people may be ambivalent about or disregard the outcomes of their action, but again this indicates the depth of their difficulty and distress, not a direct correlation with suicide.

Self-injury: types and numbers

Self-injury is often defined as self-cutting and/or taking overdoses of medication, and these are frequently believed to be the most common forms (Babiker & Arnold, 1997; Gallup, 2002; Warm, Murray & Fox, 2003). However, people hurt themselves in a huge range of ways, including burning and scalding the body (which may be done using heat, flame or chemicals); hitting or banging parts of the body; scratching, picking, biting and scraping at the body; inserting sharp objects under the skin or into body orifices; interfering with wounds; tying ligatures; pulling out hair (the medical name for this is trichotillomania – it is the only form of self-injury that has its own diagnosis); scrubbing away the surface of the skin (sometimes using chemicals or household cleaning fluids), and swallowing sharp objects or harmful substances – which is called overdosing when these substances are medications or drugs (Inckle, 2010a).

It is very difficult to get an accurate picture of rates of self-injury across any population, and research that attempts to measure self-injury is rarely reliable. Statistics are influenced by a number of factors, including the definition of self-injury used, the methods by which the information is gathered and the context from which the information is drawn – such as A&E departments (eg. National Suicide Research Foundation, 2010), university campuses (eg. Gollust, Eisenberg & Golberstein, 2008) or prisons (eg. Lord, 2008). These factors mean the data are variable and incomplete. For example, rates of self-injury are frequently calculated using data from A&E admissions (eg. National Suicide Research Foundation, 2008; 2010). However, it is widely recognised that most self-injury does not come to the attention of emergency medical services (Chandler, Myers & Platt, 2011; Gratz, Conrad & Roemer, 2002; Long & Jenkins, 2010). Thus, in Ireland in 2009 there were 12,000 admissions for self-injury to A&E departments (National Suicide Research Foundation, 2010), but these are estimated to represent a fifth (or less) of the overall incidence (National Suicide Research Foundation, 2008). The figures from A&E therefore show only a tiny proportion of actual incidents of self-injury and are not representative of the overall picture.

The Irish statistics also illustrate further problems with trying to calculate rates of self-injury. First, they do not distinguish between injuries that were made with suicidal intent and those that were not, as all self-caused injuries are recorded in a generic category of 'deliberate self-harm' (National Suicide Research Foundation, 2008; 2010). Second, only five types of injuries are included in the data: alcohol and drug/medication overdoses, attempted drowning, hanging, gunshot wounds and lacerations (ie. self-cutting) (National Suicide Research Foundation, 2010: v). Injuries that are less obviously self-caused (and more common), such as head-banging, wound interference, fractured or broken bones, burns and grazes, are entirely absent from these figures. Statistics for self-injury are therefore always affected by the definition of self-injury and the means by which the research is carried out. Thus, research that uses only five categories of injuries (ie. those that are both indisputably self caused and potentially lethal) reports much lower rates of self-injury and in different population groups than research that uses broader definitions and/or includes self-reported self-injury. For example, rates of self-injury among teenagers in Ireland range from nine per cent when using the deliberate self-harm definition (Morey et al, 2008), to 20 per cent when using the broader definition (UNICEF Ireland, 2011). Similarly, in the UK, rates vary from 6.7 per cent (Mental Health Foundation, 2006) to 47.4 per cent (Williams & Hasking, 2010) of young people, depending on the definition and measures used. In the US, figures range from 13 per cent (Moyer, 2008) to 16 per cent (Gollust, Eisenberg & Golberstein, 2008) of 'youth', 38 per cent of college-age young people, and 22 per cent of adults overall (Gollust, Eisenberg & Golberstein, 2008).

Finally, the types of self-injury that appear in the statistics are often presumed to be the most common, and are also therefore the ones that receive most attention – positive or negative. In Ireland, these are overdosing and cutting. However, these injuries only appear to be the most common because they are likely to require emergency medical attention and because their self-created nature is hardest to conceal. Other injuries such as scratches, infected wounds, burns, concussion, bruises and fractured or broken bones are either less likely to receive emergency medical attention or are more easily explained away as accidental. Self-report surveys that use the more comprehensive definition of self-injury suggest that the less visible forms are actually the most common (and least recognised). These include head-banging, wound interference and self-hitting, with people usually adopting more than one method (DiStefano, 2008; Gollust, Eisenberg & Golberstein, 2008; Heslop & Macaulay, 2009). Indeed, one piece of research reported rates of wound interference and banging the head or body at over 35 per cent, with self-cutting as low as 11 per cent (Gollust, Eisenberg & Golberstein, 2008). Similarly, in Japan, while nine per cent of female and eight per cent of male high school students reported cutting themselves, 12 per cent of the girls and 28 per cent of the boys reported self-hitting (DiStefano, 2008). Therefore, what is visible and what is known (or presumed) about self-injury may bear little relationship to its actual incidence and prevalence. What is clear, however, is that self-injury is very common, often secret and frequently misunderstood.

Terminology

Along with the diversity of measurements of self-injury, there is also a wide range of terms used to describe it. These include self-harm, deliberate self-harm, self-mutilation, self-inflicted violence, self-destructive behaviour, self-wounding, para-suicide and non-suicidal self-injury. However, these terms have a variety of meanings and can be problematic in a number of ways. Terms such as deliberate self-harm, self-mutilation and self-inflicted violence carry value judgments that often have a negative impact on people who self-injure. For example, the use of 'deliberate' in deliberate self-harm is problematic not only as a generic term for attempted suicide and self-injury (above) but also because the prefix 'deliberate' carries a blaming or pejorative connotation. To do something *deliberately* implies having done something wrong and/or bad with deviant or malicious intent – and this pathologisation has been central to medical discourse around self-injury (Cresswell & Karimova, 2010). Similarly, the word 'behaviour' has negative connotations as it is usually only applied to actions that are viewed as bad. This is particularly significant for the way in which self-injury by people with intellectual disabilities is framed as a 'challenging behaviour' rather than a coping mechanism (Heslop & Macaulay, 2009). Words such as 'violence' or 'mutilation' also have strong negative connotations allied with danger and revulsion, and words like 'destruction', 'wounding' and 'harm' are similarly negative. Other terms such as 'para-suicide' share similar problems with deliberate self-harm as a generic term for any self-created injury, regardless of the intention behind it. There are also some medical terms, such as 'non-suicidal self-injury', 'delicate cutters syndrome' and 'moderate superficial self-mutilation' (Favazza, 1996), that reflect a gendering of self-injury as a female and trivialised experience (discussed below). Likewise, self-injury is often referred to as 'attention-seeking', which not only implies that people who hurt themselves are not worthy of attention but also minimises the level of distress that underpins self-injury and fails to recognise that most self-injury is secret.

In short, all of these terms have the effect of minimising the injury and contrasting it with more 'serious' issues.

Overall then, the terminology around self-injury is problematic in that it tends to be either blaming and pathologising or minimising and invalidating towards the people concerned. These terms influence how self-injury is understood and how people are responded to. For Mark, the term 'deliberate self-harm' was particularly problematic. He felt that defining his injuries as 'deliberate' implied that he had the opportunity to 'choose' an alternative activity – such as watching TV – which in no way reflected the circumstances or the functions of his self-injury:

> One of the things I absolutely *hate, hate, hate,* is that expression *deliberate self-harm,* because it was never *deliberate,* there was no deliberation on it. I was a very young child at that stage, a young teenager, pre-teenager, who was *doing* these things because of horrendous circumstances at home.

Clare's experiences illustrate the ways in which terms like 'self-inflicted violence' create a negative impression of a person who hurts themself as violent and dangerous to others. She recounted one of her first experiences of self-injury awareness training:

> My very first training day – I'm co-training with the facilitator of my survivors therapy group. I talk a bit about my experiences of self-harm and then the group is invited to ask me questions. Janet [the facilitator] asks them to be careful not to ask any question they wouldn't want to be directed to themselves. A woman raises her hand [and asks], 'Do you abuse other people?'

Words and expressions are powerful indeed. They convey both intended and unintended messages to people about how they are viewed and valued. In this book I use the term self-injury because it is the most straightforwardly descriptive and the least value laden of the terms available. However, the term self-injury is not entirely unproblematic in that 'injury' is largely understood as something negative or bad, and it also focuses purely on the physical dimension of the experience. Ideally, I prefer the expression 'people who hurt themselves', because this expression places the person rather than the injury at the forefront, and also because 'hurt' or 'hurting' signifies both physical and emotional pain. In this definition, the person and their emotional and physical pain are at the forefront, and this is crucial to a meaningful and supportive response.

Self-harm

Self-harm is another term that is often used to describe the actions I refer to as self-injury. However, technically self-harm describes a broader category of experiences than self-injury, and it is helpful to understand the differences between the two.

Self-harm is any action that causes pain or damage to the body, but this may not be immediate or its primary purpose. Self-harming is a universal human phenomenon; some forms of self-harm are socially acceptable (and sometimes even compulsory) and others are not. Socially acceptable forms of self-harm include drinking alcohol or caffeine, smoking, comfort eating, over-exercising, contact sports and some risk-taking activities. They also include beauty practices such as plucking and waxing, cosmetic surgery and wearing high-heeled shoes. Tattooing, piercing and other forms of body modification are also a form of self-harm that may or may not be socially acceptable, depending on the individual, their age, gender and so on, the context they are in (their social class, job, as well as the wider culture in which they live) and the extent and visibility of the body marks. Socially unacceptable forms of self-harm include eating disorders, addictions/substance misuse, sexual risk-taking, fighting and non-mainstream cosmetic surgery and body-modifications that create an appearance that is outside of culturally accepted norms (Inckle, 2007).

Self-injury is best understood as one specific category in the larger pool of self-harm, and one that is not socially acceptable. Self-injury and self-harm differ in terms of their immediacy and intention, but understanding self-harm, and particularly socially acceptable forms of self-harming coping mechanisms, can be a useful route into understanding self-injury. For example, smoking, drinking, comfort eating, over-exercising and so on are commonly used as ways to cope with negative feelings and experiences and to find a degree of comfort and relief from them. Clare noted that 'most people's coping strategies *at times* are self-harming'. Other forms of self-harm that affect the appearance of the body, such as beauty practices, body modification and cosmetic interventions, can be a means by which an individual seeks to take control of their body, to express themself through their body, or to create an outer body that reflects how they feel, or would like to feel, about themself (Inckle, 2007). Self-injury functions in exactly the same ways as all these types of self-harm but at a more intense and immediate level, because the feelings and experiences are much more difficult than the day-to-day stresses and conflicts that these forms of self-harm mediate.

Eating disorders, addictions and substance misuse are also often categorised as forms of self-injury (eg. Miller, 1994), but they are more rightly forms of self-harm in that the pain and damage caused to the body is usually less direct and immediate and is also a secondary purpose or outcome. There are, however, a number of similarities and crossovers between these forms of self-harm and self-injury in that all of these practices are coping mechanisms, often in response to very similar feelings, experiences and life histories, and people commonly use a mixture of them (Murray, Warm & Fox, 2005; Gollust, Eisenberg & Golberstein, 2008; Hasking et al, 2008; UNICEF Ireland, 2011).

A number of my research participants described periods of alcohol and/or drug use, as well as troubled relationships with food. For some, these eventually became a substitute for their self-injury; for others, they intensified it. Colm, who had been self-injuring throughout his early childhood, described how, as soon as he was able to access alcohol and drugs (in his mid-teens), these began to replace his self-injury: 'It was an escape that *took over.*'

> As I got older, the alcohol addiction would have took hold and kind of blotted it out as well. It blotted *a lot* of stuff out – the alcohol addiction – it blotted *life* out, it blotted *reality* out, but it sort of blotted the self-harming out.

Like Colm, Mark, Rachel and Joseph also described periods where alcohol and/or drugs became a substitute for self-injury. In contrast, Amanda's alcohol and drug use intensified her self-injury:

> I would have abused drugs and alcohol, and the very, I think, like substances like *add* to it and make it more intense and make it worse... I had 15 admissions to hospital though drinking and self-harming and I was often locked in the padded cell.

Indeed, in Ireland intoxication is closely linked to hospital attendance for self-injury (National Suicide Research Foundation, 2010), with alcohol and drugs functioning as disinhibitors that can lead to much more serious injuries than if the person had been sober. Internationally, there is increasing focus on the dual risks of intoxication and self-injury (Hasking et al, 2008; Haw et al, 2005; Hawton, 2011; NICE, 2011; National Suicide Research Foundation, 2008; 2011; Rossow et al, 2007), and alcohol and/or drug misuse within the family can also be a risk factor for self-injury (Deliberto & Nock, 2008) (see Chapter 3).

Treatment facilities for alcohol, drug and food problems contain high numbers of clients who self-injure, and self-injury is particularly common when people have withdrawn from, or are prevented from accessing, the substances that they use as a means of coping. Once an individual's method of coping with, or 'blotting out', their feelings and experiences is gone, they often revert to direct self-injury. This makes it essential that any response to enactments of distress focuses on the underlying causes rather than the primary 'symptom'. Otherwise people remain in intense emotional difficulty but without their primary coping mechanism, and therefore become increasingly desperate for relief and another way to cope (see Chapter 6). Joseph's experience of using hypnotherapy to 'cure' his self-injury illustrates the ways in which harmful coping mechanisms are substituted for one another when the underlying issues remain unchanged. Thus, even though the hypnotherapy 'worked', to the extent that he no longer self-injured, because his psychological and emotional issues had not been addressed, he simply moved to another coping mechanism – alcohol:

> Life wasn't any better afterwards [ie. when the self-injury stopped]; I didn't miss it, but I was still the same person with low self-esteem and all that, but the cutting was gone. Then I started drinking instead! Not a conscious decision! [Laughs] No! But it's not too much of a journey from one to the other. It's the same issues that leads you from one to the other, I believe, for myself.

Likewise, if control of food is a primary coping mechanism and it is removed – which is often the case in the 'treatment' of eating disorders where people are compelled to consume a certain amount of food per day – then direct self-injury becomes a way to manage and cope with the underlying issues (see Pembroke, 1996). Issues with food are commonly experienced by people who self-injure and this was true for Colm, Emma, Elaine and Clare. Colm described how 'as I got a little bit older I started compulsively eating more'. For Colm, his use of food was particularly problematic: 'The thing that actually damaged my body and my health the most was actually food.'

Overall then, while self-injury and self-harm are distinct in a number of important ways, understanding self-harm as a mechanism for coping with, expressing and taking control of experiences and feelings can be useful in understanding some of the functions of self-injury and what are helpful and unhelpful responses to it. To illustrate: imagine someone who has been smoking cigarettes for a number of years and who, after a very difficult day at work, goes outside to have a cigarette as a way of relieving the stress and providing some comfort from the day. If a friend, colleague or their therapist rushes up and tries to take the cigarette off them, insisting that smoking is irrational, dangerous, unacceptable or even disgusting, and ordering them to stop immediately and do something more healthy and acceptable instead, it is clear that this will not produce a positive response. Nor will it lead to a meaningful and supportive discussion about either the smoking or the stress. The smoker will most likely want a cigarette even more, will probably smoke additional cigarettes in order to cope with the added stress, and will feel angry and alienated from the 'helper'. In future they will be unlikely to turn to that person in times of difficulty and more likely to use cigarettes as their only means of comfort and coping. They may even make extra efforts to keep their smoking secret to avoid negative attention.

Set out like this, a non-accepting, preventative approach is clearly unhelpful and inappropriate, yet this remains the mainstay of responses to self-injury. Elaine pointed out: '"Stopping" people self-harming isn't going to stop them doing it... I don't believe it's a behaviour that people just stop... they *can't* as they wouldn't be doing it in the first place.' Likewise, Clare pointed out that 'being told to stop is really not a constructive or meaningful response, it makes you feel worse, and you do it anyway'.

Overall then, self-injury is distinct from self-harm in that its purpose is to cause immediate and direct pain and damage to the body. However, like some forms of self-harm, it is a means of coping with, expressing and gaining relief from difficult feelings and experiences. Self-injury is often referred to as self-harm (and in quotations I leave the terminology in its original form), but it has important differences.

Gender and self-injury[1]

For a long time, self-injury was believed to be a predominantly female experience, and in particular an adolescent female experience, and rare among men and boys. This is largely as a result of psychiatric perspectives about female instability and, as noted above, has led to some of the more problematic terminology for self-injury. However, rather than depicting actual experience, this assumption further illustrates the problems with the ways in which self-injury has been defined and measured. This is based not only on misperceptions about self-injury but also on gender stereotyping and sexism. During the 1990s, feminists produced a number of publications and services that challenged psychiatric approaches to gender and self-injury and highlighted the ways in which gender inequality and physical and sexual violence against women and girls are implicated in mental ill health and self-injury (eg. Arnold, 1995; Babiker & Arnold, 1997; Miller, 1994; Newham Asian Women's Project, 1998; Smith, Cox & Saradjian, 1998). The Basement Project and the Bristol Crisis Service for Women (now Self-injury Support) were also established at this time, providing information, resources and services specific to women's needs and experiences. Today, gender inequality and violence against women and girls remain significant problems across the globe and continue to impact on women's health and wellbeing (Women's Health Council, 2007). However, this does not provide a full account of the relationship between gender and self-injury, and male experiences merit further attention.

It is, however, important to note that the discussion of gender and self-injury that follows does not take account of differences between ethnic majority (white) and Black and minority ethnic (BME) populations. Figures for gender and self-injury are complicated by issues of ethnicity. For example, rates of self-injury, attempted and completed suicide are much higher among Asian women, and especially young Asian women, than among young white women (Siddiqui & Patel, 2010; Watts, 2005). These issues are discussed in more detail in Chapter 4.

Historically, women and girls have been seen as more vulnerable to all forms of mental illness, as a result of medical and psychiatric accounts of female biology in which females were defined as biologically weaker, less stable and more vulnerable than men. This meant that any aberration from expected

---

1. Parts of this section were first published by Sage Journals as Inckle, K (2014). Strong and Silent: men, masculinity and self-injury. *Men and Masculinities 17*(1): 3–21.

female behaviour was viewed as a sickness that resulted from flawed female biology. In contrast, any male behaviour that deviated from expected male roles was viewed as deviance rather than sickness and was punished rather than medically treated – Jane Ussher (1991) describes it as 'mad women' and 'bad men'. This trend remains evident today in that the majority of prison inmates are male (Evans & Wallace, 2008), and the majority of those diagnosed with mental illness are female (Affi, 2007; Ussher, 1991).[2]

In the past, the high rates of female diagnosis arose from the view that women and girls were more vulnerable to mental disturbance due to their reproductive functions and hormonal cycles, and particularly so at times of change, such as puberty and menstruation (Frost, 2000). Indeed, some of the earliest mental illnesses, such as hysteria, were defined purely in terms of female biology: the womb was thought to have become detached and to have wandered into a woman's brain, making her insane (Ussher, 1991). Today, biological, sex-based accounts of mental illness are decreasing, although the current focus on genetics and 'brain structures' as the cause of sexed characteristics and mental pathologies means that sex-typing has not entirely gone away.

The second reason for the link between females and self-injury is based on socio-cultural factors and gender roles, rather than biology, but is also a misunderstanding of the functions of self-injury. When self-injury is defined as a form of violence or aggression, it is assumed that, because gender norms make it unacceptable for women and girls to outwardly express angry, aggressive or violent feelings and behaviour, they are more likely to turn these feelings and acts inwardly on themselves. Men and boys, on the other hand, are free to express angry and aggressive feelings and to engage in a whole range of physical activities, from contact sport to public violence, that allows them to express these emotions without direct self-injury. As Dusty Miller puts it: 'Men act out. Women act out by acting in' (1994: 6).

However, the 'acting out/acting in' analogy does not hold true for self-injury, which includes elements of both. In these crude terms, self-injury is clearly 'acting out' in that it involves externalised, physical and sometimes 'violent' actions. At the same time it is also 'acting in', since self-injury is usually a secret process through which people control and regulate their inner feelings, thoughts and memories. Therefore, linking gender and self-injury in terms of

---

2. Many writers also argue that psychiatric diagnosis is a means of social control. This is evident not only in the gendering of diagnosis but also in the prevalence of diagnosis and differences in standards of treatment given to people from BME and lower social-economic groups, as well as the 'great confinements' in mental institutions during times of social upheaval or unrest (Sedgwick, 1982).

a crude binary of 'acting out' and 'acting in' is based on a misunderstanding of the functions of self-injury and its presence and purpose in an individual's life.

Furthermore, the cultural association of violence and aggression ('acting out'), rather than vulnerability and distress, with men and boys, has significant implications for the way self-injury is both defined and perceived, and results in the neglect of male self-injury and a lack of appropriate services and responses for them. For example, if a young man hits a wall with his fist, this is seen as an outward act of aggression, whereas if he (or a girl) hits the wall with another part of his body, such as his head, then it would be more quickly recognised that he was hurting *himself* rather than aggressively damaging an object.

In my research, service-providers and service-users were keenly aware of the ways in which norms of masculinity influence the definition of self-injury and result in dismissive responses to males. Elaine felt that 'the approaches to men and women in that way, it doesn't help either'. Service-providers also acknowledged the negative effects of this kind of gendering: 'The amount of men who will punch things, hit things, we're talking about walls etc where obviously what they're hitting isn't actually going to suffer, but *they* are.' Another observed: 'All the young fellas [ie. young men] that punch the wall out of anger or kick the door or something like that, and they've *hurt themselves*.' Moreover, these kinds of incidents, to continue with the example of wall hitting, are also seen as more socially acceptable in males than females. If a female hits a wall, it would be much more quickly acknowledged that something was 'wrong' and that distress or difficulty was at the root, and not just written off as 'typical' male aggression.

The third reason for the assumed prevalence of female self-injury is also based on socio-cultural factors associated with gender, but this time focusing on the experiences that underlie self-injury, rather than its functions (eg. Babiker & Arnold, 1997; Gallup, 2002; Miller, 1994; Smith, Cox & Saradjian, 1998; Ussher, 1991). This approach rests on the contention that self-injury is most commonly a response to experiences of powerlessness, sexual abuse, lack of autonomy and control over one's life and/or body, or trauma. The norms of gender and sexuality that sexually objectify women and girls and give power and dominance to male sexuality mean that females are much more likely to be sexually exploited and victimised. Gender inequality also means that women and girls are often dependent on men or have less power and fewer resources to challenge male dominance and abuse. Therefore, the increased female vulnerability to sexual exploitation and abuse and decreased resources and autonomy to challenge it mean that women and girls are more likely to turn to self-injury as a coping mechanism.

To some extent this connection between vulnerability and self-injury is true (see Chapter 3) but, more importantly, it is increasingly recognised that these are not exclusively female experiences. There are gender differences in the *types* of vulnerability and victimisation that males and females experience, but not the overall extent. Men, for example, die on average six years younger than women, experience more stress-related illnesses and are more likely to be victims of accidents and homicide (Evans & Wallace, 2008). Males are also more likely to be homeless, to experience drug and alcohol dependency, to be imprisoned, and to be admitted under section to a psychiatric hospital (Evans & Wallace, 2008; White, 2006) – all experiences that have significant correlations with self-injury. Furthermore, males are much more likely to die by suicide – they account for 80 per cent of annual deaths by suicide in Ireland (National Suicide Research Foundation, 2008) and 75 per cent in the UK (Evans & Wallace, 2008) – and, while suicide is not directly related to self-injury, it is certainly indicative of widespread, unresolved male distress. Furthermore, males and females with physical and intellectual disabilities are more vulnerable to sexual violence and abuse than people without disabilities (Equality and Humans Rights Commission, 2011; Shakespeare, Gillespie Sells & Davis, 1998). There is also evidence from Ireland that the physical, emotional and sexual abuse of boys and girls in institutional care settings is equally common (Ryan, 2009). Finally, while females tend to be more physically oppressed and restricted in current gender structures and norms, males are more likely to be emotionally imprisoned and policed (see Evans & Wallace, 2008), and self-injury is equally bound up with both physical and emotional experiences. Therefore, it is true that experiences of vulnerability, powerlessness and abuse have a relationship with self-injury. It is also true that the norms and inequalities of gender mean that women and girls are subject to particular types of risk and vulnerability. However, this does not mean that women and girls are more likely to experience *all* of the risks and vulnerabilities related to self-injury and are therefore more likely than males to hurt themselves. The structures of gender also create a particular set of vulnerabilities and risks for men and boys that have a significant and under-recognised relationship with self-injury.

In recent years there has been increasing recognition that there is little difference in male and female rates of self-injury (Gollust, Eisenberg & Golberstein, 2008; Gratz, Conrad & Roemer, 2002; Long & Jenkins, 2010; Pattison & Kahan, 1983); we only have to consider the high rates of self-injury in prisons to realise that gendered accounts have not taken these men into consideration (Babiker & Arnold, 1997; Smith, Cox & Saradjian, 1998). Moreover, if there are differences in male and female self-injury, it is much more about the type and method of the injury and the ways in which the injuries are interpreted – or, more accurately, ignored – for men and boys than actual incidence. For example, if only cutting and overdosing are recognised as self-injury – which are not the most prevalent forms – then the majority of self-injury and the bruises, scratches, burns and broken and fractured bones that result from it will be overlooked. In the context of gender norms where it is considered socially acceptable for men and boys to have visible wounds and injuries and where damage to the body is often associated with heroic forms of masculinity – such as sports injuries – then the majority of male self-injury is simply not recognised. One service-provider explained that:

> The thing is with boys, which is really only emerging now, is that boys have been self-harming and we haven't been aware of it. We've put it down to rugby injuries or skateboard injuries, but in fact there was one young man who, he was I think about 18, and he had been in hospital 21 times with a broken foot or a broken wrist and he did them all to himself.

There is also a cultural precedent to ignore the physical and emotional vulnerability of men and boys and to interpret their experiences within traditional gender norms that invalidate their experiences of self-injury. Colm, who grew up in a very disadvantaged area and experienced violence in his home and the local community, hurt himself from a young age and yet this was never recognised. He said: 'When you're a *boy* in [name of place], being beaten up in school was a *regular thing* for most kids, it [ie. physical wounds and injuries] was just considered like *boyhood*.' In a different context, Mark also described the ways in which the culture of masculinity concealed his self-injury:

> There were times I had black eyes, busted lips – when I would hit myself I would tend to hit myself in the face a lot, quite violently, and I would have looked like somebody who had been kicked around the place by people. I always had excuses: 'What's that?' 'Oh, I fell'... I was doing martial arts at the time, or there were times when I wasn't, and people still thought I was, so I used to just say, 'Oh,' you know, 'I got it in the club.'

Female bodies, on the other hand, are much more scrutinised than male bodies and are expected to be free of blemish, imperfection or any sign of deviance from the norms of femininity – including physical injuries. Coupled with the fact that female bodies, sexuality and behaviour are much more closely policed than male bodies at all ages, and especially during adolescence, where females are seen to be particularly vulnerable to both their own biology and external threats (Frost, 2000), it is not surprising that self-injury is much more visible and problematised among women and girls. At the same time, on a daily basis, women and girls are expected to carry out painful and sometime debilitating practices on their own bodies (for example, plucking, waxing, corsetry, wearing high heels, restricting food) in order to be beautiful, acceptable and even 'natural' (Inckle, 2007). Many women and girls struggle with the contradictory demands of feminine embodiment and often experience what Liz Frost (2000) described as 'body-hatred', which she found to be closely connected with self-injury. The link between body-hatred and self-injury is not difficult to understand in that, if we don't like something, it is easy to hurt and damage it.

Likewise, 'body-hatred' is commonly cited as a reason for self-injury among people with intellectual disabilities (Heslop & Macaulay, 2009), where it also reflects the restrictions and cultural perceptions that shape their lives. For example, people with intellectual disabilities are rigidly policed in terms of their behaviour, appearance and life choices, and their sexuality is interpreted in pathological terms as either entirely non-existent or as excessive, predatory and dangerous (Wilkerson, 2002).

Finally, when considering the relationship between gender and self-injury it is important to consider the experience of trans people who hurt themselves. The term 'trans' refers to people whose sex and/or gender identity is not the same as the sex they were labelled with at birth (ie. male or female), regardless of whether they have had medical interventions to match their body with their felt identity.[3] Trans people have existed throughout history and across the world. Many small-scale cultures have much more complex conceptions of sex and gender than contemporary 'western'[4] cultures; here, trans people are

---

3. Other terms include transgender, transsexual, non-binary gender, F2M, M2F and gender variant. I use 'trans' in an attempt to be inclusive.

4. Using the term 'western' is politically contentious as it is based on an ethnocentric world view that divides the world into a hierarchy of 'western'/norm and non-'western'/Other. However, 'western' values and perspectives have had a major impact on approaches to health and illness – many of which are particularly counterproductive for understanding and responding to self-injury. Therefore, the 'western' origin of a number of ideas, beliefs and perspectives needs to be acknowledged without legitimating uncritical use of the term. Wherever the term 'western' is used in this book, I intend a critical use of it, and I place it in inverted commas and do not use a capital letter to highlight this critical use.

part of the normal range of gender identities (Brettell & Sargent, 2004; More & Whittle, 1999). However, in 'western' medicine, being trans is defined as a mental illness – usually gender identity disorder (GID),[5] but also dissociative identity disorder or multiple personality disorder (DiStefano, 2008).

The experience of being trans within a culture that pathologises any non-standard gender presentation has a significant impact on mental health and wellbeing. Research has found that as many as 76 per cent of trans people have used antidepressants and 53 per cent have self-injured (McNeil et al, 2012). A significant factor in their self-injury were issues related to gender-identity conflicts, with 63 per cent saying they self-injured more before their gender transition than afterwards. The most common ways in which they hurt themselves included cutting, punching, head-banging and biting, but 'mutilation' of the breasts and genitals was also common. Significantly, while self-castration is recognised as a specific form of self-injury (Favazza, 1996) and is frequently reported by trans people (McNeil et al, 2012), it is not included in the diagnostic criteria for GID.

McNeil and colleagues (2012) found that 60 per cent of trans people self-injured for reasons specifically related to their trans identity. These included body-hatred, problems with treatment, healthcare services and providers, and negative attitudes in society more broadly, and 20 per cent reported self-injuring directly as a result of how they were treated at the gender identity clinic to which they had been referred. They also reported a range of non-trans-specific reasons for self-injury, including lack of support, bullying, guilt and shame, breakdown of relationships, isolation, loneliness and childhood abuse. These feelings and experiences are common among those who self-injure, regardless of identity, which highlights that, while certain gender experiences promote particular vulnerabilities, there are common themes across all people who hurt themselves. These are explored further in Chapters 3 and 4.

Age and self-injury

In much the same way that femaleness has been associated with mental vulnerability and self-injury, so too has adolescence (see, for example, Gollust, Eisenberg & Golberstein, 2008; Moyer & Nelson, 2007; UNICEF Ireland, 2011). Adolescence has become increasingly associated with vulnerability, deviance

---

5. *DSM-5* is one of the two main 'western' psychiatric diagnostic manuals of 'mental disorder' (the other is the World Health Organization's ICD-10). *DSM-5* has made some revisions to its definition of GID in response to challenges to it. However, the diagnosis has not been removed altogether.

and dysfunction, to the extent that it is almost seen as synonymous with a mental illness in itself. It is 'a time of difficulties and disturbances, needing a variety of interventions and reforms' (Frost, 2000: 81). This view potentially minimises the significance of self-injury in young people and also reinforces the assumption that adolescence is the point of onset. However, many people have been hurting themselves in a variety of ways and for a significant period of time before their self-injury is discovered – as illustrated by Mark (in the section on terminology, above) and Colm (in the section on gender, above). Nonetheless, onset is presumed to be the point when self-injury comes to the attention of professional services. In Clare's experience, 'when I first came into contact with psychiatry at the age of 20, I'd been self-harming for at least 10 years. Despite this, the psychiatrist diagnosed third year nerves [ie. final year university exams].'

As such, there are conflicting attitudes towards children and young people who self-injure. Young people are often seen as particularly vulnerable to self-injury and peer pressure during adolescence, yet at the same time evidence of self-injury among younger children is often ignored. Mark and Emma's experiences highlight not only the significance of self-injury in their young lives, but also how quick adults were to minimise it. Emma described how:

> The first memory I have of hurting myself is throwing myself downstairs and knocking myself unconscious when I was about five. I did this to try and avoid seeing the person who sexually abused me. I think that this is the trigger that meant that I then turned to self-harm regularly as I grew older.

Mark began hurting himself around the same age:

> My *earliest* memory of self-harming or self-injuring, I reckon I was four, and I damaged the inside of my mouth with a lollypop stick that I had sharpened… [Later] I remember a significant period of time of hair-pulling… It got to a stage of aggression, a fair amount of bald patches, and I suppose that was probably from the age of 10 to 14… My mother was aware of the first incident but I think she put it down to just me being a kid. But there was tensions in the house at that stage... Certainly from the age of 10, I'd be sitting there pulling my hair and she'd be: 'Stop pulling your hair! What are you doing?!' But no one thought about it anymore than I was just doing something that was just really a bit silly.

Clare's self-injury became increasingly obvious during her teenage years, but she found that adults were still willing to overlook it:

> I was self-harming from round about the age of 10, but I didn't have any
> contact with services up until the age of 20... I think there was, round
> about the age of 15, it was sort of picked up on at school and something
> was said to my mother, who said something to me like, 'How did you get
> those cuts on your wrists?' And I said, 'Oh I did it on a barbed wire fence,'
> and I think there was an element of it was *much* easier for *everybody* to
> accept that explanation than to actually ask me further questions or to
> think that, 'Well that doesn't quite add up.' So, yeah, I think there were
> people who had an inkling, but nobody actually did anything about it.

Emma recounted how adults were aware that she was hurting herself during her teens but similarly chose not to engage with her about it: 'I was expelled from school at 13 for smoking cannabis and around this time my class teacher had become aware that I was cutting myself. This was not really discussed.'

Mark and Clare had mixed feelings about the way in which their self-injury was ignored. Both of them felt that a helpful response – ie. one that focused on the distress and difficulties they were experiencing – would have had a huge impact on their lives at that point. However, as adults they were also aware that it was very unlikely their self-injury would have been met with a constructive response. Clare said: 'Looking back I'm almost grateful [for it being ignored]. Well, it's real mixed emotions, 'cos I [also] think that was a *huge* failure, 'cos I think a helpful response at that age would have made a *massive* difference.' Mark concurred that:

> If somebody had shown interest and the right approach, yeah... *Me* being
> very introverted at the time, it would have taken somebody to be *interested*
> and spot it. But having said that... I would have *hated* anybody to try and
> separate the self-injury from what was going on. You know, if somebody
> had noticed the injuries or hair loss or other things and just concentrated
> on that. And *still*, that still sits very strongly with me, that that [ie. the
> self-injury] wasn't just what was going on. What was going on for me was
> how bad I felt, and all the other stuff that was going on around it. So, my
> fears, my fears about the world, loneliness, isolation at times, *all* of those
> different things of which the self-injury was *a part of* but *not all*, and
> that has stuck with me still, that, you know, self-injury is symptomatic of

something else. Yes, in itself it is important, particularly when there were times when I would have put my life in danger, but what would have been more important was, 'What's the problem?'

Overall then, young people hurt themselves for very significant reasons, yet the approaches to young people who self-injure often minimise the significance of their injuries and problematise the young person.

Finally, there is a common perception that adults and older people do not hurt themselves. However, despite only minimal research focusing specifically on older people and self-injury, there is a great deal of evidence of self-injury among adults in prisons, psychiatric and special hospitals and facilities for people with intellectual disabilities (Birch et al, 2011; Liebling, Chipchase & Velangi, 1997; Lord, 2008; Groves, 2004; Heslop & Macaulay, 2009). The research that has been conducted on the specific experience of older people (ie. over 65) who self-injure highlights similar features to other vulnerable groups: 'Loneliness, lack of support from services and poor integration in the community appear to be important factors' (Dennis et al, 2005: 539). There is also increasing recognition of the problem of elder abuse (Help the Aged, 2004; Phelan, 2013), which may, like other forms of abuse, correlate with self-injury (see Chapter 3).

Self-injury exists across all age groups, from young children to elderly people, and, while it might be more visible at certain stages in the life course, this is much more a reflection of the social structuring of age (and gender) than inherent to self-injury. One service-provider commented: 'The youngest we have seen is seven and the oldest is 68; 70 I think we've had is *the* oldest, but we have a 68-year-old at the moment. Many have been men. There doesn't seem to be any particular profile.' Overall then, as with the other issues related to defining and measuring self-injury, the assumptions around gender and age – and specifically the assumed higher rates of adolescent female self-injury – prove to be inaccurate and to stem from misleading representations.

• Chapter summary

This chapter has explored the core issues necessary for a thorough understanding of self-injury. These include the differences between self-injury and attempted suicide and the range of ways in which people hurt themselves, all of which defy stereotypes and challenge many of the assumptions about self-injury. Misperceptions about self-injury, such as those suggesting that adolescent females are most vulnerable to both self-injury and its underlying experiences, have also been challenged. The critical exploration of the ways in which self-injury is defined and measured has also highlighted the potential impacts of failing to recognise and respond appropriately to people who hurt themselves. As such, this chapter provides the basis for a broad and holistic understanding of self-injury, which is the first step to responding helpfully.

The issues explored here also emphasise the importance of understanding before intervention. It is essential to understand each individual's experiences before any useful response can be made. This understanding takes time; it cannot be achieved through a few quick questions on a diagnostic checklist or from presumptions based on statistical representations. Nor can the type or extent of the injury be presumed to tell the full story. It is essential to take time and listen to each individual, to hear their distress and what is being communicated through it. All too often people who hurt themselves end up in 'crisis response' situations where their autonomy and individuality (and often their dignity and rights) are stripped away from them as a result of misplaced fears that they are imminently suicidal. Understanding the distinction between suicide and self-injury can allay these fears and create a context where time and space is available for proper attention and understanding.

Learning into practice

Definition	Self-injury is coping and surviving
Working principles	• Understanding before intervention
	• Listening not labelling
Practice applications	• Reflection not reaction
	• Active listening

Definition: self-injury is coping and surviving

Self-injury is a way of coping and surviving and it is often a strategy that someone has been using for some time. It can be seen as an indication of resilience rather than risk, and therefore it does not need a huge crisis intervention. If someone has injuries that may put their life at risk, then medical attention should be sought. If it is not clear whether the individual was attempting to end their life, they should be clearly and directly asked.

Working principles

1. Understanding before intervention

This principle should be the foundation of all responses and services, so that no action is taken until there is a clear understanding of all the relevant details. Crisis situations can demand immediate reactions, but self-injury is not a crisis in this regard, and helpers need to take the time and space to listen to and understand the individual and their distress before they act.

2. Listening not labelling

Building on the first principle, it is essential that each person is listened to as an individual and that helpers are open to understanding the person's experiences from their perspective, rather than rushing to label and categorise them. Labels close down communication and are often based on information that does not accurately reflect the individual or their experiences. This is particularly significant in self-injury, where, as illustrated above, many of the statistics and definitions do not correspond with lived experience.

Activity

- Write down all the coping mechanisms that you have used throughout your life.
- Divide the list into three columns: healthy, unhealthy and neutral.
- Reflect on how you would feel if you were to be primarily identified as a person who engaged in one of the coping mechanisms in the unhealthy list.
- What do you think you can learn from this activity about the way in which people who hurt themselves are labelled and valued?

Practice applications

1. Reflection not reaction

Understanding requires reflection as well as information. Therefore, reflective practice is key to responding helpfully. Reflection is a way of separating our own 'baggage', feelings and needs from those of other people. It is also a way of opening up a bigger picture than the circumstances that are immediately apparent. A simple and effective way to promote reflection is to focus on the thoughts, feelings and sensations that were present in a particular situation and to explore where they emerge from. A journal can be a useful way to do this, as can dialogue with a colleague, supervisor or friend. Practising reflection can improve self-awareness and responses, even in very challenging situations. Reflective practitioners are attuned to and manage their own feelings and responses, creating time and space to focus on the needs and experiences of the other person. This practice is crucial for responding helpfully to self-injury, where interventions are often focused on resolving the fears and anxieties of the helper rather than the needs of the person who has hurt themself.

2. Active listening

Active listening is a core skill of many professions in health and social care. However, it is easily neglected in the day-to-day pressures of work. It is also a skill that can be used to great effect in all aspects of life. It is important to take time to refresh active listening skills, as listening with full attention and without prejudice is one of the most powerful responses. People who hurt themselves describe how being 'really' listened to is one of the most positive supports they can be offered.

Clare described listening as the essential element of a helpful response:

> The *only* principle that is transferable from every individual is *listen*, and sometimes that might be listening to the fact that people don't want to talk, so listen to that, and then obviously respect what you hear! Don't listen and carry on regardless!

Amanda emphasised that helpers should 'believe what's going on for the person; don't label them in any way; really hear and listen'. Nonetheless, listening is often devalued and people feel like they need to do 'more'. This was a frequent learning experience for volunteer supporters in a self-injury service, who often described 'feeling quite powerless and really questioning the value of just listening, but actually just listening *is really* powerful'. For those who have not tried active listening before, there are lots of resources available,[6] and practising at home can have very powerful results!

Activity

1. Think about a situation where you have instantly reacted 'in the heat of the moment'. This might be in conversation or in response to a text, email or tweet.

2. Now think about a situation where you paid careful attention to all aspects of the context and what was happening before you decided how to act.

    *   What do you think you can do to reduce incidence of the first situation and increase the likelihood of you responding in the way you did in the second?

---

6. See, for example, www.mindtools.com/CommSkll/ActiveListening.htm (accessed 23 August, 2016).

2

Embodying distress:
the functions of self-injury

The previous chapter established that self-injury is a coping mechanism that people use to manage their feelings and experiences. In this chapter, I explore how and why self-injury functions in this way. Understanding human experience as embodied and exploring the meaning and purpose of body rituals from around the world provide useful insight into the ways in which pain and damage to the body have powerful emotional, psychological, symbolic, social and physical effects.

> Injury to the body (by oneself or by others) is part of a long and universal human tradition, which has had important functions for groups and societies throughout all eras. Body mutilation, pain, and the drawing of blood have had (and continue to have) a range of deep and powerful symbolic meaning. (Babiker & Arnold, 1997: 20)

Recognising that direct pain and injury to the body are universal human phenomena enables a much deeper understanding of self-injury and dissipates much of the fear, confusion and misperception around self-injury.

This chapter also highlights the range of functions of self-injury and their often contradictory nature. Thus, while the functions of self-injury may be understood broadly, they are always unique to the individual and no one model of response fits everyone. Nonetheless, in order to understand the functions of self-injury, it is important to understand embodiment.

Embodiment

'Western' cultures in general, and 'western' medicine in particular,[1] have a fragmentary perception of human beings in which mind, body, emotion, and society/culture are regarded as separate entities that exist in isolation from one another and where illness is simply a mental or physical pathology. However, human experience in general, and self-injury in particular, is much more complex than this perspective allows.

> It is clear that the individual human body mirrors the collective social
> body, and each continually creates and sustains the other. Misperceptions
> of reality, feelings of guilt, negative self-images, anti-social acts, and
> all the other symptoms we associate with personal mental illness defy
> understanding without reference to the psychological, social, cultural and
> physical integrity of the communal 'body'. (Favazza, 1996: xiii)

Furthermore, the idea that it is possible, or desirable, to fragment human experience in this way is the antithesis of many older philosophies and practices, which are rooted in the interconnectedness of the physical, emotional, mental, social and spiritual/symbolic aspects of personhood. This more holistic perspective – which is increasingly being incorporated into today's therapies (see Chapter 5) – regards our body, mind, emotions and energies/spirit as inseparable from one another and as shaping and shaped by the context in which we live. In this way, all of our experiences are embodied – that is, made up of intersecting physical, emotional, social, symbolic and mental factors. Our identities, feelings and experiences are mediated and communicated through our bodies. This fundamental embodiment means that physical pain and injury to the body have powerful effects in all of these dimensions – physical, mental, emotional, social and symbolic.

An embodied perspective highlights the complex inter-relationship of our faculties, experiences and meaning-making processes, and is key to understanding the ways in which self-injury functions as a coping mechanism.

---

1. Using the term 'western' is politically contentious as it is based on an ethnocentric world view that divides the world into a hierarchy of western/norm and non-western/Other. However, 'western' values and perspectives have had a major impact on approaches to health and illness – many of which are particularly counterproductive for understanding and responding to self-injury. Therefore, the 'western' origin of a number of ideas, beliefs and perspectives needs to be acknowledged without legitimating uncritical use of the term. Wherever the term 'western' is used in this book, I intend a critical use of it, and I place it in inverted commas and do not use a capital letter to highlight this critical use.

This chapter explores the functions of self-injury through the themes of 1) symbolic and physical functions, 2) social and political functions, and 3) emotional and interpersonal functions. The final section includes an exploration of the counter-functions of coping by self-injury.

Physical and symbolic functions

Healing and medicine

The first function of causing pain and injury to the body is to provide healing and relief in physical and symbolic terms. Contemporary 'western' medicine is based on a fragmented or disembodied model that separates physical from mental (and emotional) health and considers matters of existential or spiritual wellbeing to be outside the realm of medical science altogether. However, this has not always been the case; it is only in relatively recent history that this separation occurred. Prior to the 19th century, all illnesses, be they physical (such as fever, syphilis or measles), mental/emotional (an attack of the nerves, depression or 'low spirits') or spiritual (being possessed by evil spirits), were seen as inseparable from the body and were treated with physical interventions. For more than a century (and up until the early 20th century in some parts of Europe), bleeding was the most popular of these interventions (Hackett, 1973). Bleeding emerged from the belief that humans were made up of four humours that coursed through the body and interconnected each person's physical, mental and spiritual dimensions. Disturbance arose from an imbalance in these humours and, since blood was the most powerful of them (and the only one for which there was physical evidence), bleeding was used to restore balance and bring the patient back to full health (Hackett, 1973). Bleeding, known as 'breathing a vein', was also believed to promote general good health, and regular bleeding was even recommended for pregnant women in order to strengthen the foetus. Indeed, bleeding became so popular that ornate bleeding bowls became part of the family inheritance in well-to-do families, and were passed down from generation to generation along with the family silver (Starr, 2000).

Bleeding is no longer a part of modern medicine, but blood has not lost its symbolic power (see below). Indeed, *The Lancet*, the prestigious medical journal, takes its name from the sharp-bladed instrument that was used to bleed patients (Hackett, 1973). Moreover, physical interventions have continued to be used throughout psychiatric practice to attempt to treat mental or emotional states, including electroconvulsive therapy (ECT), brain surgery and aversion therapy (Dickinson, 2015).

Self-injury functions in similar ways: it is an attempt at healing that uses a physical intervention to address mental or emotional states, and it can have very powerful effects. This was true for Joseph, who began to hurt himself during his teens in response to overwhelming anxiety attacks, during which he would often collapse, hyperventilate and partially lose consciousness:

> It would always start off with a panic attack, and I was always scared that a time would come when there would be nobody around and I would swallow my tongue and I'd – this was the logic I associated with it – and I would just stop breathing. So I thought, 'Well if I inflict the pain on myself then I won't get a panic attack and I won't faint and swallow my tongue.' So I used to cut myself so that the high level of pain would stop me from doing that.

And while, on reflection, Joseph felt that 'of course, that wasn't rational thinking', it nonetheless worked: when he began to cut himself, the panic attacks abated. Therefore, it is clear that Joseph's self-injury was functional in direct relation to his immediate difficulties. As such, a helpful response would focus on the cause of his intense and overwhelming anxiety, rather than the fact that he used self-injury as a way of managing it.

Older forms of medicine and healing, such as Chinese medicine, take a more complex approach to mind, body and spirit, and their relationship with physical and emotional pain and wellbeing. Acupuncture, for example, uses needles to tap into invisible energy flows in the body to promote emotional/mental relaxation, as well as physical healing. It is used for a whole range of conditions, from sleeplessness and chronic pain to addiction (Brumbaugh, 1993; Vickers et al, 2012). Self-injury functions in exactly the same way: a physical intervention provides mental and emotional relief in a range of contexts.

Self-injury may also have symbolic functions in transferring invisible emotional pain into a visible physical wound that can be treated and healed (Babiker & Arnold, 1997; Chandler, 2013). 'Having a physical pain to deal with was easier than dealing with the, the pain that you couldn't put your finger on [...] not that it took it away, but it was still really helpful' (in Chandler, 2013: 724). This symbolic healing can be just as powerful as the physical effects, especially when people's pain and struggles have been concealed or denied: 'When I have feelings of anxiety or panic, it feels like a logical conclusion;' 'It helps to take some of the pain away' (in Babiker & Arnold, 1997: 75–76). Physical pain can, then, provide a sense of healing, directly and symbolically.

Blood and symbolism

Understanding the symbolic nature of physical injuries, and especially the emotional effects of transferring an invisible and perhaps unrecognised inner pain into an external injury that is indisputably 'real', also illustrates the powerful symbolic functions of blood and bleeding. Today, in our high-tech societies, we consider ourselves to be rational, scientific and logical, yet our cultures remain full of symbolism, superstition and mysticism about our bodies.

> Blood is the most symbolic of all body substances [...] blood, pumped
> through the body by a beating heart is the essence of life force. The
> spilling of blood both gives life, during birth, and takes it away, at death.
> Throughout time, blood has been used in religious ritual to demonstrate
> suffering and salvation, piety and enlightenment: from blood sacrifice
> to crucifixion, mortification of the flesh to the martyrdom of saints,
> from ecstatic stigmata representing the wounds of Jesus to the drinking
> of wine representing Christ's blood at Holy Communion. Bleeding has
> always signified healing, from the bloodletting of early medicine to the
> psychological release of ill will, known metaphorically as 'getting rid of
> bad blood'. (Strong, 2000: 34)

This recognition that 'bleeding has always signified healing' is essential to understanding the powerful and transformative effects of injuries. As Strong indicates (above), this has been integral to medicine, religion and social ritual throughout history and is no less powerful for being carried out at an individual level today. Seeing and feeling blood released from the body can help people to feel calmer, cleansed/purged and restored to an uncontaminated sense of self (Babiker & Arnold, 1997; Harris, 2000; Spandler, 1996). This was true for Amanda: 'I had incidents where – when I was 13 or 14 – I would go round smashing windows so I could see the blood coming out of my hands.' Others describe how, 'When I see all the blood, it's such a relief, it's like all the awfulness is coming out, and I know I'll be alright now' (in Babiker & Arnold, 1997: 72), and 'As the blood flows down the sink so does the anger and anguish' (in Harris, 2000: 167):

> If I only cut just the once and see the blood coming out of my veins then
> it'll cleanse me – make me feel that I have released all this dirt that's
> sticking to my veins. (In Spandler, 1996: 31)

The blood that flows from self-injury has powerful symbolic functions at social, psychological and emotional levels. Many of these functions have been integrated into social and religious customs, which also have powerful psychological effects when people self-injure.

Purging and punishing

Much as in medicine, injury to the body, pain and releasing blood are hugely significant means of healing and purification in spiritual practices throughout the world, particularly in relation to punishment, redemption and salvation. Purging, purifying and punishing the body are commonly viewed as sacred practices in religions that have a negative view of the human body and are hierarchical and patriarchal – that is, they have a clear hierarchy of power, traced through a male line to a single masculine god. Here, a spiritual state of purity or grace is reached by separation from the body, either in death or through ritual practices where an individual (usually male) transcends their bodily needs by undergoing physical pain and privation.

In Christianity, the sacredness that is achieved through physical suffering, and ultimately through death, is symbolised in the torture and crucifixion of Jesus and its re-enactment during Easter festivals across the Christian world. The Christian tradition is also replete with saints and martyrs who underwent torture, privation and self-sacrifice in order to atone for their sins and enter a state of grace (Favazza, 1996; Synott, 1993). The historic Christian practice of self-flagellation is used not only to atone for the flagellator's individual sins but also to gain redemption for the sins of the wider community, or even the whole of humanity. And even in secular culture, we show great admiration for people who subject their bodies to punishing regimes, including sports and fitness training or extreme diet/make-over routines. People who overcome the needs and impulses of their body are admired as exceptionally worthy and heroic.[2] Thus, powerful religious and social discourses equate physical pain and suffering with elevated social status, as well as with individual and collective purification and atonement.

---

2. Professional sports people who become debilitated or disabled at a young age as a result of their high-impact training and lifestyle are also held in high regard. Their permanent injuries and/or disabilities are not considered 'deliberate', 'irrational', 'attention-seeking' or indicative of mental illness, even though this might be an apt description of them – and certainly more so than for those who hurt their bodies in order to survive deep distress and trauma.

Self-injury may equally fulfil these functions: people commonly describe their self-injury as a form of self-punishment and purification and a means of atoning for their 'badness', or getting the 'bad' out of them (Harris, 2000). Likewise, an individual's self-injury may also be an attempt to intervene and redeem badness in another person or context (Babiker & Arnold, 1997), particularly where boundaries and culpability are blurred, as is often the case with sexual abuse.

Joseph identified that, as well as directly alleviating his anxiety, his self-injury also functioned in this more symbolic, punitive way:

> Growing up, I didn't like myself so maybe it was also a form of
> punishment, I don't know. Punishment and control are two words that
> I would associate with what I was going through and what I did, and
> *ownership* as well, I guess.

Colm also described a punitive element to his self-injury, resulting from his internalisation of the shame and hatred from the abuse he experienced:

> I really started kind of pinching myself and like sticking myself with
> compasses and banging my head, and punching myself. And, like, looking
> back at it, I know *now*, it wasn't just low self-esteem, it was self-hatred.

An embodied approach to the functions of self-injury highlights the meaning and purpose of body wounds and their similarities with a whole range of belief systems and practices. This view of the functions of self-injury also clarifies why certain responses are unhelpful and counterproductive – and in many cases exacerbate the underlying feelings and beliefs of the person who is hurting themself. For example, if someone's self-injury functions as a form of punishment because they feel bad or wrong in some way, then a punitive response will only increase those feelings and lead to more self-injury. Amanda's experiences in a psychiatric hospital illustrate this. For Amanda the feelings associated with self-injury were primarily self-blame and punishment:

> When those feelings [to self-injure] come up it's usually about pulling me
> up about that I made a mistake in my day, and it will become [huge]. My
> mind will try and add to that and make that *worse* and more intense and
> give myself a hard time.

However, despite her self-injury being connected with feeling bad or wrong, Amanda was hospitalised in a system where self-injury was also regarded as 'bad' behaviour and punished:

> It makes out that you're *wrong* in some way and that you need to be punished for it… It was like you had committed a *crime* and you were made to feel *wrong* doing it.

Clearly this kind of environment would not have a positive impact on Amanda's wellbeing, and it increased the negative feelings at the root of her self-injury. She described how 'I was actually locked up for six months in [name] hospital… In those six months I had learnt really negative ways of dealing with my emotions'. Nonetheless punitive responses to self-injury are commonplace:

> Women who self-harm are expressing such deep pain that punishment seems absurd and inappropriate. Too often, both correctional and mental health staff are concerned that women will self-harm again if not punished […] This is faulty thinking that needs to be eradicated. Punitiveness and feelings of guilt are what often led to this behaviour, and more punitiveness […] is not going to reverse it or establish a climate to address the dynamics and pain that self-harm is indicating. (Lord, 2008: 933)

It is essential, therefore, that any response to self-injury does not reinforce the underlying feelings and experiences and thereby produce further distress and injury. Thus, understanding the functions of self-injury for each individual provides insight into not only the issues that self-injury is addressing but also how to respond helpfully. However, it is also essential to recognise that the functions of self-injury vary from person to person, as well as for each person over time. These functions may sometimes completely contradict one another, as the example below illustrates.

Pain, presence and reality

Inflicting pain and injury to the body has also been integral to sacred practices in indigenous spiritual belief systems, which tend to be more body positive and less hierarchical and patriarchal. In these cultures, pain and injury function not as a form of punishment but as means of spiritual advancement or evidence of the individual's ability to undergo feats of endurance. Some rituals require the individual to go through an extended period of pain in order to leave the earthly realm and enter the domain of the spirits, from where they will eventually return with deep wisdom and insight (Favazza, 1996). These effects can be understood in both symbolic and direct physical terms: extended periods of physical pain and/or injury cause the body to release endorphins (natural painkillers), which can induce an altered state. Self-injury can function in exactly the same ways: the pain of the injuries and their physiological effects can provide immediate relief or escape from an unbearable reality. This was true for Colm, who, as a child, had no control over the physical, emotional and sexual abuse he endured but discovered that, by causing pain to himself, he could achieve some relief from his circumstances. He described his injuries as 'a form of escapism':

> I used them [injuries] to distract me from my life, and distract me from what was going on. Like when I'd cause myself *pain* I'd be focused on the pain of my *body* and how disturbing and distressing it was, and that was an escape into that moment.

For Colm, causing pain to his body provided respite from unbearable circumstances. However, people's relationship with pain and self-injury varies widely. An individual may or may not perceive pain at the time that they hurt themself and it may or may not be important to them (Chandler, 2013). Thus, for some people injuring the body may have the completely opposite effect: drawing them back into their body and the reality around them, rather than providing an escape from it.

> Some people cope with their uncontrollable stress response by disassociating [ie. leaving the body/reality], and harm themselves in order to disassociate [ie. to leave their body] [...] Paradoxically other people self-harm in order to end a period of disassociation, using the pain and physicality of injuring themselves to bring their awareness back to their body. (Cameron, 2007: 83)

If an individual feels numb, disassociated or disconnected from reality or their body – which is a common response to trauma – causing pain to their body can help to make them feel alive and real again. These injuries can ground people in their bodies and their immediate reality (Babiker & Arnold, 1997; Cameron, 2007; Chandler, 2013; Gallup, 2002). Some people describe this process as a way of rejoining themselves:

> Like being detached from your own feelings as if you are looking at someone else hurting rather than it being yourself. Cutting is a way of bringing the two together or to feel some pain even if it is mainly physical, with the physical pain comes emotional pain so you do end up feeling on both levels which to some extent is better than not feeling. (In Horne & Csipke, 2009: 659-660)

> Sometimes it's just frustration that I just can't feel something solid, that everything's sort of jumbled, so that's [self-injury] the only solid thing that I can sometimes feel. (In Chandler, 2013: 725)

Injuries, then, function in direct and yet often contradictory ways. Thus, a meaningful response entails supporting an individual to explore the ways in which their self-injury functions for them. In doing so, it is important to remember that injuries have both direct and symbolic functions: self-injury 'provides temporary relief from a host of painful symptoms such as anxiety, depersonalization and desperation [...] It also touches upon the very profound human experiences of salvation, healing and orderliness' (Favazza, 1996: xix). These symbolic functions are also present in the rituals of many indigenous cultures, which illuminates the social and political dimensions of self-injury.

Social and political functions

In order to explore social and political functions of self-injury, it is important to understand that many life experiences are 'political', in that they are connected to social structures. The sociologist C Wright Mills (1959) argued that what are often experienced as 'private troubles', such as unemployment, are actually 'public issues' related to wider economic and social structures. Likewise, vulnerability to distress and self-injury is as much a public (ie. political) issue as a private trouble: 'Mental health in general, and self-injury in particular, are political as well as personal issues. Self-injury is inextricably related to the social conditions within which it occurs' (Babiker & Arnold, 1997: 56). This is explored further in Chapter 4 in relation to social structures and minority stress. Here, it is enough to note that social structures have a powerful impact on wellbeing as well as influencing which bodily practices are considered acceptable and which are considered pathological.

Warrior marks: survival and endurance

In many traditional cultural practices, ritual bodily injuries that cause permanent scars have important social functions. Symbolic wounds that are created through ritual tattooing or scarification indicate an individual's strength and capacity to fulfil their role and function within that society (Brain, 1979; Rubin, 1988). For example, in Maori culture, when young men reach the age and the requisite knowledge to fulfil an adult male role in their society, they undergo a process of facial tattooing. The tattoo, called a Moko, covers the full face and is unique to each man, with the designs following the specific contours of his face (Brain, 1979). The Moko is inscribed by hand, using ink and a special chisel, and it creates a tactile as well as visual effect (see Gathercole, 1988 for more detail). Obviously, to have one's whole face tattooed with a chisel takes a long time and requires a huge amount of physical, emotional and psychological strength. Thus, these ritualised warrior marks[3] quite literally embody the individual's strength, capacities and social status – both during the process of inscription as well as in their symbolic representation.

Self-injury can function in very similar ways: these 'warrior marks' can provide evidence that the person is a survivor who is able to overcome the most challenging circumstances in order to continue with their life. This was true for Joseph, who described how the welts on his body after he had cut himself held special significance: 'It was like you had come through a battle and there were the scars to prove it.' Others report that, 'I was very proud of my scars, they were like battle-scars – proof of what I had been through' (in Babiker & Arnold, 1997: 79).

In 'western' cultures, however, we regard body marks as negative and indications of sickness, deviance or social alienation, rather than powerful symbols of endurance, social integration and the desire to survive. Nonetheless, understanding injuries and the scars they leave behind as warrior marks is crucial to a deeper understanding of self-injury, as well as helpful and unhelpful responses. For example, if, as a result of their injuries, a person is placed in a situation (hospital, care unit etc) where self-injury is a very common but also stigmatised experience, it can have the effect of minimising and normalising

---

3. Alice Walker and Pratibha Parmer (1993) used the term 'warrior marks' to refer to female genital mutilation. In Alice Walker's novel *Possessing the Secret of Joy* (1992), the protagonist, Tashi, voluntarily undergoes female genital mutilation at a much older age than is customary in her culture, despite the excruciating pain of the ritual and the resulting sexual dysfunction. For Tashi, this symbolises her commitment to her culture and irrevocably marks her allegiance to it.

injuries that have been a unique and powerful articulation of the individual's experience (see below). Likewise, a well-meaning response to an injury, along the lines of, 'Don't worry, that will heal up soon, and you'll never know it was there,' can have invalidating effects. If that wound is the embodiment of the horror that someone has endured and their attempt to 'do battle' with it and overcome it, then these kinds of responses are counterproductive. In both instances, there is a suggestion that more severe injuries might perhaps be recognised as having greater validity. These contexts convey very confusing messages about self-injury, with potentially devastating consequences. For Elaine, mixed messages about self-injury, coupled with the social isolation of life in an adolescent unit, had disastrous consequences, and her injuries escalated very quickly from scratches to wounds that required stitches, and then skin grafts: 'In a period of three years you can go from very minor to very severe.'

> There were times when, you know, I would just feel really, really awful
> if the scar was really small because at the time self-harm is a form of
> communication about something. It's about something that you can't
> express in any other way and when it's *gone* or it's really *small*, it's not right,
> you know.

The culture of the unit reinforced the meaning and purpose of Elaine's wounds:

> I had all kinds of sets of rules: it was only self-harm if it was over 10
> stitches. I upped it, and I upped it, and I upped it. It was only self-harm if I
> was stitched, or it was only self-harm, you know, to the point where at the
> *end* it was only self-harm, it only mattered, it was only *worthy*, it was only
> important if it was *big* injury, or, you know, a *small* scar that didn't require
> a skin graft wasn't good enough.

Elaine's experiences illustrate the devastating impacts of minimising self-injury and failing to recognise its meaning and purpose (see also Crouch & Wright, 2004). Therefore, it is essential that, while self-injury is understood as a coping mechanism, it is not 'normalised' to the extent that the significance of the underlying distress is ignored. Normalisation of self-injury in an unhealthy/ minimising way may also be an indication that staff in such services are unsupported, desensitised and vulnerable to burnout.

Control and self-identity

In many indigenous cultures, body marks and the accompanying pain and injury have important social symbolism and status – indeed, they have been considered 'marks of civilisation' that demonstrate the human capacity for culture, a capacity that, many argue, is what distinguishes us as unique among other animals (Rubin, 1988). However, in 'western' cultures, body marks are associated with low social status, deviance, criminality and 'madness'. Historically, both criminology and psychiatry have defined all body marks – be they tattoos or the wounds of self-injury – as indicators of mental illness and/ or criminal tendencies (Shrader, 2000). Body marks were also associated with 'primitive' cultures and the 'lower' social classes and used to designate those who did not have full human rights or status. For example, enslaved people were branded to mark them as the property of the person who held them in captivity. In more recent history, during the Holocaust, concentration camp prisoners were tattooed with a number. Today tattoos have become less stigmatised (depending on the type and extent of the tattoos and the gender, social class and occupation of the tattooed person), but the legacy of associating both badness and madness with marked or scarred bodies remains strong. Thus, the 'good' body is pristine and unmarked, while scars remain a common defining feature of the 'bad guys' in Hollywood movies (Parker, 2000). Therefore marked bodies are still viewed as 'deviant', undesirable and something to be avoided.

However, where people already occupy stigmatised status or are marginalised and excluded, the body is often the only site where a person can exercise power and control. Here, body marks can function to reclaim control over the body or to subvert the meaning of a stigmatised identity. This is true in criminal gangs, where tattoos signify status, and in prisons, where homemade tattoos are common (Schrader, 2000). Another example is the 'borstal spot', which took the form of a homemade tattoo beauty spot worn just below the left eye by young women who had been in local authority care or the youth offender system (Inckle, 2007). Therefore, marks that once derogated an individual's status can be reclaimed and invested with new meaning as the individual attempts to take back some power and control over their identity.

Self-injury can function in exactly the same way: it can be a means by which an individual re-stakes their control over their body and their pathologised identity. This is particularly common where people have been stripped of their own sense of their identity and autonomy (such as in prison, hospital or local authority care), or where their boundaries have been violated and their body treated as the property of others (common experiences for people with disabilities). Here, self-injury can be a means of reclaiming the body and self-identity. For Clare it was a means to 'try and impact *somehow* on circumstances in a setting where your power is absolutely minimal', while others report that 'I scar myself as a sign that it's *my* body' (in Babiker & Arnold, 1997: 77).

Reclaiming and control can have immediate material functions as well as effects at emotional, psychological and symbolic levels. For Joseph, 'control' and 'ownership' were important elements of his self-injury:

> The ownership of something that it *would* give me, that it was mine...
> Control also came into it, and control doesn't have to be about attention
> [ie. controlling others], it can be about your own self-possession.

Joseph's injuries thus had a positive, reclaiming function and also, simultaneously, impacted negatively on his self-identity: 'They were *mine*, even though at the same time I felt like a *freak*.'

Control is particularly significant for those who have little power, choice or autonomy in their lives (this is discussed further in Chapter 3), as highlighted by young people in Helen Spandler's research: 'I think control's a big thing, when you can't control what's happening around you [...] you can't control pressure from the outside, from society, but you can to yourself' (1996: 32). Likewise, people with intellectual disabilities often highlight lack of choice and control as integral to their self-injury: 'Sometimes I just want to be on my own and I can't get on my own' (in Heslop & Macaulay, 2009: 39).

For Rachel and Emma, the control and ownership functions of their self-injury operated at a more psychological and symbolic level. Rachel grew up in an environment with no boundaries around her space and privacy. She described an 'invasive' and 'absolute' regime where her parents' ethos was, 'You *belong* to us.' The emotional and psychological consequences were such that self-injury became the only 'thing that was *mine*'. When she cut herself, Rachel took control of her body and her feelings:

> The point of me cutting myself is for me to take control of *my* body, and
> to have something that no one else had anything to do with, that was *mine*
> that I kept in a *neat package*, that kept everything, all of my problems
> safely away from other people, so that I didn't have to talk to anyone or
> *share*. I didn't *want* to tell anyone, because I didn't trust anyone.

For Emma, the control element of her self-injury was a complex psychological and symbolic response to a series of devastating life experiences throughout her early years. In an unsafe world where she was continually hurt and betrayed, her self-injury became her only means of redress and control:

> I felt like the easiest thing to do would be to try and not care and so
> I would cut myself to show myself that I didn't care, to express my
> frustration with myself for feeling all the things I felt, and to try and take
> some control back over my life.

When self-injury is an act of control or reclaiming self-possession, any response that aims to prevent the self-injury is counterproductive. Attempting to remove the last means of self-control a person has will only intensify their need for it. Likewise, an environment where an individual's needs and experiences – as well as their self-injury – are ignored or invalidated only exacerbates its reclaiming functions. Unfortunately this is a common response in hospitals, prisons and local authority care, where individuals who have already endured many traumatic and invalidating events experience further erosions to their autonomy and identity. This is illustrated by Clare's experience as a psychiatric inpatient:

> Some hospitals take away *absolutely everything* that people have, but they
> *still find a way to self-harm*. And it's not rocket science to see why you
> would do that worse as a result of having *every* bit of individuality and
> autonomy and everything taken away from you.

Responding to an individual's attempt to maintain control by imposing tighter regimes of control on them only creates a destructive cycle. It produces more harm and does nothing to address the underlying causes of the distress and self-injury. The impulse to control is particularly strong – and counterproductive – where young people are concerned, and this is evident in the general pathologisation of young people (see Chapter 1), as well as in specific responses to self-injury. One service-provider noted that:

> It often feels like people don't take children's and young people's distress
> seriously, you know; they kind of focus on their behaviour, not what might
> be hurting them *inside*. But the other thing is that it is even harder for
> people to accept that, with children and young people, however much you

might *want* to, you *cannot* control everything they do, and you *can't* base an approach to helping a young person on preventing every single possible incident of self-harm. You've got to base it on trying to help them with their distress.

Finally, understanding the control and reclaiming functions of self-injury also highlights why it is essential that self-injury elicits a *response* rather than a *reaction*. A reaction is fast, impulsive, panicked and counterproductive, because it is based on crisis feelings rather than a deep understanding of the individual and their needs. A response, in contrast, is slower; it is thought out and based on consideration of the multiple aspects of the injury. Very often the most helpful *response* is the opposite of an immediate *reaction*. This is particularly true of the desire to control: when self-injury functions as a form of control, it is *less* external control that is required, not more – no matter how challenging this may be.[4]

Youth cultures, 'contagion' and 'learned behaviour'

The impulse to control young people is particularly evident in beliefs that young people are unduly susceptible to negative peer influence and peer group cultures. Indeed, this often creates anxiety about peer support groups for people who hurt themselves, because of misplaced concerns that they will just teach each other increasingly severe and devious ways to self-injure. Yet, as we will see in Chapters 5 and 6, peer support can be one of the most effective resources for people who hurt themselves, and it is usually in mainstream, prevention-based services that self-injury worsens.

The anxiety around peer influence is evident in 'moral panics' (Cohen, 1972) about youth cultures and their supposed propensity to encourage self-injury. Historically, this anxiety has been attached to punks, followed by Goths and currently Emos. And, while the practices of these subcultures may indeed share some of the functions of self-injury, in that they use visible and sometimes painful body practices to create a specific identity that marks out the individual as different or at odds with mainstream society (and which certainly constitute self-harm), this is not the same as self-injury. Furthermore, the sense of 'being different' embodied in subcultural imagery and practices may well result from difficult life experiences or from feeling particularly sensitive to, or at odds

---

4. Control is not the same as boundaries. We all need clear boundaries that are upheld and respected, but few of us benefit from enforced control by others.

with, the wider world. Indeed, the term Emo stands for 'emotionally open' or 'emotionally unstable' and Emos often describe themselves as feeling things more deeply than others.[5]

Youth cultures also reflect that, as social beings, humans tend to group together with others who share similar world views, life experiences and feelings. Therefore, people who feel that they are different in some way will identify with one another and often make that difference visible – not unlike people who wear the shirt or jersey of the sports team they support, spend time with others who support the same team and wear its shirt, and, indeed, often engage in risky and dangerous behaviour (such as binge-drinking) while doing so. It is therefore essential that, rather than a youth subculture or group being viewed as the reason for self-injury, there is deeper consideration of the experiences and feelings that have brought the group together. One service-provider emphasised that young people self-injure for exactly the same reasons as adults, rather than simply succumbing to peer pressure. 'They self-harm because they are in emotional pain, and because they feel like they can't cope with something – something in their lives, or something in their feelings.'

Furthermore, despite the fact that we live in the age of mass communication, self-injury (and the related underlying trauma or distress) is often experienced in secret and isolation. As such, finding others with similar experiences can be a powerful relief. When Rachel ran away from home at the age of 17, she became flatmates with a young woman who also self-injured. 'I moved in with this girl and *she* did it… I went, "Ok, it's *not just me*". Prior to this, Rachel was unaware that what she was doing had a name or that others did it too:

> When I started doing it I *didn't know* what it was. It was like scissors, it was scissors, I can remember the first time I did it was scissors on my window ledge... I just picked up this pair of scissors and I honestly didn't know what it was... I didn't know anything about it. So it [the label self-injury] wasn't really relevant; it was about *me*, I was in my room and it was nobody's business.

Mark, who had been hurting himself in different ways throughout his childhood, adolescence and into adulthood, described how it was only in his adult life that he identified his coping behaviours as self-injury and began to access information about it:

---

5. See Chernoff & Widdecombe, 2015 for an outline of Emo culture.

> I mean the fact that I hurt myself, *never* throughout my life, until probably
> that significant episode, that time of my life, I never knew what the word
> self-injury was or self-harm, *never*. I *never* knew. At that stage of my life
> this stuff was just going on, and I can't remember *how* but I looked it up
> and I read about it. And I found out it was all these different things and
> I was bowled over by finding self-injury, self-harm, is this, if you do self-
> harm, blah, blah, blah.

Even today, people can live in chronic isolation with their self-injury, with
research indicating that two-thirds of people who self-injure believe it is
unique to them (Hodgson, 2004).[6] Moreover, as is evident from the experiences
contained in this book, it is not uncommon for children as young as three
or four to hurt themselves (see also LifeSIGNS, 2004; Spandler, 1996), and
obviously this cannot be simply attributed to peer pressure or internet sites.
Many people who hurt themselves do not label what they are doing as self-
injury or identify with others who self-injure. Mark felt that the labels of self-
injury (or self-harm) did not fit his own experience and they affected him in a
number of ways:

> Depending on the day and how I was feeling at the time, [it] would have
> a different sequence of impact on it. Stuff like being linked to things like
> borderline personality disorder was always scary.

There is, then, a frequent mismatch between assumptions about self-injury
and individuals' experience of it: isolation and confusion around self-injury
are much more commonly people's experiences than peer-pressure, 'contagion'
and 'learned behaviour'.[7]

From this perspective, a group of people with the experience of self-injury
clustering together could be viewed as a 'natural' and potentially supportive
social process rather than a deviant aberration. Groups and youth cultures that
allegedly 'promote' self-injury should not be judged by surface appearances.
Such groups could, rather, be viewed as potentially indicating the presence of
deeper underlying issues, their members' sense of difference or isolation from
the rest of the world, and their need for connection with others with similar

---

6. While some aspects of the research findings in Hodgson's report are useful, much of the analysis tends to
be uncritical and to reinforce the beliefs and stereotypes that I challenge throughout this book.

7. This mismatch between the labels about self-injury and individuals' experience of it was a frequent
theme in my research and is explored in the story 'normal' in *Flesh Wounds* (Inckle, 2010b).

experiences. Simplistic judgments only fuel unhelpful stereotypes and do nothing to promote understanding of self-injury or the underlying distress. This is illustrated in the response to the publication of a Canadian study (Lewis et al, 2011) in which young people gave high ratings to YouTube posts depicting self-injury. The media interpreted this as the glorification of self-injury that young people mindlessly copied. However, the report was actually careful to state that the clips were rated positively *not* because the young people learned a new behaviour to copy but because the videos broke through some of the isolation and freakishness many felt about their self-injury.

Nonetheless, challenging these common assumptions about 'group culture' and 'learned behaviour' is not to dismiss that sometimes people do learn coping mechanisms from each other sooner than they might have otherwise discovered them. This may occur where people in distress are artificially grouped together in settings such as psychiatric hospitals or local authority care facilities. These settings often exacerbate distress by placing individuals in close contact with others with significant and possibly more challenging difficulties. As Clare points out:

> I've never understood the whole sort of psychiatric set up of putting
> distressed and anxious people into a ward full of distressed and anxious
> people. It just doesn't seem right! You know, imagine if you yourself
> are feeling down or anxious, saying, 'Oh well, I will just put myself in a
> situation where I'm completely surrounded by incredibly distressed and
> anxious people!' Of course you wouldn't do it – it's completely counter-
> intuitive. It makes you feel worse. I have often thought there is no logic to
> it! (Shaw & Hogg, 2004: 174–175)

In these (or other) situations, people may well discover self-injury as a means of coping. One service-provider explained: 'It [self-injury] does work if people have the underlying pain and distress.' She described how people may come across self-injury 'in some form... and they've thought, "Oh I wonder would that help?" You know, and for some people that do it, it doesn't help, so they stop, but for an awful lot of people it *does* help.'

It is possible, then, that people may discover coping mechanisms such as self-injury through contact with other people. However, that is not to imply that people simply copy behaviours without a significant underlying reason for doing so. People will only self-injure if it functions for them, which indicates a pre-existing distress that self-injury alleviates. After all, if hurting one's own body feels *better*, then clearly there is significant pre-existing pain. Moreover, none of the people who have attended any of the training and courses I run, or who have read any of my work, have reported that they have begun self-injuring as a result of learning more about it. Likewise, if I instructed that, having read this chapter, readers should send me all their money and then gouge out their eyes, I don't expect that anyone would do so. People who hurt themselves need to be respected as having the same discernment and intelligence as anyone else, and not viewed as likely to irrationally mimic harmful practices for no other reason than someone else has done it. Finally, if there *are* such risks of learned behaviour, it makes little sense to confine people who are self-injuring – or, indeed, suicidal or homicidal – in close quarters in one institution. At the very least, this violates a basic duty of care.

Injustice and protest

Thinking critically about notions such as 'learned behaviour' also highlights the importance of critical reflection about the context in which people hurt themselves. This awareness should extend to formative and current environments as well as where people are placed as a result of their self-injury (or other issues). The context that people are in has an intricate relationship with their self-injury, both in terms of the original causes of the distress and in either compounding or alleviating those experiences (see Chapter 4). For example, in situations where people experience profound and ongoing injustice without recourse to redress, their own bodies are often their last resort of protest and resistance. This is evident in the use of hunger strikes throughout the history of political struggles, including in Northern Ireland and India. More recently, in 2002, hunger strikes were used to protest about the inhumane conditions by asylum-seekers held in the Woomera detention camp in Australia. A number of detainees also sewed up their lips, eyes and ears in a symbolic protest against the ways in which their rights and humanity were denied by the detention camp and asylum application procedure (Groves, 2004). (The camp was closed in 2003.)

Self-injury can function in similar ways. When both the immediate context and/or the broader social environment are unjust or create a sense of confinement (physical, psychological or symbolic), then wounds and injuries can function as a protest. Gender roles are often particularly significant here, and a number of writers have explored the ways in which women and girls use the bodily pain and privation of self-injury (Babiker & Arnold, 1997; Frost, 2000) and eating disorders (Bordo, 1993; Orbach, 1986) as a means to protest against the confines of traditional femininity. Susie Orbach (1986) explicitly refers to anorexia as a 'hunger strike', and direct bodily pain and damage can speak powerfully against structures of oppression: 'In injuring her own body, a woman spoils the thing that society both values and despises' (Babiker & Arnold, 1997: 40).

Bodily protest is a powerful human resource against injustice and inequality at social-political levels as well as at more intimate, individual levels. Mary, who grew up in a 'small town' culture, described how the authority figures in her young life colluded to scare and isolate her because of her self-injury. 'I was told that, at 13, "You can't go to school here while you do that".' Mary's GP informed her (incorrectly): 'That's GBH [grievous bodily harm] and that's illegal, even to yourself, so stop or you'll be arrested.' She described how: 'My father also got a *gard* [police officer] to say it to me one day when he was at the house.' However, these authoritarian responses only strengthened Mary's resistance and reinforced the functions of her self-injury: 'It had the complete opposite effect of course!'[8]

Emotional and interpersonal functions

Emotional functions

One of the more commonly recognised functions of self-injury is its role in regulating and expressing emotions. This is often framed in terms of providing relief or release of overwhelming or unmanageable feelings (Babiker & Arnold, 1997; Chandler, 2012; Spandler, 1996; Spandler & Warner, 2007). Both Colm and Rachel spoke explicitly about emotional release. Colm described how his self-injury 'started as emotional pain' from which hurting his body provided an 'escape'. For Rachel, self-injury was her means to release feelings for which she had no other outlet: 'For me cutting myself is when I have wound myself up so tight that I can't – that I *have to* release it.' In Helen Spandler's research, young people also spoke about the ways in which hurting themselves provided release and escape from their feelings: 'It's like a release. It feels better after I've taken tablets and I feel better after I have cut myself to pieces' (1996: 27); 'Cutting myself kind of creates a haven. I don't think about what else has gone on' (1996: 28). Physical pain has an important survival function in that it dominates our consciousness, demanding all of our attention and temporarily extinguishing all other thoughts or feelings. Thus, the pain of self-injury can provide immediate

---

8. This is taken from a personal communication that Mary gave consent for me to use in my work, rather than from a research interview.

mental and/or emotional relief in quite straightforward ways. (It is, however, important to note that not everyone feels the pain when they hurt themself.)

Needing to find relief from overwhelming emotions also has cultural significance. For example, avoidance of overt emotional expression is integral to many 'western' cultures that favour rational, dispassionate ways of being. Overt displays of feeling (other than at major sports or life events or, indeed, when drunk) are regarded with suspicion. We are expected to hide our feelings, not to have major fluctuations in them (especially not visible ones), and to avoid being influenced by them.[9]

In some cultures around the world, however, the opposite is true. Here, emotions and intense emotional experiences are much more accepted and integrated into the norms and practices of the social group. These cultures recognise the life-changing effects of experiences such as bereavement, and do not expect people to promptly 'get over it', 'get back to normal', or 'put on a brave face'. Instead, these emotions are embodied and ritualised. In India, for example, 'by beating and tearing at their own bodies, female mourners displace emotional pain onto their physical selves and transform their bodies into ongoing testimonies of loss' (Mallot, 2006: 170). In other cultures, significant emotional experiences are permanently inscribed on the body during ritual practices. Thus, life-changing events become visibly embodied so that everyone in that society can recognise and respond to an individual's experiences in accordance with their customs and traditions. For example, in the Chimbu Province of New Guinea, women who experience the death of a male relative amputate a finger joint in mourning and permanent recognition of their loss (Brain, 1979; Favazza, 1996).[10] The amputated finger joint means that it is not possible for a woman's loss and grief to be ignored or hidden, and it is recognised and responded to by all members of her society. Indeed, it is not uncommon for bereavement to be experienced as a physical sensation, as if some part of the self is missing. As such, marking the loss on the body articulates the experience in a way that both reflects the emotional intensity of it and simultaneously invites social recognition and support.

Self-injury functions in similar ways and is also commonly associated with grief and loss (Chapter 3). Self-injury may also be a means to permanently express feelings and experiences that have been minimised, invalidated or

9. Jack Barbalett has pointed out that the dichotomy between reason and emotion is an oxymoron since 'without appropriate underpinning emotions, reason soon turns into its opposite' (in Inckle, 2007: 86).

10. Embodied mourning practices tend to be gendered – ie. enacted on female bodies (Mallot, 2006).

ignored. People often describe their wounds as visible markers of something unseen: 'It is something I can look at. Somehow it makes the pain I feel inside real and important' (in Babiker & Arnold, 1997: 79). Rachel described her scars as permanent mementos of events that have shaped her into the person she is today:

> There are a few of them that I look at and like, [remembering] '*That* was that,' and '*That* was that,' and you know, and my memory is shit so it's almost like this catalogue that to me has this purpose, and in a way it fascinates me, and you know, it reminds me of things that have happened, and have happened and I'm a better person for it.

Likewise, Monique (in Strong, 2000: 201) described how 'seeing each scar was like a marking of what I went through at the time [...] I could point out each one and remember what happened'. The relationship between emotional experiences and the wounds that express them is both literal and symbolic. In literal terms, human beings experience emotions through physical sensations in the body (which we later learn to name and interpret through language). In symbolic terms, wounds, injuries and permanent scars may give voice to deep but invisible emotional hurt and loss. In many cultures these functions are recognised in social norms and practices that powerfully integrate an individual and their traumatic experiences within the cultural milieu. In 'western' societies, this process is seen in memorial tattoos, which are one of the most common designs requested of tattooists (Benson, 2000). Here, rather like the amputated finger joint, the tattoo literally inscribes the lost person onto the body of the mourner, creating both a physical and symbolic memento that is read and responded to by those around them (see also Davidson, 2017).

Understanding the physicality of emotions and their physical expression and management through self-injury is essential to responding helpfully. Similarly, exploring the feelings behind the physical injuries, rather than focusing on the injuries themselves, is absolutely essential in providing meaningful support. It is also important to recognise that an injury can have more than one function and may operate simultaneously at both the direct and symbolic levels. For example, Heslop and Macaulay (2009) found that self-injury often made people feel better and worse at the same time.

Comfort

Another apparent paradox of self-injury is that physical wounds and injuries can provide a source of comfort and self-soothing (Gallup, 2002; Harris, 2000). And while, at first glance, taking comfort from pain may seem counter-intuitive, it is also integral to our cultural beliefs about healing, medicine and beauty practices. If a treatment is invasive, painful or has uncomfortable side-effects, then people often rate its outcomes more highly than those that do not. Moreover, finding comfort in pain may also reflect the quality of early formative relationships: if emotional formation takes place in contexts where security and care are experienced simultaneously with hurt and pain (such as neglect or abuse), then it is likely that an individual's relationship with themself will reflect this. During her time in an adolescent unit, Elaine's self-injury both communicated her need for love and also allowed her to access the only form of care available to her:

> Self-harm is really a form of communication. I mean I'm *not* saying that people do it to *get* attention, but when you're in that environment, you know, quite often the only time that anyone has got time for you is when you need a bandage. And, quite often, for me, the only time I got care was when I was having my [part of body] stitched up. So that, you know, *care* came for me, as someone without a family, in the form of a nurse *having* to give me *medical* care. And that was the closest I got to, to I guess what felt like parental care.

Rachel described her self-injury as 'a pet' that provided her with love, comfort and safety:

> It used to be like a *pet*, do you know what I mean? It used to be this thing that I had that was mine that no one else knew about and that I trusted and confided in. 'Cos I really, really didn't, and still don't, really, trust people with my feelings a lot of the time… and it used to be like this little creature that I kept with me that comforted me. And now I feel almost like it's a creature that comes in every now and again when I need comforting.

The functions of self-injury, then, like the appropriate responses to it, may seem counter-intuitive, but are no less significant for being so.

The body: physical, symbolic and social

If, as a culture, we struggle with emotions, then we fare even worse when it comes to our bodies and body literacy. This chapter has already illustrated how the body is deemed problematic in most of the major world religions: the site of sin, sexuality and the failings and weaknesses of human beings, which must be transcended through privation or death. But negative ideas about the body are not confined to spiritual belief systems; they also permeate 'western' philosophy, science and medicine. Here the body is seen in mechanistic terms as an inanimate object that is subordinate to and powered by superior mental processes (Lupton, 2003). More importantly, the body is also framed as a flawed object, particularly in its (unavoidable) variability, mortality and vulnerability. As such, humans are positioned as dependent on science to improve and control our bodies and eradicate natural variations and the effects of natural processes, such as ageing.

This general alienation from, and disparagement of, our bodies is compounded by experiences that further stigmatise or problematise the body. These may be experiences such as sexual abuse, which often leaves survivors feeling dirty, ashamed or somehow culpable. Or they may be experiences that are connected with social inequalities (which are discussed in more detail in Chapter 4), such as racism, homophobia or disablism, which target an individual because of their perceived physical difference.

The impact of body-negating experiences relates directly to the functions of self-injury in that, if we don't like something or if we see it as responsible for something terrible or shameful, then it is very easy to hurt it and treat it badly (see Chapter 1). Body-hatred was significant for Colm, who became alienated from his body because of the chronic physical, emotional and sexual abuse he experienced:

> I started really kind of just, just being very ashamed of my body, and
> like starting to, like even as a *small child* of maybe eight or nine or ten, I
> starting pinching myself and getting very ashamed, and very shy and not
> wanting to be *touched* or whatever.

Self-injury, then, can directly reflect an individual's experience of the world and their place in it. Once again, this highlights how essential it is that the response to an injury does not reinforce any of these underlying issues, such as by shaming. Any response needs to be grounded in awareness of the impacts of negative and punitive reactions and must never replicate them.

A language of the body: communication

Understanding embodiment is key to understanding the communication functions of self-injury, whether as a purely private articulation for the individual themself, or as a means of attempting to communicate and express something to others. Physical communication is especially significant when people have feelings or experiences that are beyond words or, indeed, when someone does not or cannot use language/verbal communication (Mallot, 2006). Here, 'the act of wounding oneself *embodies* – literally – an implicit connotation of something unbearable, unutterable, that is communicated in this act' (Babiker & Arnold, 1997: 1). Amanda described her self-injury in precisely this way:

> I just *couldn't* talk, and I couldn't express what was going on… It [self-injury] was like trying to express what was going on, I didn't know how to word it, but I could put it into physical words.

Clare also spoke about her self-injury in terms of communication, where it functioned as a physical metaphor for what could not be spoken:

> It's such an articulate metaphor, self-harm, that's the sort of power of it. When I look back at *what* I was trying to do, I was trying to communicate *intense distress*, that I felt I just didn't, that first of all I didn't have the *vocabulary* to put into words, and I didn't have the sort of *entitlement* to put into words.

The point that Clare emphasises about not being *entitled* to speak is particularly significant. Many people who hurt themselves have survived traumatic and stigmatising experiences; experiences where, although they are the ones who have been hurt, it is they who are seen to be diminished, rather than the person who hurt them. This may be the case when someone is harmed in a (presumed respectable) middle-class household (Babiker & Arnold, 1997), or a disabled person is hurt by their (presumed saintly) carer (Wendell, 1996). It can also be the case where people have been hurt by members of the medical profession (Morris, 1996) or the clergy (Ryan, 2009). Indeed, just 20 or 30 years ago the possibility of sexual abuse by clergymen or other esteemed figures was quite literally unspeakable, and those who spoke out were often silenced or punished. The need to express such experiences does not just disappear however; rather, it manifests in non-verbal forms. For Clare the unspeakable was articulated 'through *wounds* and *overdoses* and they were incredibly articulate ways of expressing distress, and desire and need for support and comfort'. The language of the body, then, speaks powerfully when words are not possible.

Bodies and injuries are also powerfully symbolic and may communicate much about the meaning and function of the self-injury. This is particularly true when helpers are sensitive to the conscious and unconscious messages conveyed through the type and location of the wound. For example, if someone has experienced sexual abuse, it is not uncommon that they will damage the part of the body that is associated with the abuse, as a form of punishment and an enactment of shame. At the same time, these wounds might also be intended to 'make ugly' the feature that was identified as 'attracting' the abuse, and thereby function as an attempt to repel it (Babiker & Arnold, 1997; Smith, Cox & Saradjian, 1998).

Finally, it is also notable that, while on the one hand we are culturally oblivious to the language of the body or the 'physical words' of self-injury, at the same time, the English language is full references to self-injury: 'I was tearing my hair out;' 'Don't beat yourself up about it;' 'It's like banging your head off a brick wall;' 'It was bleeding me dry;' 'I'd rather stick pins in my eyes.' These expressions hold currency because they reflect the deep, embodied (and often unconscious) level at which we understand that sometimes feelings and situations are so overwhelming that only an externalised physical response can fully express and release them.

Functions and counter-functions: the consequences of coping

Self-injury clearly has a wide range of deep and powerful functions in physical, psychological, emotional, social and symbolic terms. However, while self-injury meets a range of needs, and often provides an individual's primary means of coping and surviving, this does not mean it is problem free. The most obvious concern is the physical risk and damage of the injuries, which in some cases may cause irreversible or fatal harm, and these are explored in Chapter 6 on harm-reduction. However, self-injury may also have social consequences, including marginalisation and stigma (explored in Chapter 4), as well as negative long-term emotional effects. Thus, while functioning as a response to emotional difficulties, self-injury also brings its own emotional challenges and consequences. Therefore, notwithstanding that self-injury is usually the very best resource that a person has in their situation, given the choice of not being in circumstances that make self-injury necessary, most would happily do without it. As one service-provider explained:

> I know *so* many clients who are saying they just, even in the middle of self-injury, they want to do something else. And I'm aware even as I said that, that in some ways implies that those who *don't* are somehow *less than*, I don't mean that. If somebody has a choice of, 'You can self-injure or not,' that's quite different to, 'Would you like to be in a position where you don't *feel* the need or, have to, self-injure?' And I've never known anyone saying, 'Ah no.' It's ways [in an aspirational tone], 'If I didn't feel I *had* to do it.'

Clearly, no one wants to feel so bad that hurting their own body is the only way that they can feel better. Indeed, while self-injury provides some relief or comfort in the moment, many people also described how, in the longer-term, it adds to negative self-feelings and closes down emotional processes. Elaine spoke at length about the more ambivalent emotional impacts of self-injury that she experienced over time:

> Self-harm is shutting off. Whilst it might be a vent for the emotion like while you're cutting your [body] you're not *feeling* the emotion you're suppressing it, it's not dealing with it. It's just pushing it back down, which you don't realise, obviously, at the time when you're doing it.

Elaine experienced self-injury as a means of simultaneously 'dealing with' and 'suppressing' emotions:

> Even though self-harm is visibly expressive in terms of the scar that it creates, the *point* of self-harm is visibly expressing with a scar an experience. The whole point of self-harm is to dumb down, to *stop* feeling. Even though you think at the time that you're expressing it, you're just passing off the emotion, you're not actually getting it out. You're *not* dealing with it, you're turning it into an injury. You're not *dealing* with the emotions. The emotion is still there, you just create a physiological reaction in your body – adrenaline, pain – which effectively cuts off what you feel. You might think the scar's expressing whatever you feel but a scar at the end of the day is only really a scar, because what you actually feel is still there, you just had an injury to distract you from what you feel, otherwise self-harm would be a wonder cure!

Amanda also recognised that, although self-injury provided relief from difficult feelings in the moment, it did not eradicate them over time: 'It was just a temporary relief to a lot of very negative emotions that was going on. But you're still left with the emotions, it just takes you away from it, just temporarily.' Therefore, while self-injury is a powerful intervention in the immediacy of emotional distress, it does not provide emotional resolution in the long term.

The power of self-injury also makes it almost too effective as a way of coping, and the fact that it functions so effectively can also make it increasingly necessary. Elaine described how, 'once it becomes part of your coping mechanism, you might have done it for something severe in the beginning, but then you then do it for all kinds of emotions'. Many service-providers echoed Elaine's experience: 'It replaces not just *one* emotion but eventually it replaces nearly *every emotion*.'

> Once you have sort of *found* something like cutting as a way coping, is that it does it better than anything else... The difficulty is that you have got this kind of, for a time anyway, this *magic* solution, and people say the relief is sort of short lived, but actually it can be more effective than anything else, and I would be quite interested in how that can prevent you from being able to find other things that might be helpful.

Thus, while self-injury can help people to cope and survive in the moment, it can shut down long-term emotional healing processes and move from being an 'emergency' coping mechanism to one with increasing use. Finally, self-injury in itself can reinforce negative self-feelings and isolation, as Mark described:

> I *didn't* tell people. I didn't show it, I didn't *want* anyone to know. I went to *so many* great lengths that nobody knew, and that was through embarrassment and shame. Not just embarrassment and shame because I self-injured, but embarrassment and shame about how I felt about myself *anyway*. And I just thought that this was just another thing that, you know, really, like, makes me worse than others again.

Elaine similarly felt that, while self-injury helped her to survive, it also diminished her:

> Whilst it might have positive implications in that you're *coping* at the time... the way that I would see self-harm, certainly after stopping using it as a coping mechanism, is it kind of takes *away* from you.

In summary, then, these consequences, alongside the risks of self-injury, are characteristic of its complexity and the multifaceted ways it functions as a coping mechanism. Self-injury has both positive and negative impacts in the immediate and long term. For example:

- self-injury enables people to cope and survive, but it also may endanger their life and physical wellbeing
- self-injury provides relief, comfort and control, but in the long term it may also add to negative feelings and isolation
- self-injury enables life to continue, but can impact negatively on the quality of that life.

Overall then, like so much of what makes us human, self-injury is contradictory and complex and there is no easy answer to it. Thus, it requires an equally humane and complex response that is specific to the needs, feelings and experiences of each individual.

• Chapter summary

Self-injury is essentially embodied, and embodiment provides a key to understanding the way in which self-injury functions for each individual. As infants our bodies are the first medium through which we learn to communicate, feel and experience the world around us. Our bodies are also where we experience emotions, intuition, memory, trauma and all of our senses. Our bodies are also full of social meaning and symbolism and are replete with cultural messages and values. Understanding self-injury requires an awareness of the power and complexity of embodiment and the multiple functions, meanings and experiences that are mediated through and stored within our physical selves.

Self-injury is a fundamentally embodied experience: it is physical, emotional, psychological, social and symbolic, and it has meaning, purpose and functions at all of these levels. Therefore, self-injury needs to be responded to in equally multifaceted ways. It is crucial to remember that the meanings and functions of self-injury are always specific to each individual, and they may vary and be contradictory between individuals as well as for the same person over time. For example, self-injury may be a form of self-punishment or a form of self-comfort; it may be about leaving the body and escaping reality, or it might be a way of becoming grounded after a period of disassociation; it might be a form of control or a means of release. These functions can never be simply read off from the type of injury or its perceived severity and, furthermore, one injury may simultaneously have a number of both practical and symbolic functions. As Elaine described it, 'Self-harm is very complicated because it can serve many different functions for the person doing it.'

As such there is no one model that fits all. Nor is an embodied approach going to provide quick answers or instant solutions. It will, however, enable helpers to communicate meaningfully with people who hurt themselves and to work with them to explore the meanings and purposes of their self-injury and the kinds of support they require.

Finally, an embodied approach also highlights that self-injury is, in many ways, a normal part of the range of human behaviour and not an aberration. People who use self-injury as a means to cope with and express their experiences 'are drawing not on some deviant and idiosyncratic idea born of their individual pathology, but on profound traditions of human belief and religious and social practice' (Babiker & Arnold, 1997: 26). However, understanding self-injury in this way is not the same as normalising self-injury to the extent that individuals in distress are ignored. Situations where self-injury is considered 'normal' to the extent that it is not recognised as the embodiment of deep distress are unhealthy and unsafe for everyone.

Learning into practice

Definition	Self-injury has meaning and purpose, it is the embodiment of distress
Working principles	• Self-injury is part of the 'normal' range of human experience • There is no one model that fits all
Practice applications	• Explore the meanings and functions • Body sensitive, body literate

Definition: self-injury has meaning and purpose, it is the embodiment of distress

In self-injury, bodily pain, wounds and injuries express and manage difficult feelings, thoughts and experiences. Bodily damage has both practical and symbolic functions. These functions are unique to each individual, and their meaning and purpose reflect each person's life experiences and needs. Nonetheless, an embodied approach enables an understanding of the range of possible functions in each person's self-injury and the possibilities of engaging with their meaning and purpose.

Working principles

1) Self-injury is part of the 'normal' range of human experience

Self-injury is often framed as an aberration from 'normal', healthy human behaviour. However, self-injury engages with human embodiment and shares many of its functions with acts that have been ritualised throughout human societies. Nonetheless, self-injury is a reflection of distress, and it should not be 'normalised' so that no concern is shown for the person who is hurting themself.

2) There is no one model that fits all

Self-injury is a response to and a reflection of an individual's life context and experiences. As such, self-injury functions in different ways for different people, and it may also have a number of different functions for the same person. Therefore, there is no one model of intervention, diagnostic checklist or formula for understanding that can be applied to everyone. Each person is unique and so are the functions, meaning and purposes of their self-injury. However, the broad themes outlined in this chapter can be used to develop an individualised understanding of each person's self-injury and the support they need. Developing an understanding of the functions of self-injury should be collaborative rather than based on an assumption that the helper is an 'all-knowing expert', with ready-made solutions (see Chapter 5). One service-provider described this approach as follows:

> I deal with *people as individuals,* and I see them as an individual, working with what's going on with them, in their circumstances, in their context, through their history, where they are now… you have to understand the individual. But our education at a broader level should lead us to respond to self-injury with compassion and understanding in a *knowledgeable* way.

Activity

- Make a note of two or three different occasions when you have been helpful to another person in specific, tangible ways. For example, this might have been helping someone in housing need to find accommodation, swapping shifts with a colleague to enable them to deal with a family matter, or practising assertiveness skills with someone who felt very disempowered in their life.

- Now consider the impact of applying your first response to all of the different situations – how would people feel and how effective would it be?

- Reflect on the implications of this for self-injury – people hurt themselves for vastly different reasons and yet it is very often assumed that there is one single effective intervention.

- Finally, think about what made you feel confident about helping the people in the situations that you identified above. What do you need in order to feel equally confident to respond helpfully to people who hurt themselves?

Practice applications

1. Exploring the meanings and functions

Some of the most important work with someone who hurts themself is to explore the meanings and functions of their self-injury. This requires awareness of the range of ways in which self-injury can function and a sensitivity to what the wounds might be expressing. However, as noted above, there is no shortcut or simple model to determine how self-injury is working; this process takes time, patience and sensitivity. Furthermore, since the 'physical words' of self-injury may be the only way someone can articulate their experiences, a breadth of communication tools is essential. These tools can include creative and symbolic forms of expression (see Chapter 5), and it is important that they are grounded in body-awareness (see below).

2. Body sensitive, body literate

Sensitivity to the body is alien to much of 'western' culture and medicine. However, to fully understand self-injury, helpers need to be attuned to their own bodies and the embodied nature of human experience. Bodies and bodily actions communicate in powerful ways, both directly and symbolically. To help someone explore their self-injury in meaningful ways, and to support them as they do so, requires that helpers have a sensitivity to embodied expression and become attuned to what could be described as embodied communication, or body literacy. Clare highlighted the importance of a holistic or embodied approach to listening:

> Listening is not always about your *ears* listening to somebody talking, it might be listening to their *behaviour* or their other ways of expressing themselves, but just *engage with* and try and understand where somebody is coming from, and respond to that with *caring* and *kindness*.

Activity

- List as many different negative feelings as you can.
- Now think about how self-injury might function in respect of each of those feelings in turn.
- How might understanding the feelings beneath self-injury and the functions of it impact on your response to someone who hurts themself?

3

The inner world:
what is it like being you?

In the previous chapter I highlighted the range of possible functions, meanings and purposes of self-injury. This chapter explores some of the life experiences that may underlie self-injury. Exploring these experiences promotes a deeper understanding of the functions of self-injury and how best to support those who self-injure. It does not suggest a simple 'cause and effect' approach; likewise, nor does knowing why an individual hurts themself stop their self-injury.

The themes explored in this chapter are abuse, neglect, loss, institutionalisation and bullying. However, this is not an exhaustive list of experiences that may underlie self-injury, and nor should someone be treated any differently (ie. worse) if there is no apparent reason for their self-injury. Rather, these experiences highlight how an individual's inner world and relationship with their body/self is shaped and how self-injury becomes the vehicle through which they navigate the world around them.

This chapter also highlights why an individualised response to self-injury is essential; no two people are the same and therefore no two interventions will be the same. It is crucial that each individual is allowed the time, space and flexibility that they need in order to deal with their experiences in their own unique way. Moreover, it is paramount that helpers do not recreate the invalidating and damaging environments that were formative to self-injury – a theme I explore further in Chapter 4, with reference to the wider social context.

Inner worlds and self-injury

Experiences such as sexual abuse and bullying are often acknowledged as significant factors in self-injury, while other experiences, such as hospitalisation and loss, are less well known. However, in all cases it is essential that the problems with measuring and defining self-injury outlined in Chapter 1 are also recognised in relation to these issues. The difficulties of accurately quantifying acts of self-injury are equally relevant to the underlying experiences. For example, issues around definition, disclosure, stigma and measurement mean that it is incredibly difficult to gather accurate data on the extent and types of sexual violence in society (see Walby & Myhill, 2001). Likewise, research throws up contrasting findings about experiences that underlie self-injury. For example, some argue that physical neglect and sexual and emotional abuse in the family home are the most significant underlying factors (Glassman et al, 2007), while others suggest that these impacts are gendered, and that peer victimisation (bullying) is much more significant (Jutengren, Kerr & Stattin, 2011).

This chapter aims, therefore, to be informative rather than definitive. It gives an outline of a range of experiences that are frequently reported by people who hurt themselves, with the intention of promoting an informed response, rather than making definitive claims about the prevalence and significance of particular experiences. This approach also reflects best practice in response to self-injury, which is informed but open, rather than fixed and definitive. It is important to remember that the purpose of exploring the underlying experiences is not to enable a quick diagnosis – 'Oh, she was sexually abused, that's why she self-injures' – but, rather, to promote a deeper understanding of how self-injury functions for an individual and what kind of supports may be useful for them.

Abuse

Physical, emotional and sexual abuse are widespread, although there is reluctance to acknowledge their full extent (Breggin, 1991). As such, the experiences themselves, as well as the social stigma and secrecy surrounding them, have a significant relationship with the functions of self-injury.

In recent years, sexual violence has come to public attention through revelations of the sexual abuse of children and young people by public figures and lenient sentencing in rape cases (eg. Pollard, 2012; Ryan 2009).[1] The term 'sexual abuse' is generally used to refer to violations of a dependent person by a

---

1. See, for example, the Independent Inquiry into Child Sexual Abuse in England and Wales (https://childsexualabuseinquiry.independent.gov.uk/ – accessed 24 August 2016), and (for example) the BBC news coverage of the five-year sentence given to a man who raped a 13-month-old baby (http://news.bbc.co.uk/1/hi/uk/3080502.stm) (accessed 24 August, 2016).

perpetrator who is in a position of authority over them, such as a parent, carer or care worker. Sexual violence is a broader term that includes all acts of sexual abuse, sexual assault and rape. Sexual abuse and sexual violence are commonly cited as an underlying cause of self-injury (Babiker & Arnold, 1997; Gallup, 2002; Glassman et al, 2007; Gratz, Conrad & Roemer, 2002; McAllister, 2003; Murray, Warm & Fox, 2005). It is not difficult to understand the ways in which the violation, deceit, manipulation and threats of, or actual, physical violence that may accompany sexual violence relate to many of the functions of self-injury, such as purging and cleansing, punishment and control, as described here:

> I felt I was bleeding the bad bits out. (In Babiker & Arnold, 1997: 81)

> I can feel her on my skin... I can't explain... I suppose it's like... as if we are in some way melted into each other. I scrape and scrape at my skin but I cannot get deep enough into myself to get rid of her. (In Smith, Cox & Saradjian, 1998: 33)

> I've never said anything to my father about what he did to me. But he hates my scars. It's like they're a reproach to him – he can't pretend that nothing has happened, or that it hasn't hurt me. (In Babiker & Arnold, 1997: 83)

While it is indisputable that a significant proportion of people who hurt themselves have experienced sexual violence, this needs to be understood in a broader context. Between 25 and 51 per cent (Kelly & Regan, 2001) of the population experience some form of sexual violence during their lifetime, and therefore any manifestation of distress is going to include a significant proportion of people who have experienced sexual abuse. As such, sensitivity to the possibility of sexual violence needs to be balanced with caution about over-generalising the correlation between sexual violence and self-injury. Overly focusing on sexual violence can be invalidating and confusing to people who self-injure who have not had this experience. For example, Rachel minimised her own distress because it did not fit stereotypical assumptions about the 'causes' of self-injury:

> I think they kind of made me feel like I was *faking* because I know such a lot of people who had such *crazy* experiences, and I wasn't, I was never

69

physically abused, I've not had anything in a classic sort of life-wrenching way happen to me.

In contrast, Emma's experiences demonstrate how ignoring the possibility of sexual violence – alongside the difficulty of disclosing it – added to, rather than alleviated, her difficulties. Emma experienced sexual abuse as a young child, and sought help for her self-injury as a teenager. However, the service response, coupled with a further incident of sexual violence, meant that, as she became increasingly distressed, the interventions became increasingly problematic:

> I saw someone for a few sessions and then they went on maternity leave. I starting seeing an occupational therapist and then a few weeks into this I was attacked and raped by stranger in the streets near where I lived. I had been wondering if I could talk to the occupational therapist about my memories of the abuse but felt that being raped was some kind of warning to stop me from doing this. It was easier to believe that I had made it happen than to believe that these things just happen randomly because I wanted to believe that I could stop it happening – eg. if I didn't tell anyone about the abuse I wouldn't be raped again. This, combined with my mum warning me not to say anything, meant that, although I continued to see this occupational therapist weekly for about a year and a half, I never felt safe to talk about the things that had happened.
>
> I took my first overdose a week after this attack and the doctors in the hospital pumped my stomach, told me off and told me that they didn't want to see me again. I felt like I was being told off for feeling suicidal and also that the best way to not get told off would be to not let people find out that I wasn't OK.

As a result Emma increasingly turned to self-injury in order to survive:

> At this point I felt like the easiest thing to do would be to try and not care and so I would cut myself to show myself that I didn't care, to express my frustration with myself for feeling all the things I felt, and to try and take some control back over my life. From the age of 14 to 16 I cut myself very regularly and mostly managed to keep this secret.

The interventions Emma received are clearly antithetical to the kind of support, understanding and services that young people require. Emma's experiences also highlight the complex ways in which traumatic experiences are internalised and reformulated. This is crucial for understanding how self-injury that emerges from abusive environments has both direct and symbolic functions.[2]

However, it is also important to remember that there are other forms of abuse, such as physical and emotional abuse, and these can be equally traumatic, and connected with self-injury (Glassman et al, 2007; Murray, Warm & Fox, 2005). Indeed, forms of abuse commonly intersect: physical and sexual abuse are usually accompanied by emotional abuse, where the individual is manipulated into feeling that there is something wrong with them rather than the perpetrator, and that they are responsible for what is happening. Abuse also creates feelings of guilt and culpability, induces fear, undermines trust in the self and others and confuses boundaries and self-protection – all of which are essential survival tools. Social stigma around abuse has added to a culture of secrecy and shame for those who have been hurt, while protecting the social standing of perpetrators.[3]

Furthermore, because abuse is often carried out by someone who has either a caring and/or authoritative role over the individual, it creates an experience where being cared for, or being 'treated right', is associated with hurt and pain: eg. 'Families where a backhand means discipline, where inappropriate sexual attention means love' (Strong, 2000: xix). In this context, self-injury can function as a form of self-comfort, care or protection, and can provide a calming intervention when no other means of 'self-soothing' have been learned (Gallup, 2002).

Self-injury functions in complex ways for those whose formative environments have been abusive. It may be an attempt to normalise or work through traumatic experiences and integrate them in some kind of meaningful way that enables the individual to survive their world. For example, self-injury may allow the person 'to play out the roles of victim, perpetrator and, finally,

---

2. Dusty Miller (1994) has focused on the impacts of trauma and its relationship with self-injury through what she calls trauma re-enactment syndrome (TRS). TRS is where physical and/or emotional self-wounding functions as an attempt to take control of, heal or integrate a traumatic experience through symbolic or actual repetition. There are many different manifestations of TRS, including self-injury, repeated violent relationships and self-harm.

3. Domestic violence is also a form of abuse and has a significant relationship with both self-injury and suicide. Domestic violence is also subject to community shame and secrecy, which tends to protect the perpetrator rather than the victim (see Siddiqui & Patel, 2010). Amanda witnessed intimate partner violence against her mother, and her self-injury was her attempt to take control and prevent further occurrence: 'Rather than carrying on the violence, I always had a fear of going to or following in my mum's patterns and ending up in those sort of violent relationships – and instead I turned it in on myself rather than follow the pattern of my mum. It was the only way I knew how to deal with the situation.'

loving caretaker, soothing self-inflicted wounds and watching them heal' (Strong, 2000: xviii). Here, self-injury functions psychologically, emotionally and physically as a survival mechanism. However, these survival processes that attempt to integrate and manage traumatic experiences may appear strange to an outsider, and may also confuse and distress the individual themself. Colm's experiences illustrate this as he describes his treatment by his father, and then his treatment of himself:

> He [father] was quite violent a lot of the time. He would beat us up and he would *abuse* us, physically and sexually, but he would erm he used to kind of, he did very, really, really strange and deranged things, like he would burn us with cigarettes, and he'd, he used to watch documentaries on the television about World War Two and torture and, and like he used to then, when he'd watched this documentary where they'd stick like paper or like wood, or matches under people's nails, he used to do that then when we'd done something wrong. But, I seemed to – and all my brothers and sisters would agree with this – I seemed to get the *worst* of it.

Colm then recounted that:

> I used to replicate some of the things that my dad used to do, which was the things I was most ashamed of, because I used to burn myself with cigarettes, and I used to stick matches under my own nails, and I could never really *understand* why I was doing that, to this day. I think that maybe I was replicating the self-hatred that I had.

Colm's experiences illustrate the complex ways in which human beings survive and explore their experiences through self-injury and why depth and sensitivity are essential in any response to it. The shame and confusion that Colm feels are entangled in his awareness of his father's abusiveness and his own mimicking of these acts.

Shame, stigma and confusion around self-injury are common experiences. Joseph and Mark also highlighted the shame and secrecy that characterised their self-injury. Joseph described how 'I was deeply ashamed, *deeply* ashamed, if I had scars I was deeply ashamed and *deeply* embarrassed', and secrecy remains important to him: 'Most of my closest family members do not know… They would be *horrified*, and I wouldn't *want* them to know.' Mark experienced similar feelings:

I *didn't* tell people, I didn't show it, I didn't *want* anyone to know, I went to *so many* great lengths that nobody knew and that was through embarrassment and shame. Not just embarrassment and shame because I self-injured, but embarrassment and shame about how I felt about myself anyway. And I just thought that this was just another thing that, you know, really, makes me worse than others again.

Stigma around self-injury can also exacerbate existing shame and secrecy. Rachel described her self-consciousness about her scars and the extensive efforts she has to undertake to 'repair' situations if someone becomes aware of her self-injury:

You *have* to cover them [scars] up because they don't look at *you*, they look at the scars and it's such a hindrance. From that, you know, you then have to work to pull it back… It's almost like someone has to completely reassess who you are as a person, they have to completely redefine you in their minds, and then *you* have to work on going, 'No I'm still here, *nothing's changed*, it's okay,' and you have to sort of baby people back into your space.

Elaine and Amanda were similarly reticent. For Elaine: 'When people comment on scars, you feel little, you feel like you can't quite speak up for yourself.' Amanda always made sure that her scars were hidden:

I always wear long sleeves now. I would just rather not have to be questioned for why I have scars. As far as I'm concerned it's a healing journey that I have come through to not going down that route anymore, and I don't want to have to explain myself.

Overall then, self-injury can be a response to and a reflection of abusive environments and experiences. In many cases these have been the formative context for an individual's sense of self and the way in which the world functions. Formative experiences are not always conscious or easy to articulate; rather, they manifest themselves in ways that may discredit or stigmatise the individual who has been hurt (Babiker & Arnold, 1997). It is therefore essential that the complex ways in which bodily injuries speak of these experiences are understood, so that an individual is not further shamed or stigmatised. The following two contrasting approaches highlight the impacts of negative and positive responses to self-injury. In the first instance a service-user's shame is compounded by the professional's apparent attempt to manipulate her into stopping self-injury:

> My psychiatrist said to me, 'What you're doing to yourself is as bad as what your father did to you.' I can't explain why, but it made me feel very ashamed. (In Babiker & Arnold, 1997: 80)

In the second instance Clare describes a profound personal epiphany that emerged from genuine personal and intellectual engagement:

> I remember… first coming across the idea that maybe I *wasn't mad*, that maybe I had just lived through a certain set of circumstances and I had kind of learnt to see the world in a particular way, and [then] that *absolutely transforming realisation* that there were *other ways* of looking at the world and they might be a bit more *useful* and constructive for me.

Neglect

Neglect is frequently cited as a commonplace experience in relation to self-injury (Babiker & Arnold, 1997; Cameron, 2007; Glassman et al, 2007; Gratz, Conrad & Roemer, 2002; Jutengren, Kerr & Stattin, 2011; McAllister, 2003; Spandler & Warner, 2007). There are various forms of neglect, including emotional neglect (Gratz, Conrad & Roemer, 2002), physical neglect (Glassman et al, 2007) and 'poor parenting and invalidation' (Jutengren, Kerr & Stattin, 2011: 251). However, 'neglect' is defined in different ways: it might be how often a child was smiled at, spoken to in a warm voice, or made to feel wanted, or degrees of 'security and comfort' in relationships with parents (Gratz, Conrad & Roemer, 2002: 136). Neglect might also be measured by harshness of punishment and criticism, or 'lack of care and protection' (Jutengren, Kerr & Stattin, 2011: 251).[4] As such, studies of neglect often explore quite different experiences, ranging from forms of neglect that are quite deliberate and targeted – such as harsh criticism (Jutengren, Kerr & Stattin, 2011) – to neglect that emerges as a side-effect of other issues, such as parental illness or alcoholism (Babiker & Arnold, 1997).

---

4. Jutengren, Kerr and Stattin (2011) found that peer victimisation was a more important correlate than neglect in terms of self-injury, but also that harsh parenting may have a gendered impact, being more detrimental to girls than boys – see also Gratz, Conrad and Roemer (2002) for further discussion of the gendered impacts of neglect.

Neglect is best understood as a context where an individual's physical, emotional, psychological, social and/or sexual needs are not recognised, validated or met. Like abuse, neglect is both under-reported and difficult to define (Breggin, 1991), but it is also less widely recognised as a problem – partly because of the varying definitions. However, there is evidence of profound emotional and psychological impacts of neglect that directly relate to self-injury.

> People who self-injure are very likely to have been emotionally abused or neglected as children; to have suffered significant separation from their main carer or to have been ignored or responded to in an invalidating rather than an empathic way. (Cameron, 2007: 82)

In Arnold's (1995) research with women who self-injure, neglect was reported at an equal rate (49%) to sexual abuse (in Babiker & Arnold 1997).[5] However, some studies indicate that gender mediates the impact of neglect (Gratz, Conrad & Roemer, 2002; Jutengren, Kerr & Stattin, 2011). For example, it has been suggested that maternal emotional neglect has a significant correlation with female self-injury, while paternal emotional neglect does not. For males in this study, emotional neglect from either parent was not significant, but separation from the father or physical abuse was (Gratz, Conrad & Roemer, 2002). Other studies indicate that the type of neglect is more significant than gender, with some research suggesting that physical neglect is the most significant in relation to self-injury (Gratz, Conrad & Roemer, 2002), while other research suggests that emotional neglect is most significant (Cameron, 2007; Glassman et al, 2007). However, as with abuse, rather than getting caught up in the specific correlations of neglect and self-injury, the purpose here is to highlight its impact on a person's sense of self and relationship to the world, in order to understand their self-injury and helpful ways to respond.

Mark described a context where his needs were not met because his father was very ill 'physically and psychologically'. In this situation, all of the family were experiencing stress, but the focus of concern was Mark's father. As such, Mark's self-injury, which at one stage involved pulling out clumps of his hair, was neglected: 'No one thought about it anymore than I was just doing something that it was just really a bit silly to be doing. But then everybody's attention was elsewhere.'

---

5. Women could report more than one underlying experience, therefore both sexual abuse and neglect were reported at 49 per cent (Babiker & Arnold, 1997).

Like abuse, neglect can undermine 'the ability to self-soothe during periods of distress' (Spandler & Warner, 2007: xvii). As such, childhood neglect is implicated not just in self-injury but in all forms of self-destructive behaviour, where it provides a means of calming and regulating feelings and coping with trauma (Cameron, 2007). Child neglect also impacts on developmental processes and can damage an individual's sense of self-worth, as well as their ability to love and care for themself (Babiker & Arnold, 1997). Moreover, the fact that neglect, like abuse, is often stigmatised and secret can lead to shame and self-blame:

> When I'm feeling really empty and frightened I'll sometimes hurt myself. It seems like the only thing to do. It's horrible, but it also comforts me somehow. (In Babiker & Arnold, 1997: 79)

Neglect may also lead to self-punishment and harsh and excessive self-criticism. Glassman and colleagues found that harsh self-criticism was closely related to the functions of self-injury for those who were subjected to 'repeated insults or excessive criticism' (2007: 2484). Here the self-injury clearly mirrors the formative environment and the person's beliefs about how they should be treated. Neglect can also confuse a child's perception of what is normal and what constitutes acceptable behaviour towards them (McAllister, 2003). This is compounded by the normalisation of problems in the home: 'Incidents of abuse and neglect are often kept secret within the family. Indeed, the child may see this as normal' (McAllister, 2003:180):

> Sometimes no one spoke to me for weeks. We would pass on the stairs like strangers. There were never any hugs or love, just ice-cold looks, no conversations. (In Babiker & Arnold, 1997: 59)

In these contexts, providing emotional support and a safe and nurturing environment are important elements in supporting the person who self-injures (McAllister, 2003). Engagements that help an individual to move away from self-criticism and self-blame are also important (Glassman et al, 2007). At the same time, family interventions that decrease mistreatment can be significant in preventing further harm to young people (Glassman et al, 2007).

Finally, neglect and its consequences also need to be understood in a wider context of family systems and mental ill health. It can be difficult to categorically distinguish between neglect and more insidious dysfunction in family systems. For many people, family life consists of difficult relationships, poor parenting, 'alienation' between family members, 'harsh parenting', 'angry outbursts' and 'coldness-rejection' (Jutengren, Kerr & Stattin, 2011: 251–253). These experiences are detrimental to children (and other family members), but may fall outside statutory definitions of neglect. As such, self-injury may emerge from families where there are officially 'no problems', but which are nonetheless unhealthy environments (see Rachel's story in Chapters 2 and 4). Moreover, because experiences of neglect can be difficult to articulate, sensitivity towards what might be 'normal' for someone who self-injures is paramount.

'Chronic invalidation' also has a significant relationship with self-injury (LifeSIGNS, 2004: 25): one of the impacts of neglect is the way in which it invalidates a person's sense of self, emotions, needs and desires. Adams, Rodham and Gavin (2005) found that self-injury related to a view of the self as invalid in significant ways. Their research found that external injuries could validate internal pain but, more significantly, that they occurred where there was invalidation of self-worth. 'Invalidating family environments' (Jutengren, Kerr & Stattin, 2011: 251) may be much more commonplace than is commonly recognised, and invalidation may emerge as much through rigidity and expectations as through rejection (see Chapter 4).

Chronic invalidation can also occur outside the home – in school, the workplace, or hospital. Here, 'chronic invalidation' occurs when 'a person's emotional expressions (wishes, preferences, desires etc) are ignored or prohibited' or 'a person is made to feel that their ideas, desires, thoughts and feelings are wrong, stupid or not worth considering' (LifeSIGNS, 2004: 25). Self-injury can reflect and express this undermining of self-worth, as well as the desire for validation (Adams, Rodham & Gavin, 2005). It may also be an outlet for the frustration and distress provoked by invalidating environments or a way of turning these feelings against the self (LifeSIGNS, 2004).

It is also important to remember that society can be an invalidating environment for many people, with structures of gender, ethnicity, sexuality and disability impacting negatively on how a person is valued and treated (see Chapter 4). 'Self-harm tends to occur in the context of past (and present) abusive and neglectful social relationships' (Spandler & Warner, 2007: xvii). Spandler and Warner (2007) emphasise how these structures create oppressive and invalidating environments for many service-users, and that anti-oppressive and anti-discriminatory practice is therefore essential in any helpful response to self-injury. Indeed, all forms of validation are integral to responding helpfully to people who hurt themselves.

Finally, the family home and symptoms of 'mental illness' (such as anxiety, depression, post-traumatic stress disorder as well as self-injury) are rarely correlated in mental health services or psychiatric practice. The definitions of mental illness that have most currency in these settings define it as arising from biological, chemical or genetic imbalances in the individual. However, evidence indicates that mental illnesses and 'behavioural disorders' are actually responses to childhood mistreatment (Breggin, 1991; Gallup, 2002): 'The whole spectrum of so-called psychiatric and psychological disorders in children can be traced to child abuse and neglect' (Breggin, 1991: 274). This is all the more important when neglect is understood as a form of chronic invalidation, because if people are simply defined by an illness, rather than having their underlying pain and distress attended to, then this becomes another form of neglect and invalidation. This is true for a whole range of mental distress, as well as self-injury:

> In children, as in adults, there is no evidence that any of the common psychological or psychiatric disorders have a genetic or biological component. The typical school-related diagnoses – attention deficit disorder and learning disorder, as well as so-called hyperactivity, depression, autism and schizophrenia – tend to cover up the abuse, neglect, miscommunication, and family conflict that drive children to despair and failure.
>
> Psychiatric labelling inflicts additional humiliation and injury on already damaged children. It can rob them of all self-esteem, shatter their identity among their peers, and relegate them to inferior status in the eyes of parents and teachers. Often the stigma remains for a lifetime. (Breggin, 1991: 291)

Breggin's point is reinforced by young people's own descriptions of how psychiatric labels reinforce their own (and potentially others') negative perception of themselves (see also Timimi, 2008; 2010):

> I have been depressed for the whole of my life (so the psychologists tell me). I've been self-injuring since I was nine.

> I'm bipolar... my doctors have actually told me that on the dissociative scale, I'm dangerously close to MPD [multiple personality disorder]. (In Adams, Rodham & Gavin, 2005: 1302)

Overall then, it is important to remember that self-injury (and other harmful practices) emerge from unhealthy and damaging environments. Therefore, many of the meanings and functions can appear 'upside down' to someone from a more healthy environment. For example, hurting the body as a form of self-care or self-soothing can be difficult to understood at face value. However, when understood in the context of emotional formation, in which love may have been enmeshed with pain, or where one need may be met only at the expense of another, then self-injury clearly reflects the formative environment. When viewed in this way, self-injury is a powerful reflection and communication of an individual's life context. It is also clear why a sensitive, in-depth and caring response is essential. Indeed, a response that doesn't involve genuine attention, care and validation will only compound experiences of neglect and invalidation (see 'Hostile care', below).

Loss, bereavement and grief

Chapter 2 highlighted that grief is a powerful emotional experience that is embodied in a variety of ritual practices in many societies. Just as grief and loss are associated with ritual body practices, they also have a significant relationship with self-injury. Loss and grief following the death of a parent, close relative or friend can be particularly significant for young people (McQueen, 2007; Samaritans, 2003), but so too is the loss of a parent through divorce, separation or illness (Babiker & Arnold, 1997; Cameron, 2007; Hurry, 2000; Sadler, 2002; Strong, 2000). Loss of a close relative can also have a profound impact in adult life:

> If I sat in the house I would just be upset all the time. I mean, I'm getting alright now but it's just sometimes... like I can't get on a bus, and I can't look at his house... and that's why I tend to go out... that's why certain things [self-injury] happen. (In Heslop & Macaulay, 2009: 43)

In Arnold's (1995) research, 42 per cent of women who hurt themselves reported some form of loss or separation during childhood, including through parental illness or addiction. Babiker and Arnold (1997: 59) also reported: 'Significant losses in childhood included the death of parents or siblings, and prolonged or total separation from one or both parents.' Significant loss in early life can have a huge emotional impact. In Strong's research, people who hurt themselves commonly described feeling 'empty inside, unable to express emotions in words, afraid of getting close to anyone, and wanting desperately to stop their emotional pain' (2000: 26). These feelings can be overwhelming and, for young people, a catalyst for self-injury, especially when appropriate supports are not available. Stephanie described how:

> Parents were getting divorced [...] I can't really take my anger out on somebody else; I take it out on myself. And when you are upset and you cut yourself, you don't feel it. (In Moyer & Nelson, 2007: 44)

For young people and adults alike, loss through bereavement, relationship break-up, death of a child or any traumatic experience that creates loss, including institutionalisation, has a significant relationship with self-injury (Babiker & Arnold, 1997; Gratz, Conrad & Roemer, 2002; Kirk, 2007). Loss may also result from life events that radically transfigure a person's identity or place in the world, and it may also be cumulative. For example, the end of a relationship may mean the loss of a home, the loss of other familial and social relationships and the loss of an identity. This is suggested to be particularly significant for men, since current gender norms mean that a man's intimate female partner is also likely to be the primary source of his emotional support, and male identity is closely bound up in gendered familial roles (Williams, 2009). Therefore, a man can find himself suddenly bereft of all of the anchor points in his life and adrift from his usual support mechanisms. Gender may also increase the impact of parental separation, so that separation from the father may be more closely associated with self-injury for boys than it is for girls, and also more significant for boys than experiences of neglect and physical abuse (Gratz, Conrad & Roemer, 2002).

The feelings of grief and despair that result from all of these experiences can be overpowering, and self-injury can provide relief and a means to express them (Babiker & Arnold, 1997; Strong, 2002). Moreover, bereavement and separation are also often accompanied by feelings of distress, rejection and self-blame, especially for young people, all of which can compound the functions of self-injury (Sadler, 2002). One young person described how: 'I blamed myself for my dad leaving and not being the ideal child' (in Spandler, 1996: 67).

The ways in which loss and grief are responded to are also significant. Jutengren, Kerr and Stattin (2011) found that parental neglect of a child's sadness made it more likely that a young person would hurt themselves. Indeed, a key feature of self-injury is not just the impact of the underlying experiences, but also the context in which they occurred. For example, it has already been highlighted that there is often assumed to be a causal relationship between self-injury and sexual abuse. However, not all people who self-injure have experienced sexual abuse, and not all those who have been sexually abused self-injure as a result. The key factor in the development of self-injury seems to be the context of the experience and its aftermath (Babiker & Arnold, 1997). Thus, if a person has had a traumatic experience such as sexual abuse, but it is responded to appropriately and the person is supported in their recovery from it and their feelings and needs are validated, then it is less likely that they will self-injure. However, if a person experiences sexual abuse, or any other traumatic experience, and it is not responded to appropriately, and the person, their distress and their emotional needs are ignored, mistreated or invalidated, then it is much more likely that they will self-injure.

Likewise, interventions that attempt to address one issue in a person's life can result in other losses that impact just as harshly as the original issue. For example, if a young person is placed in a care facility as a result of violence at home, then not only do they have to contend with the feelings that result from their initial experience, but they have additional experiences of loss and separation, lack of control and autonomy, institutionalisation, alienation and stigma to contend with – all of which are significant factors in self-injury. This is not to suggest that a young person should never be removed from their home, but rather to emphasise that the solution to one problem often brings with it a collection of additional problems that are just as significant. Helpers need to be attuned to these issues and aware that the 'side-effects' of many interventions can be problematic, and not view them simplistically as a catch-all remedy. Babiker and Arnold (1997) refer to this trajectory as a 'legacy of distress', where one experience is compounded by another, culminating in overwhelming distress and self-injury:

> Many people who self-injure report having experienced since childhood overwhelming and unbearable feelings of sadness, grief, betrayal, anger, shame, powerlessness and anxiety. The intolerable nature of their distress leads them to a desperate search for ways of alleviating and coping with their feelings [...] A frequent trigger for self-injury is overwhelming feelings of emotional pain or anger. (Babiker & Arnold, 1997: 62)

Responses to self-injury can have huge impacts on an individual's immediate and long-term wellbeing, and they can either exacerbate or alleviate the underlying causes of self-injury.

Hospitalisation/institutionalisation

The experience of hospitalisation and enforced medical treatment in childhood and adolescence has been linked to self-injury (Babiker & Arnold, 1997). Indeed, institutionalisation in any form, such as in a psychiatric hospital, prison or a local authority care facility, has a close relationship with self-injury (Birch et al, 2011; Groves, 2004; Liebling, Chipchase & Velangri, 1997; Mental Health Foundation, 2006) – despite these settings operating stringent 'no-harm' policies (see Chapter 6 on harm-reduction).

Institutionalisation removes control and autonomy from the individual and often places them in an alien and frightening environment, where their personal safety may be at risk (Groves, 2004; Jones, Davies & Jenkins, 2010; Shaw & Hogg, 2004; Shaw & Shaw, 2007). Institutionalisation may also increase feelings of guilt and/or shame. These factors in themselves have a close relationship with self-injury, as well as exacerbating the feelings emerging from the underlying circumstances. Indeed, as noted above, in many cases the response to one of the underlying circumstances can result in situations that compound other significant experiences related to self-injury.

Similarly, medical interventions in childhood to 'correct' physical conditions and features can also be detrimental to the young person (Babiker & Arnold 1997). For example, parents of young children with Down's Syndrome are increasingly requesting extensive facial surgery to 'normalise' their child's appearance (Davis, 2003). There is evidence that enforced medical treatments of young people with physical disabilities are particularly damaging and have a significant relationship with self-injury. For example, disability research has highlighted that medical treatments during childhood and adolescence can be experienced as dehumanising, humiliating and even abusive (Kennedy, 1996; Shakespeare, Gillespie-Sells & Davis, 1996). These enforced treatments can not only include extremely painful and often traumatic physical procedures, but can also often involve young people being stripped naked or semi-naked against their will or having private parts of their bodies displayed to groups of adults (Kennedy, 1996; Shakespeare, Gillespie-Sells & Davis, 1996; see also Bob Flanagan in McRuer, 2006 and Wollach in Sandahl, 2003). These experience violate the body/self, with very similar impacts on the individual as sexual abuse. For example, in Kennedy's (1996: 125) research a disabled woman described how medical practices 'groomed' her for sexual abuse:

It [sexual abuse] did not seem anything out of the ordinary. The way the
porter looked inside my nightie and lifted it up and touched me seemed,
I think, just like what had been done to me a thousand times before by
doctors and other people who wanted to look and prod and poke and
talk – all as though I did not exist. All of my early hospital experiences had
'groomed' me for abuse. If you have never been given the opportunity to
object to a doctor taking off your clothes just to look at your leg or if you
objected to a doctor pulling down your knickers just to measure your leg
but the doctor carried on regardless, then how do you recognise that what
a porter does to you in a lift is called sexual abuse and that you could/
should say no? It all seemed the same to me.

These kinds of experiences have led to calls for a broader definition of child
abuse that incorporates the specific experiences to which many disabled
children are subjected (Bass & Davis, 2002; Kennedy, 1996). These include
enforced passivity and compliance with 'treatment' or 'care' regimes that inflict
painful, humiliating and violating practices on children in order to 'make
them better', such as 'force feeding; photographing children's impairments
in intrusive, insensitive ways; medical rehabilitation programmes which are
experienced as painful and oppressive; physical restraint; misuse of medication;
depriving of visitors; opening letters; listening to telephone calls; open days
where strangers intrude on children's privacy' (Kennedy 1996: 177). Similarly,
survivor-led recovery programmes for people who have experienced child
abuse are increasingly defining 'unnecessary medical treatments' as constituting
abuse (Bass & Davis, 2002). These practices harm children in multiple ways:
they violate their bodily and emotional integrity and self-determination, and
they also give out very powerful messages about what that child is worth, what
is an acceptable way to treat them, and that they should remain passive when
feeling hurt or violated. Like many of the experiences connected to self-injury,
these kinds of medical interventions create an association of 'being good' and
'being helped' or 'cared for' with being hurt and violated. They create an inner
world that is antithetical to self-protection and self-care and place children in
traumatising environments:

It was the worst time of my life because it was when I was in hospital that
I remembered something else that happened to me when I was a kid.
A similar experience – being locked up, not being allowed out, and not
having any privacy or anything. (In Spandler, 1996: 76)

The connections between enforced medical treatments and self-injury by people with disabilities are increasingly being articulated in survivor forums.[6] For example, Fred describes his experiences of traumatic medical interventions as an infant and how he later dealt with the trauma through self-injury:

> I was very obsessed (and in a very private way) about the 10 x 3cm scar on the middle of my body left by surgery for pyloric stenosis only a couple of weeks after my birth. I wanted to experiment what would have caused this scar, what the cutting and stitching must have felt like, how the wounds healed, and what kind of tissue this kind of scar consisted of on and below the surface. Like most self-harmers I did all this without anybody knowing or even noticing, in high secrecy. I did not slash my arms, legs, or torso: I just worked on my scars.

His parents never acknowledged the surgery and this invalidated his experience and increased his trauma and confusion. By wounding his body, he attempted to both heal and express his traumatic experiences:

> The trauma of my surgery and all that went with it had been experienced by my body even though my mind was incapable of recording and recalling it. I believe my self-harming was part of my instinctive self-healing, as I re-imagined, re-experienced and explored what happened to my self so that I could integrate and calibrate my body's memories and my powerful emotions.

Understanding his self-injury in this way enabled him to identify further functions of it:

> It is only in recent years that I have come to understand my self-harming more fully. My experimenting and attempts at re-experiencing were in fact only the tip of a kind of iceberg [...] My self-harming expressed my loneliness and alienation, frustration and even anger and hatred, and indeed self-punishment. It was also a coping mechanism to relieve my emotional pain.

---

6. See for example http://survivinginfantsurgery.wordpress.com/2011/06/30/self-harming-a-pain-filled-subject/ (accessed 17 August, 2016).

Deborah described similar treatment-induced trauma, which left her increasingly confused and distressed by her own actions:

> I had many, many eye operations as a young child, yearly, 'til I was 15 and old enough to say 'no more!' Over the years I have bashed myself, threatened to cut myself, threatened my partners with knives, and I never knew why for years. I was in a constant state of hyper-reaction. I couldn't rest and at any moment, triggered by one thing or another, I would run, scream, get confused, walk for miles, cry hysterically or for years drug myself out with anything I could.

In all of these instances, bodily trauma and violation co-exist with the powerlessness of the child. This is further complicated by a context that frames it as 'good' for the child and demands compliance, regardless of how disturbing the procedure is. There is little understanding of the impacts of these kinds of experiences, which further alienates and isolates the young person. Peter Levine (1997) is unusual among trauma specialists in paying significant attention to the ways in which children can be traumatised by hospital treatments and operations.

Finally, there is some awareness of sexual abuse perpetrated by medical practitioners on patients, with indications from Ireland that the extent of medical abuse may far exceed the level of clerical abuse that has recently come to light (Ring, 2012a). Likewise, the recent British investigations into the abuses perpetrated by Jimmy Savile also revealed that hospitals have been environments where abuse can flourish and where those who make allegations of abuse are discredited and disregarded (Pollard, 2012). Finally, the experience of self-injury may itself result in negative treatment and 'hostile care' (Harris, 2000).

Hostile care

Trauma may also occur as a direct result of medical interventions around self-injury. Official medical guidelines (eg. NICE, 2004) are increasingly recognising that there are significant problems with the ways in which people who hurt themselves are treated in medical settings. Negative, punitive and abusive attitudes and 'blatant mistreatment' (Simpson, 2006) of patients are so commonplace that they have been labelled 'hostile care' (Harris, 2000), and medical settings have been found to be 'institutionally prejudiced' (Simpson 2006: 435) against people who hurt themselves. Much of this emerges from stigma and a lack of understanding about self-injury, which create 'dysfunctional attitudes' towards people who hurt themselves (Clarke & Whittaker, 1998: 135; see also Taylor et al, 2009). This lack of understanding may give rise to feelings of anger, irritation, fear, impatience, intolerance, helplessness, frustration and revulsion, which then impact on the treatment of patients (Clarke & Whittaker, 1998; Cresswell & Karimova, 2010; Favazza, 1996; Hadfield et al, 2009; Harris, 2000). Moreover, service-providers may fear that their own physical and mental integrity is threatened by a service-user's self-injury, and therefore maintain a distance from them (Favazza, 1996; Hadfield et al, 2009). Critical self-reflection and supervision are not part of conventional medical practice, and so staff remain unchallenged when they act out their own fears, prejudices and lack of understanding (Hadfield et al, 2009).

Adults and young people who hurt themselves experience similar mistreatment in medical settings. For example, one woman reported: 'When I was in A&E getting self-injury treated, the consultant psychiatrist on call told my husband: "Your wife has the mental age of a 15-year-old attention-seeker and is best ignored"' (in LifeSIGNS, 2004: 92). Kirsty, another woman who attended A&E for stitches after hurting herself, was asked: 'Can we use a student nurse on you? It's not like it matters' (in Sadler, 2002: 18). As reported at the beginning of this chapter, Emma also experienced hostile care in A&E as a teenager after she had been raped and taken an overdose:

> I felt like I was being told off for feeling suicidal and also that the best way to not get told off would be to not let people find out that I wasn't OK.

Being told off is a consistent feature of medical intervention:

> I was told off by nurses and the doctors. I just felt small. They do treat self-harmers different to accident people [...] The hospital staff look at you as though you are wasting their time. (In Harris, 2000: 168)

> Treated like shit. They were really laying into me saying I was wasting someone's bed, just a waste of time. They didn't listen, didn't take notice of what I said. I tried to tell them why I did it. (In Spandler, 1996: 79)

Amanda described how judgmental and punitive treatment of those who self-injured was also the norm in an inpatient setting: 'It was like you had committed a *crime* and you were made to feel *wrong* doing it.' Criticism, punishment and being 'told off' is particularly worrying, given that people who hurt themselves are already likely to be overly self-critical (Glassman et al, 2007; see also above), and this kind of response can only exacerbate that self-criticism and feelings of shame. Hostile care may also be a particular problem in services for specific groups: for example, many people with intellectual disabilities report particularly negative treatment (Heslop & Macaulay, 2009 – see also Chapter 4).

Hostile treatment is deeply damaging to service-users and, moreover, compounds many underlying feelings and experiences and reinforces self-injury. Louise Pembroke describes this as a 'cycle of degradation' (1996: 36) that is so commonplace in regard to self-injury that she has created specific terminology for it: 'iatrionic traumatic stress' (in Inckle, 2010b).[7] This trauma is not only detrimental in itself but also places individuals at further risk by reducing the likelihood of their seeking help – even if they have life-threatening injuries: 'Even if my life was in danger I'd rather sit at home and sit it out and see whether I survived than risk the humiliation' (in Simpson, 2006: 434; see also Pembroke, 1996; Spandler, 1996).

Overall then, experiences of institutionalisation and enforced and/or abusive medical treatment have a significant relationship with self-injury, and highlight key issues in providing meaningful services for people who hurt themselves. These are, first, that 'hostile care' is commonplace, and that institutionalisation and enforced or abusive treatment can violate the individual in just the same way as physical, emotional and sexual abuse – which can also occur in hospital settings. Second, it highlights that sensitivity and understanding are integral to helpful responses to self-injury. What is normal to each of us reflects the environment that has shaped our world; 'normal' cannot simply be imposed or transferred from one experience and belief system onto another. Injuries speak of formative experiences and their impact, and may be the 'language' through which the unspeakable is articulated (Babiker & Arnold, 1997). As David Pitonyak (2005) points out, 'all behaviour is meaning-full,' and the injury itself, as well as the type, place and location, can often have significant meaning and purpose for the individual. Therefore, to really understand and support an individual requires a willingness to enter their world as they have experienced it – something that many helpers remain reluctant to do. Indeed, it is not an easy task and it requires great sensitivity, commitment and engagement. Likewise, for an individual to rework their entire world-view, emotional formation, beliefs and values is an enormous task.

---

7. Iatrogenesis, or clinical iatrogenesis, refers to physician-induced harm (Illich, 1976).

As such, on both sides, it takes courage, trust and a safe and supportive context to begin to explore the inner world of self-injury. If this is not in place, helpers risk compounding trauma and distress, rather than alleviating it.

Bullying

Experiences of being treated with hostility or being stigmatised and treated in negative ways have a significant relationship with self-injury wherever they occur, and bullying is increasingly recognised as related to self-injury. For young people in particular, bullying is often cited as a key underlying factor (Jutengren, Kerr & Stattin, 2011; King & McKeown, 2003; McQueen, 2007; Mayock et al, 2009; Mental Health Foundation, 2006; Samaritans, 2003; UNICEF Ireland, 2012). However, the significance of bullying varies from study to study, with some reporting bullying as only a minor contributor to young people's distress and self-injury (Samaritans, 2003), while others find that bullying has a highly significant relationship with self-injury (Jutengren, Kerr & Stattin, 2011; UNICEF Ireland, 2011).

Jutengren, Kerr and Stattin (2011) suggest that bullying, or 'peer victimisation', is one of the key predictive factors in self-injury among young people, and argue that bullying may have more impact on the likelihood of self-injury than parental neglect. They also argue that the impacts of bullying are overlooked: 'The psychological consequences of peer victimisation may be even more extensive than normally recognised' (2011: 260). Their findings also highlight that many school strategies to deal with bullying are ineffective, and that significant development needs to take place in this regard. This finding is reinforced by young people, who frequently report that it is they, not the perpetrator/s, who are problematised at school following a disclosure of peer victimisation. For example, Eoghan described how, after he reported homophobic bullying to his head teacher, it was suggested that he, not the bullies, should leave the school (in Ring, 2012b). Rachel also highlighted how inappropriate responses to bullying at school can be particularly damaging, as school 'is your entire life when you are a teenager'. The reaction to Rachel's victimisation implied that she was responsible for it: 'This whole thing of, "Well, if you look weird then you *will* get bullied won't you?!"' She felt acutely that this kind of response '*make[s] you* [culpable]… diminish[es] you'.

Bullying is also commonly experienced in conjunction with other difficulties, adding to 'the legacy of distress'. This was true for Emma and Mark, who both experienced bullying alongside other issues:

I started cutting myself when I was 11 which I think was to do with being unhappy about getting attention from men generally and from being bullied in school (Emma).

My father was very ill when I was young, and his illness affected him physically and psychologically so – I'm not going into any of the details of that – but it was hugely, hugely difficult. So that was going on and, probably because I was vulnerable, I was also getting bullied at the time, so there was nowhere safe in the world. So a lot of things were internalised (Mark).

It has also been suggested that perpetrating bullying may increase the likelihood of a young person self-injuring (LifeSIGNS, 2008). Indeed, it is often stated (but unproven) that bullies themselves are being victimised in other contexts. Therefore, as with all of the other experiences that underlie self-injury, the important factor is the way in which these experiences impact on a person's sense of self and their psychological and emotional wellbeing, rather than a simple causal relationship. For example, one young person described how bullying resulted in the internalisation of self-blame and feeling 'like I must have done something really bad to deserve it – that it was all my fault' (in UNICEF Ireland, 2011: 12).

Moreover, the fact that bullying is often not addressed at all, or is addressed inappropriately, adds to the stress, even for those who are not directly targeted. For example, in Colm's school and local community, bullying and violent peer victimisation were the norm, and Colm had a heightened awareness of his own vulnerability and the need to protect himself: 'Being beaten up in school was a *regular thing* for most kids, and erm, it was just considered like *boyhood*.' As a young gay teenager, Colm knew he was at significant risk of peer victimisation and worked hard to maintain a 'macho image' as a means of defence. 'You *had* to maintain a *tough* exterior to like fend some of the bullies off. It was really, really rough and violent.'

It is important to remember that bullying is not something that is just experienced by young people. Bullying can also take place in adult life, and there is increasing recognition of the extent and impact of workplace bullying, which has in some cases culminated in suicide (Beale & Hoel, 2011). Bullying may also occur across the social sphere, and people from minority groups are particularly at risk of this kind of victimisation in adult life. People who are disabled (Heslop & Macaulay, 2009; Equality & Human

Rights Commission, 2011), or from BME groups (Martins, 2007), or who are gay, lesbian, bisexual or transgendered (King & McKeown, 2003; Mayock et al, 2009) often experience bullying and harassment, as well as physical and verbal violence. People with intellectual disabilities often report being subjected to significant bullying, and self-injure as a way of coping with it: 'People, it's the people make me do it... 'cause I hear things, saying they hate me and all, they don't like me, you know? And I got bullied all my life' (in Heslop & Macaulay, 2009: 41).

Bullying, violence and abuse that targets an individual's identity highlights the relationship between social structures and wellbeing in general and self-injury in particular (King & McKeown, 2003; Mayock et al, 2009; Siddiqui & Patel, 2010). Indeed, 'negative life events' related to minority status, including bullying and discrimination, are so widely recognised as a factor in mental ill health that they have been labelled 'minority stress' (King & McKeown, 2003; Mayock et al, 2009). Minority stress and its relationship with self-injury are explored in more detail in the next chapter. Here, it's enough to say that the experiences that hurt people and lead to their self-injury result from circumstances outside them, rather than an inner pathology. This is crucial in understanding that, while all instances of self-injury are specific to that individual, and as such require an individualised response, the source of the distress lies outside the person. Therefore, any effective intervention with someone who hurts themselves needs to be holistic and tackle both their inner pain and the external causes of that distress.

• Chapter summary

This chapter has explored a range of experiences that may underlie self-injury, including abuse, neglect, bullying and loss. However, its purpose is not to make definitive statements about cause and effect but, rather, to explore how these experiences impact on an individual's inner landscape and are mediated through self-injury. All of these experiences are about being hurt, unheard, powerless and invalidated. It is therefore essential that responses do not recreate these feelings with punitive and invalidating interventions.

The experiences highlighted in this chapter may be formative to an individual's emotional and psychological development. In these instances, what is normal for an individual is hurt, pain and powerlessness. Therefore, while self-injury may seem counter-intuitive or incomprehensible to someone whose formative environment has been nurturing, it may directly reflect an individual's inner world and the context that has shaped it. As such, sensitivity, empathy and non-judgment are essential features of a helpful response.

Furthermore, it is not just the experiences themselves that lead to self-injury but also the context within which they are experienced. Integrating and healing traumatic experiences is dependent on an individual being listened to, validated and supported in exploring and expressing their feelings through whatever medium and within whatever timeframe is meaningful to them. When people are not allowed this opportunity, when their experiences are minimised, ignored or invalidated, healing is prevented and more hurt and damage is perpetrated – often reinforcing the original trauma. Sadly, hostile care is all too common, and a real commitment to anti-oppressive and anti-discriminatory practice is essential if there is finally to be an end to the mistreatment of people who hurt themselves

This exploration of some of the underlying experiences of self-injury has also reiterated the meaning, purpose and functions of self-injury. It highlights how self-injury has a deep meaning and purpose and can directly or symbolically articulate an individual's experiences. It also demonstrates how self-injury functions as a response to very real difficulties in a person's life, and that a helpful response should address these issues, rather than simply focus on the self-injury. In the same way, it is essential to explore and understand the feelings that led to the injury, rather than pathologise the injury.

Finally, it is important to remember that, while the distress underlying self-injury often begins in childhood, traumatic experiences can occur at any point in the life course and are often cumulative. Self-injury has often been a part of someone's life for a long time. As such, both the underlying experiences and the self-injury itself are a significant part of their life history, and it may take an equally long time for their life to move away from it. Patience and realistic expectations are therefore crucial: 'The fact that self-injury is highly functional, and that it serves a variety of complex purposes at the same time for any individual, means it is not going to be easily and simply overcome' (Babiker & Arnold, 1997: 85). Moreover, to undertake the journey of working through deep pain and distress takes time, courage and trust, and requires a safe and nurturing environment and relationship/s.

Learning into practice

Definition	Self-injury reflects inner-world experiences
Working principles	• The injury is not the problem • Individual experiences, individual response
Practice applications	• Validation and respect • Focus on the feelings not the behaviour

Definition: Self-injury reflects inner-world experiences

Self-injury is the embodiment of distress, and it has powerful functions that often mirror formative experiences. Negative formative experiences have powerful effects, and self-injury articulates and expresses them. Injuries can directly and symbolically depict how an individual has been treated and/or has experienced the world.

Working principles

1. The injury is not the problem

The principle that the injury is not the problem should be clear at this point: the problem is the experiences that the individual has been subjected to – such as bullying, sexual violence, institutionalisation and hostile care. Far from being the problem, the injury enables an individual to survive, cope and carry on. Mark described his injuries as 'something I did, to deal with things… I'm not saying it's a well thought out one, but sometimes it's the very, very best one you can possibly do'. Rachel reflected that, 'I think for me *that's* why I do it: because it works.' More often, self-injury is a problem for others, such as those around the person or those they seek help from. Focusing on the injuries only adds to invalidation and stigmatisation. This is why developing an informed response, rather than a fear-based reaction, is essential in responding helpfully. In short, self-injury emerges from deep distress and any response should focus on the causes of the distress, not the fact of the injury.

2. Individual experiences, individual responses

There are a number of experiences that have a relationship with self-injury, some of which have been explored in this chapter. However, it is essential to understand that the relationship between a difficult experience and self-injury is complex. Each person has their own, unique set of experiences, beliefs, strengths, difficulties and desires, as well as a specific context in which their experiences occurred. As such, each response needs to be equally individualised and unique. This means that, while there are broad principles for understanding and responding to someone who hurts themself, there is no simple, formulaic solution. Joseph described self-injury as 'a very deep, personal thing… It's one of those things that you *cannot* generalise. You cannot have a text book and say "Da, da, da, da – *everybody* is like that or like this".' Likewise, Emma highlighted that 'self-harm is very complicated because it can serve many different functions for the person doing it.'

Activity

- Write down all the people who might be affected by someone's self-injury, starting with the person who hurts themself. Affected people might include teacher, social worker, nurse, GP, friend, partner, child and so on.

- Then write down all the ways in which self-injury is a problem for each of these people. For example, as well as providing a coping mechanism, self-injury might also be a source of shame for the person who hurts themself. They may also be afraid of negative consequences if their self-injury is discovered at school or in the workplace. It might also be a problem if their wounds have become infected and they don't know how to treat them. Another person who is affected – for example, a nurse – might perceive self-injury as a problem because they are expected to report, and prevent, every incident of it that occurs on their shift. A nurse might also find self-injury confusing and distressing and may not have any professional support or training in how to deal with it.

- Next, contrast the ways in which the self-injury is a problem for the other people affected with the ways in which it is a problem for the person who hurts themself. Reflect on these differences, their implications, and whose needs are likely to be prioritised.

Practice applications

1. Validation and respect
This chapter has highlighted the ways in which a range of difficult experiences affect an individual and relate to self-injury. These experiences diminish an individual's sense of self-worth and violate their self and bodily integrity. As such, any meaningful response not only needs to recognise the pain and gravity of these experiences but must also counter them by providing the individual with an alternative experience of themself and their place and value in the world. This requires an ethos based on validating and respecting every individual, as well as sensitivity to their individual needs and experiences. Much of what is therapeutic is not about the specifics of the intervention but is much more about the quality of the relationship.

For example, Emma described the most significant elements of a helpful response in terms of the genuineness of the relationship: 'She [the therapist] responded positively and truthfully to the questions I asked and really seemed to have faith that I could be ok and that I could feel positive about myself. She seemed to believe me and she seemed to respect me as a person.' Conversely, disrespectful and punitive responses only serve to further traumatise people and reinforce their negative experiences. Hostile care seems endemic to medical responses to self-injury, as well as to institutionalised settings. Mark highlighted the illogic of responding to distressed people in distressing ways: 'People say, "Well, self-injury is *mad*," but then responding to somebody who is self-injuring to deal with very distressing things in a way that distresses them more is *completely insane!*'

2. Focus on the feelings not the behaviour
A helpful response to self-injury is based around supporting a person to explore and express their feelings and the experiences that led to them. Crucial to this is understanding that there is no such thing as 'normal'. This means that each human being has their own, unique perception of what is normal and how the world works, based on their own formative experiences. As such, there is no 'normal' way to respond to life experiences. What may seem strange and counter-intuitive to one person will be perfectly obvious and straightforward to another.

However, most human beings share the same potential range of feelings and emotions. Thus, while the context or the reason for the feelings may be difficult to understand, the feelings themselves may be perfectly comprehensible. Therefore, focusing on the feelings is important in terms of responding to the underlying issues for self-injury and also in finding a place of connection and empathy.

Emma described how recognising and validating feelings was crucial to a helpful response: 'I would like people to acknowledge the pain of the self-harmer without reacting with anger/fear. I would like people to try and understand/empathise with the self-harmer.' Colm's experiences of self-injury and others' (largely unhelpful) reactions to it informed his own response to people who hurt themselves: 'When I meet people who self-harm, whether it's with, like, physical self-harming, or drugs, or alcohol, or food, I would *never* talk to the actual *process* of what they're doing, I would talk to the emotional part.'

Activity

- Think about some of the people that you know who hurt themselves, or some of the people in this chapter, and try to identify how they might be feeling when they hurt themselves.

- In day-to-day life how would you respond to someone who has one or more of those feelings? For example, would you be gentle, compassionate, calm, kind etc?

- Now reflect on why it is that self-injury so often seems to prevent people from responding with these qualities.

4

A social model:
context is everything

Self-injury functions as a mechanism to cope with traumatic feelings and experiences. In the previous chapter, I explored the ways in which individual experiences of abuse, neglect, bullying, invalidation, hospitalisation and lack of autonomy relate to self-injury. This chapter explores the ways in which factors outside the individual also impact on self-injury: 'Self-injury must be understood, not as a symptom of individual intrapsychic disorder, but as a coping response that arises within a social context' (Alexander & Clare, 2004: 83). Understanding how structural or contextual factors impact on life chances, wellbeing and distress is integral to a social model approach. In line with a human rights perspective, a social model recognises that lack of social status, power and autonomy can have profoundly detrimental effects on mental and physical health. Therefore, context awareness and a commitment to social justice and anti-discrimination are essential to working meaningfully with people who hurt themselves.

The concept of 'minority stress' is used throughout this chapter to explore the ways in which social status impacts on wellbeing and self-injury. The four minority contexts explored are sexual orientation, disability, social class, racism and ethnicity (I discussed gender and age in Chapter 1). The focus on minority stress highlights key issues for understanding and responding to self-injury: first that society itself is an abusive or invalidating environment for many people; second, that the outer contexts and the inner world intersect in complex ways; third, that individual and contextual experiences underlie self-injury, not some inner pathology or mental sickness; fourth, it is essential that responses do not mirror the formative context (by being racist or homophobic, for example), and fifth, that human identity is complex and all of these identity categories and experiences intersect in complex ways (eg. Seng et al, 2012).

Overall then, a social model highlights the role of social structures in creating minority stress and the possibility of self-injury:

> Individual experiences and circumstances may *underlie* the distress of self-injury, but social relations *shape* such experiences [...] Social factors are reflected in individuals' views of themselves and their own bodies. They influence their relationships with other people. Social and political realities also affect the availability to individuals of material and environmental support, which may make them more or less likely to need to turn to self-injury as a means of coping and expression. The 'language' of injury then, may be a means by which some individuals 'speak' about what are social and political as well as personal experiences. (Babiker & Arnold, 1997: 37)

Sexual orientation

Research consistently points to much higher rates of all distress behaviours – including alcohol and drug abuse, risk-taking, suicide and self-injury – among the LGBT (lesbian, gay, bisexual, trans) population (Babiker & Arnold 1997; Cochran, 2001; Mayock et al, 2009). In Ireland, for example, 25 per cent of LGBT people have self-injured (Mayock et al, 2009). These high rates have been attributed to 'minority stress', which is the particular anguish that emerges from occupying a stigmatised or marginalised position in society: 'Stigma, prejudice and discrimination create a hostile and stressful social environment that causes mental health problems' (Meyer, 2003: 674; Kessler, Mickelson & Williams, 1999).[1]

It is commonplace for the experiences of LGBT people to be grouped together in a single category, but this creates a number of problems in terms of accuracy and understanding (Balsam et al, 2005; Gavriel Ansara, 2010; Klesse, 2010). Being transgendered/transsexual is a gender identity, not a sexual orientation; many trans people identify as heterosexual and share few interests with the LGB community. Additionally, lesbians, gay men and bisexual people have very different experiences because of the differences in their genders and sexual identities. For example, research with bisexual people has found much

---

1. Minority stress was originally conceptualised specifically in relation to the experiences of LGBT people, but it is equally useful for understanding a range of minority experiences.

higher levels of self-injury in comparison with lesbians and gay men, but lower rates of suicide attempts (Balsam et al, 2005; Mayock et al, 2009). Moreover, bisexual and trans people tend to come out later than lesbians and gay men and are therefore likely to experience longer periods of identity conflict (DiStefano, 2008; Klesse, 2010). In addition, bisexual (and trans) people often experience prejudice and discrimination from gay and lesbian communities as well as from mainstream heterosexual society.[2] As a result, bisexuals experience 'greater invisibility and lack the within-group support than lesbians and gay men have begun to enjoy in recent years' (Balsam et al, 2005: 474).

Likewise, the experiences of lesbians and gay men may have more in contrast than in common. For example, as *men*, gay men may have more social and economic power and autonomy than women. However, as *gay* men they experience issues that are specific to gay male culture – including the notorious image obsession and 'body fascism' (Blyth, 2010). At the same time, gay men are also particularly disadvantaged by the norms, pressures, expectations and limitations of masculinity (see Chapter 1). Likewise, while lesbians may experience higher levels of economic marginalisation and decreased social mobility than gay men (because of gender inequality), it is easier for women than men to maintain social intimacy, and lesbian culture has historically been less consumerist and more positive about personal development, support and therapy than gay male culture (Cochran, 2001).

These brief points illustrate how generalisation can obscure important differences in relation to self-injury. Nonetheless, an understanding of the impact of homophobia (ie. prejudice and discrimination targeted at non-heterosexuals) and its relationship with self-injury is important (Alexander & Clare, 2004; Babiker & Arnold, 1997; DiStefano, 2008; Mayock et al, 2009).

Homophobia pathologises the individual's intimate, physical and emotional desires and inflicts a deeply personal attack on both the inner self and outer identity. Like many forms of prejudice and discrimination, homophobia positions the individual's 'difference' as the cause of the stigma, marginalisation and hostility. This is reflected in the historic criminalisation and medicalisation of homosexuality; the association of homosexuality with paedophilia in popular discourse; the condemnation of homosexuality as sinful in many religions, and more generalised homophobia that dismisses lesbians and gay men as not 'real' women or men, and as flawed, predatory or sick.

---

2. Prejudicial attitudes towards bisexual people include that they are sexually promiscuous, that they won't commit to either a specific partner or sexual orientation and that bisexuality is not a real identity (Klesse, 2010).

Lesbian, gay and bisexual people are at risk of discrimination and violence both in their immediate context, be that the family home, prison, hospital or care facility, and in wider social contexts, such as employment, school and social and religious communities (DiStefano, 2008; Mayock et al, 2009). This kind of identity-based vulnerability is at the core of minority stress: 'Social inequalities arising from sexual orientation, including incidents of victimisation and discrimination [...] [alongside] social stigma is a risk factor for psychological distress' (Cochran, 2001: 934). Furthermore, because prejudice is experienced in wider social structures as well as in day-to-day interactions and relationships, it can easily become internalised and directed against the self: 'Divisions in power and experiences generate dissimilar assessments of the self and social relationships' (Rosenfield, Vertefuille & McAlpine, 2000: 209).

Internalised hostile social attitudes and beliefs can result in the kind of distress that culminates in self-injury by exacerbating body alienation, self-hatred and shame. One young person described how: 'I was still depressed about the fact I was gay [...] the cutting kept getting worse and I couldn't stop cutting' (in Mayock et al, 2009: 88). Likewise, Colm's environment and his experiences of sexual abuse, coupled with the awakening of his own sexuality, compounded his confusion, shame and distress:

> When I started to get into teenage years so then I started kind of thinking about *girls* and stuff like that, and realising how I wasn't attracted to them, and realising that I was becoming attracted to the other boys in class, and not really wanting to be gay. And that's when it really took off for me, like I really started kind of pinching myself and like sticking myself with compasses and banging my head, and punching myself. And, like, looking back at it, I know *now,* it wasn't just low self-esteem, it was self-hatred, I didn't *want* to be gay, I didn't want to have had that *life,* didn't want to be at *home...* I just wasn't comfortable with *me.*

It is common for young people to be aware of their sexual (or gender) identity for a significant length of time before they 'come out' to those around them (Mayock et al, 2009). This means that many young people spend their formative years feeling conflicted and deceitful, as well as anxious about the consequences of coming out:

> I was afraid of everyone else and what they thought of me and I didn't like myself. I was, you know, shit and this and that. It was just basically self-

loathing, I didn't like myself [...] I was my own worst enemy. Then there was part of me that was proud, I was different being gay. I wasn't like everyone else in that respect but I probably didn't like that either. Like, I probably shouldn't be feeling proud about it because it's crap basically. So that's why I cut and covered it up, to justify myself, I guess. (In Mayock et al, 2009: 90)

Feelings of being in some way 'wrong' or 'different' have close links with self-injury (Alexander & Clare, 2004; Babiker & Arnold, 1997) and can be internalised, even when the immediate context may be supportive:

I know personally that it [self-injury] was to do with my sexuality because there were times when, you know when I came out, I'd been out maybe a year and I still had a problem with it even though no one else had a problem with it. So I hurt myself through myself. Then there was the whole problem of internalised homophobia. (In Mayock et al, 2009: 90)

Furthermore, while coming out may resolve some of the identity conflicts, it can also leave people more vulnerable to prejudice and discrimination in both the immediate and wider social contexts (Cochran, 2001; Mayock et al, 2009; DiStefano, 2008). Rejection by family, friends and peer group is not uncommon, and the workplace or school may also prove to be a hostile environment. Indeed, coming out is one of the most stressful periods in LGBT life (Mayock et al, 2009), and the highest rates of suicides occur immediately after people have come out (DiStefano, 2008).

The fact that LGB people also often experience prejudice and hostility in their immediate context is equally significant. They may be born into a family with negative and hostile beliefs about their identity. They may experience homophobic violence from members of their family (Beckett, 2010), and it is not uncommon for parents to expel young people from the home on discovering their sexual orientation. As one service-provider explained:

A lot of men who are gay would have talked about it, a lot of that was about shame in the family, feeling different, isolation, confusion, those types of things, but one or two was violence, actually violence that was physical.

There are also particularly high rates of self-injury (and suicide) among LGBT young people who are homeless, and even higher rates among those who get drawn into sex work (DiStefano, 2008). Thus, many LGBT people have no safe and accepting environment and very limited opportunities to develop a positive relationship with their inner self. Therefore: 'Self-injury can be understood as a coping response that arises within a social context characterised by abuse, invalidation, and the experience of being regarded as different or in some way unacceptable' (Alexander & Clare, 2004: 70).

As such, it is essential that helpers not only avoid reproducing prejudice but also actively challenge stigma and discrimination. However, research shows that, rather than challenging homophobia, services tend to exacerbate it (Cochran, 2001; DiStefano, 2008). For example, 'conversion therapy' (the attempt to use psychological techniques to change a person's sexual orientation) has been recommended in publications (Cochran, 2001), and research in the UK as recently as 2009 found that 17 per cent of mental health professionals admitted having tried to 'reduce or change their client's same-sex attraction' (in Butler, das Nair & Thomas, 2010: 106). The training of mental health professionals often ignores issues of sexuality, or underplays the complex, intersecting needs of LGB people, or simply reproduces stereotypical attitudes and beliefs (Alexander & Clare, 2004; Cochran, 2001). As such 'services, and individual professionals, often contributed to the sense of invalidation and difference'.

> Negative and homophobic attitudes and assumptions are widespread [...]
> By mirroring the negative social and contextual processes that contribute
> to self-injury, services could fuel the continuation or exacerbation of self-
> injury, or even trigger onset. (Alexander & Clare, 2004: 83)

As an inpatient on a psychiatric ward, Emma experienced frequent homophobia from both service-users and service-providers:

> In hospital another patient kept warning me that 'God doesn't like
> lesbians' and that I would 'go to hell'. Workers were aware of this and
> nothing was done. Staff would always ask questions about boyfriends even
> though I'm obviously a lesbian. One psychiatrist wrote down something
> about 'unstable self-image' when I described coming out and getting my
> hair shaved to a number 2. A member of staff repeatedly asked me if I was
> a girl or a boy. There were loads of ridiculous things like this.

Emma's experience highlights social and institutional forms of discrimination. 'Unstable self-image' is one of the diagnostic criteria of borderline personality disorder (BPD), and statistics show that lesbians, gay and bisexual men disproportionately receive this diagnosis (Clark & Peel, 2007). Therefore, while homosexuality no longer exists as a mental illness in its own right, it is still subject to psychiatric pathologisation through this kind of diagnosis (see also Cochran, 2001). As a result, lesbians and gay men are often reluctant to attend services and seek help (DiStefano, 2008), or, if they do use services, they protect themselves by concealing their sexual orientation, which can reduce the efficacy of therapeutic interventions (Cochran, 2001).

Thus, homophobia has similar effects to abuse, bullying and invalidation, and may include some or all of these experiences. It is also closely linked with self-injury through the distress and complex self-relation it causes, which has been expressed in the concept of minority stress. Finally, rather than being alleviated by services, homophobia and the damage it causes are very often compounded by 'problems with delivery of care' (Cochran, 2001: 940), and the negative consequences related to both concealing and revealing sexual identity.

Disability

The experience of people with disabilities is rarely addressed in publications on self-injury. Historically, self-injury among people with intellectual disabilities was defined as 'challenging behaviour', and was seen to result directly from the person's mental 'limitation'. More recent research has challenged this view and demonstrated that self-injury among people with intellectual disabilities functions in exactly the same way as it does for non-disabled people – as a means of coping with overwhelming feelings and experiences (Heslop & Macaulay, 2009; Kissane & Guerin, 2010; Jones, Davies & Jenkins, 2004). The high rates of self-injury among people with intellectual disabilities does not result from their disability but, rather, from the stress and powerlessness that is structured into their lives as disabled people, their increased vulnerability to all forms of victimisation, and their lack of opportunities for self-determination, self-expression and self-protection (D'Eath & Walls, 2010; Heslop & Macaulay, 2009; Jones, Davies & Jenkins, 2004; Kissane & Guerin, 2010; McCarthy, 1996; Pitonyak, 2005). Recent research into the quality of life of people with intellectual disabilities has indicated that they lack the essential components for a basic quality of life and wellbeing, such as autonomy, self-determination, economic and social opportunities and inclusion (D'Eath & Walls, 2010).

Lack of autonomy and control, particularly in institutional settings, is a significant factor in self-injury for people with intellectual disabilities:

I wanted to get out basically; I was craving to get out. … and because there was only one person on, there was supposed to be on that night. … they couldn't take me out. … I just felt (makes a sound of frustration and swears). And that's when I just went like I was gonna cut myself. (In Heslop & Macaulay, 2009: 40)

People with intellectual disabilities also report bullying in their day-to-day life as another key trigger for self-injury: 'People, it's the people make me do it… 'cause I hear things saying they hate me and all, they don't like me, you know? And I got bullied all my life' (in Heslop & Macaulay, 2009: 41).

For those who experience abuse, the effects can be longlasting, and self-injury may be the only means to alleviate the distress: 'You know the way that I was abused… it would be like the thoughts of him doing it and hurting me and stuff, those kinds of thoughts and they'd be constantly in my head;' 'Sometimes… my eyes are all over, if I see somebody in the corridor I automatically think about that tutor' (in Heslop & Macaulay, 2009: 43). The communication functions of self-injury are heightened for people who are not verbal or who use non-standard ways to express themselves when this is not supported in their environment. However, it should be emphasised that 'it is not the inability of the individual to use verbal expression that leads to self-harm but rather the inability of the wider world to accurately interpret and respond that results in self-harm' (Jones, Davies & Jenkins, 2004: 494).

In society more broadly, people with physical disabilities, like those with intellectual disabilities, experience higher levels of abuse, bullying, marginalisation and powerlessness than non-disabled people (Gannon & Nolan, 2003; Morris, 2004; Shakespeare, Gillespie-Sells & Davis,1996). These experiences are significantly linked with self-injury and can also be understood in terms of minority stress.

Finally, when disabled victims of abuse, bullying and hate-crime do seek redress, they are often disbelieved, because of their disability. An Equality and Human Rights Commission investigation into the abuse and murder of a number of disabled people who were in receipt of statutory services found repeated 'institutional failures' and a 'culture of disbelief' had resulted in a number of preventable deaths (Equality & Human Rights Commission, 2011). The following section therefore focuses on two further themes that have largely been ignored for people with disabilities who hurt themselves: sexuality and sexual abuse, and disablism and discrimination.

Sexuality and sexual abuse

People with physical and intellectual disabilities tend to have their sexuality (and their gender identity) either ignored and downplayed or pathologised as predatory and out of control (Shakespeare, Gillespie-Sells & Davis,1996). Consequently, when people with disabilities do not live independently, their bodies, appearance, relationships and opportunities for sexual exploration are rigidly controlled and policed – and, historically, many disabled people have been forcibly sterilised (Wilkerson, 2002). People with disabilities may have little or no choice about where and with whom they live and share a bedroom, or who they form relationships with. And, while there is some evidence that heterosexual expressions of desire by disabled people are becoming tolerated, expressions of same-sex desire or transgendered identities are often actively discouraged and seen as resulting from the 'impairment', rather than their gender identity or sexual orientation (Blyth, 2010; Gavriel Ansara, 2010). It is perhaps not surprising, then, that 'body hatred' is commonly cited by people with intellectual disabilities as an underlying reason for self-injury (Heslop & Macaulay, 2009): 'I didn't like myself, I didn't wanna know and I hated my body, the way it was and that's why I sort of did it' (in Heslop & Macaulay, 2009: 44).

The lack of rights and stigma that people with disabilities experience around their gender and sexuality has powerful effects on their mental and emotional wellbeing: 'Individuals' conceptualisations of themselves affect well-being […] mental health is damaged especially by situations [which] challenge valued identities or [produce] identity-relevant stressors' (Rosenfield, Vertefuille & McAlpine, 2000: 211).

The fact that the sexuality of people with disabilities is pathologised and ignored has made disabled children and adults much more vulnerable to sexual abuse. It also results in inappropriate responses to abuse – both of which have a high correlation with self-injury. Because sexual abuse is often assumed to be about sexual desire (rather than power, violence and humiliation), and because disabled people are largely viewed as asexual, ugly and undesirable, there has been a longstanding assumption that disabled children and adults are not vulnerable to sexual assault (Kennedy, 1996; Shakespeare, Gillespie-Sells & Davis, 1996). At the same time, there is evidence that points to much higher rates of sexual abuse of disabled adults and children (Kennedy, 1996; McCarthy, 1996). An international review of data indicated that more than 80 per cent of women with intellectual disabilities had experienced sexual violence (Baladerian, 1991). Moreover, when people with intellectual disabilities communicate their experience of abuse through non-verbal methods, such as sexualised actions, self-soiling or radical changes in behaviour, then these – like self-injury – are interpreted as a pathology of the disability, rather than evidence of abuse (Kennedy, 1996). This is further complicated by the fact that disabled people may be dependent on the people who are abusing them, and face an additional range of physical, social, material and communication barriers to reporting the abuse and getting it stopped. In addition, as noted above, when disabled people do make complaints they are less likely to be believed or viewed as credible complainants (Equality & Human Rights Commission, 2011; Shakespeare, Gillespie-Sells & Davis,1996).

Disablism and discrimination

Self-injury often reflects what the person has learned and experienced: 'What is carved in human flesh is an image of society' (Douglas, in Strong, 2000: xviii). Disability may not only lead to many of the experiences that underlie self-injury; it also influences the kind of treatment people receive and how their distress is interpreted. Jenny Morris (2004) found that mental health services tend to be obstructive towards people with physical disabilities and that disability services are insensitive to mental health needs. Most significantly, however, a mental health diagnosis changes how disability is perceived and responded to. In Morris's (2004) research, people with physical disabilities often faced extremely hostile attitudes and poor clinical practices in psychiatric facilities. It was not uncommon for people with disabilities to be refused physical assistance, on the grounds that they were 'really' able to manage by themselves. Staff also frequently emphasised that their role was to provide psychiatric support and not physical care. Moreover, symptoms such as pain and immobility were often regarded as part of the mental illness: ie. as psychosomatic or attention-seeking, rather than as arising from the physical disability.

Morris illustrates this with the experience of a disabled patient who, because she was not given physical assistance, fell and broke her leg while trying to use an unadapted bathroom. But she was then refused care because she was known to have a history of self-injury: 'They thought I had done it deliberately, they thought I had self-harmed and they didn't x-ray it for 24 hours' (2004: 20). After breaking her leg, this patient was moved from the psychiatric ward to an orthopaedic ward, but there she was often refused painkillers, because staff 'assumed that she could cope with pain because she had a history of self-harm' (2004: 32). This experience highlights the ways in which prejudices towards disability, self-injury and diagnosis of mental illness intersect and produce highly problematic attitudes that can result in significant physical and emotional harm.

Morris's research also highlighted a lack of awareness about and sensitivity towards self-injury in disability services, and participants were often reluctant to seek support because of these attitudes. For example, one service-user 'put off having new wrist splints made or seeking other treatment […] because of reaction to the scars caused by self-harm' (2004: 21). Likewise, another research participant described how 'having blood tests also provokes remarks from the person taking blood' and 'it's never in a private room and you don't want to have to go into discussions when there are other people in the room' (2004: 21).

In summary, the experience of disability is not just an individual 'challenge'; it is, rather, a minority social identity with a significant relationship with self-injury. This includes social marginalisation, institutionalisation and limited opportunities for work, education, social participation and forming positive relationships, which are essential to basic quality of life, self-esteem and wellbeing. People with disabilities are also particularly vulnerable to the experiences that are linked to self-injury, such as abuse, bullying, stigma and invalidation, and often lack opportunities for self-determination and redress. As such, disability increases vulnerability to many of the experiences connected to self-injury, and influences how services respond to the self-injury.

Social class

Social class (ie. differing levels of material and social resources and opportunities) also has a significant relationship with self-injury. However, there are often quite conflicting perceptions about whether self-injury is more likely to occur in people from privileged or disadvantaged backgrounds. Historically, psychiatry has defined self-injury (and eating disorders) as predominant in young women from privileged backgrounds (Favazza, 1996). On the other hand, services such as homeless and addiction facilities emphasise that social marginalisation and deprivation are closely linked to self-injury (Tyler et al, 2003). However, social status impacts in similar ways to gender in that, while social class (eg. privilege or disadvantage) affects the *type* of distress people experience, it does not ultimately determine or prevent it. Social class also impacts on help-seeking and the type of services people receive, with people from disadvantaged backgrounds faring badly in this regard.

It is important to note that 'social class' is a contentious issue and people rarely identify themselves with a social class in the same way as it is defined in research and policy. Most people tend to refer to their class background as 'ordinary', regardless of whether they would be empirically defined as working class or middle class (Bufton, 2004). Therefore, throughout this chapter I refer to social class in terms of privilege (for those with material and social advantages) and disadvantage (for those who face economic and social deprivation and hardship).

Disadvantage

Social marginalisation and disadvantage create a number of stresses related to self-injury. Poverty, unemployment, poor educational opportunities, low social status, poor work environments and lack of power and autonomy all impact on physical and mental/emotional wellbeing, and limit access to the means to articulate, challenge or escape those experiences. 'Socially disadvantaged groups are doubly disadvantaged in that they experience higher levels of discrimination and are more adversely affected than others by these experiences when they occur' (Kessler, Mickelson & Williams, 1999: 226). People from socially and economically disadvantaged areas experience poorer mental and physical health and die younger than those from more privileged and secure backgrounds (WHO, 2008). They also have fewer opportunities to develop their personal potential or to make changes in their lives (Fein, 1995; Kaplan, 1996; Sedgwick, 1982; WHO, 2008). These factors limit people's life chances and the possibilities for escaping stressful situations, as well as their opportunities for redress – all of which are linked with self-injury.

Disadvantaged localities can be stressful environments where people feel powerless and unsafe. A service-provider working in the North of Ireland highlighted some of the community issues that made self-injury a significant concern in 'areas where there were high levels of stress, histories of violence within the community: political violence and domestic violence, [and] significant use of alcohol and drugs'. Away from political violence, community deprivation can create similarly stressful environments, as both Emma and Colm described. Emma grew up in a sexualised environment that compounded the trauma of sexual abuse she experienced as a young child:

> I started cutting myself when I was 11 which I think was to do with being
> unhappy about getting attention from men generally and from being
> bullied in school. I grew up in a red light district and would get hassle off
> men on my way to school.

Colm's formative environment also had a significant relationship with his self-injury:

> It was kind of like a strange environment, I know it sounds a bit surreal *now*, but it was almost *taken* for *granted* that everybody had abusive, drunken parents. It was like this sea of alcohol where everything was like really *rough* and working class, and there was robbed, burnt-out cars everywhere, and *gangs*, and drunks on the street, and people begging at the shops – they'd ask you for odds [coins] and stuff – and after nine o'clock it was a no-go area. You daren't go down [to the shops] or out of the house, you might not make it back! It was that rough.

Colm related this deprivation directly to his self-injury:

> There was a real sense of desperation. There was a real sense of no hope and that added to the low self-esteem, that used to go even lower than that which was self-hatred. And then added to that, I couldn't handle being gay, I couldn't handle being in such a violent environment, and the kind of no hope and no future, sort of turned in on myself, and started reflecting in, 'I *hate* myself, and I *hate* where I am, and I *hate* my life, I hate that I'm not attracted to women, I hate that I'm not normal.' So I started l literally *attacking* myself with lots of physical actions.

However, in the midst of these difficulties there are also strengths, such as a sense of community, which can have positive impacts on mental/emotional wellbeing (Gale et al, 2011). Recognising the strengths within every suffering individual or community is essential to promoting self-determination and empowerment. Community and strengths-based responses that allow people to retain their autonomy, that educate and empower individuals and communities, are increasingly recognised as best practice responses across a range of issues and contexts, and especially self-injury (Green, 2007). Colm also recognised the importance of community spirit in the midst of deep suffering:

> The other *mothers* on the block of houses, like they'd help each other out – they had no money – so they'd help each other out with *food* and with clothes and stuff, and hand-me-downs, 'cos everyone was *dirt poor*, and all their husbands drank and beat them up. It was like Misery Street. It was just kind of almost accepted.

Disadvantage also impacts on the way individual distress is interpreted and responded to. For example, people from disadvantaged backgrounds report higher levels of mental/emotional difficulty but have reduced access to support services. When they do access services, they tend to get the most limited interventions, such as medication, compulsory hospitalisation and behaviour-oriented programmes. In contrast, people from more privileged backgrounds have access to a much wider variety of support services (both public and private), including talking therapies and approaches that tend to be more holistic and progressive (Rogers & Pilgrim, 2003; Sedgwick, 1982). Moreover, as one service manager pointed out, the structure of the public health system means that psychiatrists rotate every six months, thereby preventing continuity of care:

> What causes *great distress*, and it's not the services' fault, they have no choice, but it's the lack of continuity between the client – the patient – and the doctor. The continuity is one problem, but the *consistency* is another problem, the lack of consistency, you know, you're told to come back in six weeks, that type of thing, but you're coming back to a different person and you have to retell your story all over again. So it is really not a pleasant place to go to.

Overall then, the social and material context has a profound impact on the distress that people experience, as well as the support and interventions available to them and their ability to take up what is on offer. Poverty and marginalisation impact on all areas of an individual's life in ways that speak directly to many of the functions of self-injury. However, social and material advantage may bring its own particular set of stressors.

Privilege

Social and material privilege certainly create buffers against many of the specific stressors and vulnerabilities experienced by those in disadvantaged contexts. However, material wellbeing and social status can be merely facades that gloss over a range of significant challenges – as evidenced in the media exposés of troubled celebrities. Indeed, John Bradshaw (1988a; 1988b) has suggested that personal difficulties may be the driving force towards material and/or social achievement as a means of, for example, attempting to overcome a sense of shame and personal inadequacy.

A socially and materially privileged environment may also create its own challenges. It can be highly restrictive and constraining, shaped by rigid expectations. There can be intense pressure (internal and external) to maintain certain appearances, and limited opportunities to pursue personal goals, interests or aspirations. Rachel described being raised in an environment where her life was regimented in strict accordance with her parents' values and world-view: 'They brought me up with this kind of, [dictatorial tone]: "You do that because you *do*, because that's what other people do".' Here, privilege functions as 'golden handcuffs' that limit and restrict the individual while creating an appearance of abundance. This is poignantly illustrated by the life-story of the late Diana, Princess of Wales. Diana married into one of the most wealthy and powerful families in the world, and was idolised as embodying feminine perfection, yet she also experienced deep distress and powerlessness and harmed herself in a number of ways (Morton, 1998).

Furthermore, material wealth and high levels of education do not necessarily create emotional health. Many privileged households struggle with communication, feelings and emotions (Bradshaw, 1988a; 1988b). As one service-provider pointed out, loneliness and isolation exist even in homes that appear to have it all: 'We have become so isolated, and it's enforced isolation, and even within the family home.' Moreover, experiences of sexual victimisation, homophobia and prejudice around disability are not distributed on a class basis. And, while social and material privilege may provide some cushioning against the worst health inequalities, it does not prevent issues such as parental illness, addiction, separation and death – all of which are related to self-injury (see Chapter 3).

Furthermore, just as social and material privilege make it less likely that issues such as abuse will come to the attention of social services, it also impacts on how people interpret their experiences. Privilege is often seen to neutralise difficult experiences, as Rachel described in relation to her parents' struggle to come to terms with her self-injury: 'They can't acknowledge the fact that they made this person that is broken. They're like, "But we brought you up *well!*".'

A materially secure environment can also cause people to minimise the difficulties that they experience and/or define them as personal failings. Both Joseph and Rachel emphasised that they came from relatively advantaged backgrounds when they spoke about their self-injury. Joseph felt that: 'It [self-injury] came out of nowhere, because I come from a very stable, solid background, there is no emotional dramas in my family, you've got the kids and you've got the two parents.' Likewise, Rachel described her formative experiences in a way that downplayed the difficulties that she experienced: 'I was never physically abused, I've not had anything in a classic sort of life-wrenching way happen to me. But it was all completely psychological.' However, the psychological regime in her family was intense and invasive. Rachel described the ethos as:

> 'You *don't* shut your door, because what do you have to hide? We don't knock when we walk in because we are your *parents* and you have nothing to hide from us.' And I have real issues with privacy because that was very *invasive*. It's not nasty, it's not even really that *stern*, it's just *so absolute*, that they have this policy of complete invasive of 'You *belong* to us', that I think for me to *have* that [self-injury] was a thing that was *mine*. This whole kind of thing like, reading your diary when it's hidden in a teddy bear's head on the top shelf, you know, things like that. They *are* subtle but they are *so* psychological, like, 'We don't ground you, but we *will* hide all your shoes.' And you know in retrospect it almost seems *silly*, but to a teenage girl it can be really, *really* powerful.

Overall then, social and material privilege can create its own specific set of difficulties, as well as those that are not determined by social background – such as abuse or disability. Moreover, privilege can create a facade that makes it less likely that issues will be recognised within a family system and the services beyond it. The invalidation and minimisation that are often characteristic of these environments add to the hurt and confusion that self-injury expresses.

Ethnicity and racism

In Chapter 1, I noted that rates and patterns of gender and self-injury differ between BME and white groups, and this is also true across mental ill health in general. People from BME groups have much higher rates of mental ill health, longer periods of inpatient and involuntary treatment, lower rates of recovery and higher unmet needs than the white population (Bhui et al, 2005; Karlson & Nazroo, 2002; Leese et al, 2006; Shefer et al, 2013; Williams, Neighbours & Jackson, 2003). At the same time, people from BME groups also report significantly less satisfaction with mental health services and are less likely to seek help than white people (Leese et al, 2006; Shefer et al, 2013). This makes all the more significant the over-representation of BME groups, and especially young Black men, in mental health and secure mental health facilities (Leese et al, 2006).

It is consistently reported that rates of self-injury, suicide and attempted suicide among BME groups are much higher than in the white population, and significantly so for young BME females (Cooper et al, 2010; Newham

Asian Women's Project, 1998; Siddiqui & Patel, 2010; Watts, 2005). There are, however, conflicting accounts of rates of self-injury between different BME groups, with some research reporting that young South Asian women have the highest rates (Newham Asian Women's Project, 1998) and others that young Black women self-injure most frequently (Cooper et al, 2010). Some of this discrepancy may result from the source of the data – for example, whether they are A&E statistics (Cooper et al, 2010) or community-based research (Newham Asian Women's Project, 1998). This is further complicated by the fact that people from BME backgrounds are half as likely as white people to seek medical attention following self-injury (Cooper et al, 2010). BME groups are also reported to have lower rates of repeat presentations for self-injury at A&E, and, when they do attend, they are also less likely to be referred to follow-up services than white patients (Cooper et al, 2010).

Despite the conflicting data on the rates of self-injury among BME groups, two themes emerge from community-based research that are consistently recognised as significant in relation to incidence of self-injury. These are, first, the effects of racism towards BME people and communities, and second, within-community experiences of powerlessness, and exploitation within the family.

Racism

Discrimination and racism have significant negative effects on both physical and mental/emotional wellbeing (Bhui et al, 2005; Karlson & Nazroo, 2002; Newham Asian Women's Project, 1998; Williams, Neighbours & Jackson, 2003). Interpersonal racism (verbal and physical attacks on the individual and/ or their property and possessions) and institutional racism (restricted access to employment, education and leisure opportunities) have a direct relationship with anxiety, depression and stress, as well as physical effects such as high blood pressure, heart disease, hypertension and cardiovascular disorders (Bhui et al, 2005; Karlson & Nazroo, 2002; Williams, Neighbours & Jackson, 2003). Stress behaviours such as alcohol and cigarette use and food issues, and the related consequences such as diabetes, are also directly linked with experience of racism (Bhui et al, 2005; Williams, Neighbours & Jackson, 2003). Moreover, it is not just social and material disadvantage (poverty, poor housing, dangerous neighbourhoods, lack of access to education) resulting from institutional racism that is responsible for poor levels of physical and mental/emotional health; when the health status and outcomes of BME groups are compared with those of the white ethnic majority who experience similar material and social disadvantage, the BME groups still have much higher rates of physical and mental ill health (Bhui et al, 2005; Karlson & Nazroo, 2002). Therefore, the structures of inequality result in not only minority stress and mental ill health for BME groups but also poor physical health.

The situation for new arrivals also has very significant mental health implications, especially for those who arrive as a result of involuntary displacement. They not only have to deal with the traumatic events that displaced them, including persecution, torture, rape, trafficking, genocide and war; they also have to endure punitive asylum and immigration procedures, including detention. Moreover, they are often subject to discrimination and hostility in the 'host' country, and are refused access to health services (Mudiwa, 2009).

Both interpersonal and institutional racism can have powerful effects on self-identity and cause feelings and experiences related to self-injury. However, because interpersonal racism is individualised and unpredictable, it often has the most negative effects on mental health (Karlson & Nazroo, 2002). Interpersonal racism also tends to be very body-focused: skin colour and bodily characteristics become a target for attack, humiliation and violence. This can create a sense of shame and a desire for escape from the self, which self-injury can provide. Utam, an 11-year-old Muslim boy of Pakistani heritage, described how he scrubbed his skin raw as a result of the racism he experienced:

> It follows me everywhere, in the classroom, in the playing field, on the
> bus, it is there all the time and with it come the jibes and the jeers and the
> spittle and the shit and every night I scrub it and scrub it and scrub it and
> it won't go away. (In Martins, 2007: 125)

Services often compound the difficulties experienced by people from BME groups, through institutional policies and processes and the attitudes and beliefs of staff. Young people from ethnic minorities who are taken into local authority care often face alienation from their own culture, alongside marginalisation in services where staff and other clients are from the ethnic majority. They can find this a 'strange environment' (in Martins, 2007: 127), and they may also experience bullying and racism (both overt and subtle) from staff and other service-users. This led one Black teenager to describe feeling 'isolated and abused' in the very context that was supposed to be protecting her from her family's abuse (in Martins, 2007: 127). She described how remaining in the family home would have been preferable to the local authority care setting, where she was the target of racist abuse, because at home 'at least I knew the signs when trouble was brewing' (in Martins, 2007: 127–128). In the context of the constant racist abuse, the blood from her self-injury functioned to prove that she was a human being, 'the same as the rest of them' (in Martins, 2007: 128).

Within-group issues

Unequal social structures produce disadvantage, minority stress and health inequalities for people from BME groups. However, there are also issues within some cultures that can increase distress and self-injury, and these are particularly significant in relation to gender.

In some BME communities, gender roles and expectations of females can be very prescriptive. These can include attitudes towards education, employment, domesticity, marriage and relationships (Newham Asian Women's Project, 1998; Siddiqui & Patel, 2010; Watts, 2005). This often results in intergenerational conflict, especially during adolescence, as young women move towards their adult female role. This is often described as a 'clash of cultures' between the values of the home and the school, with each environment offering a different range of opportunities and limitations. This can often leave young women feeling conflicted and alienated from their own community, as well as from their school and wider white society, and self-injury has been closely linked to these experiences (Newham Asian Women's Project, 1998).

Some communities have a strong focus on family honour, and see upholding it as the responsibility of women. As such, the need to maintain family honour can take precedence over the woman's individual needs and wellbeing. For example, leaving a marriage to escape domestic violence, or leaving the parental home to flee abuse and exploitation may be seen as inappropriate because of the dishonour it would bring to the family. These pressures to maintain family honour and the lack of freedom women and girls often experience in these situations have significant consequences for both their mental and physical health, including increased risk of self-injury and suicide (Siddiqui & Patel, 2010).

> So it was sort of like taking control of yourself, like you think okay, if everyone else can hurt me then at least I can hurt myself more than they can... it's this whole thing about you have control over what you put into your body, if nothing else. When you cut yourself you can control that because you decide how deep, how much, how many, how often. (In Newham Asian Women's Project, 1998: 18)

Finally, members of minority communities may be reluctant to seek help from mainstream services, not only because they fear institutional racism and poor services but also because of within-community stigma: families may stigmatise the individual; communities may stigmatise the family; the medical profession may stigmatise the whole community, and wider social stigma against the BME community may be reinforced (Shefer et al, 2013). As such, help-seeking maybe viewed negatively as 'disclosing personal and self-denigrating experiences' (Newham Asian Women's Project, 1998: 11), as this young woman described: 'My parents, they think if I'm going through any kind of problem I shouldn't go and share it with other people, like outsiders' (in Newham Asian Women's Project, 1998: 22).

One way of coping in such contexts is to adopt an attitude that minimises the impact and power of external forces and emphasises personal responsibility. However, while this approach might offer some sense of control and/or self-protection, in the long term denying the impact of external forces only increases individual vulnerability and distress (Karlson & Nazroo, 2002). Moreover, 'personal responsibility' can equate with the kind of self-blame that is often at the root of self-injury (Babiker & Arnold, 1997), as well as culturally prescribed female culpability (Siddiqui & Patel, 2010). However, it is also important to recognise that attitudes and stigma around self-injury, mental illness and help-seeking varies *within* BME communities, in just the same way that it does within the white majority culture. The same range of attitudes can be found across all communities, from those that are supportive of individuals to those that are hostile and condemnatory (Shefer et al, 2013).

Overall then, people from BME communities experience a number of issues that are endemic to minority stress and have a significant relationship with self-injury. They are also less likely than the white majority to seek help for self-injury, and, when they do seek help, they are less likely to be referred to follow-up services. People from BME groups who use mental health services are less likely to have their needs met and more likely to be unsatisfied with their treatment.[3]

---

3. As a result of difficulties with uptake and delivery of services, some BME communities, such as Irish Travellers, have developed their own services (see Pavee Point Traveller and Roma Centre (www.paveepoint.ie/ – accessed 18 August 2016); All Ireland Traveller Health Study Team, 2010). However, that is not to assume that within-community support is always the most appropriate intervention. Service-users report very real fears about breaches of confidentiality, and belief-based responses from community services that can be detrimental to their wellbeing (Newham Asian Women's Project, 1998; Siddiqui & Patel, 2010). Cultural sensitivity within mainstream services, together with partnerships with specialist organisations (such as Southall Black Sisters – see Siddiqui & Patel, 2010), are essential in meeting the needs of people from BME groups who self-injure.

Unsatisfactory service provision may result from institutional and/or individual racism, but it can, in some cases, result from misplaced attempts to be 'culturally sensitive' (see Siddiqui & Patel, 2010).

• Chapter summary

In the last three decades there has been increasing awareness of the way in which distress in general and self-injury in particular are 'political as well as personal issues' (Babiker & Arnold,1997: 56; Alexander & Clare, 2002; Sedgwick, 1982; Spandler & Warner, 2007). As such, self-injury needs to be understood as 'inextricably linked to the conditions in which it occurs' (Babiker & Arnold, 1997: 56).

In this chapter I used the concept of 'minority stress' to explore the social factors that create the conditions for self-injury among marginalised populations. Experiences of discrimination, prejudice, disadvantage and abuse give rise to feelings that directly relate to the functions of self-injury, as illustrated in the table below.

Minority stress feelings	Functions of self-injury
Powerlessness	Agency Protest
Frustration	Control
Shame and self-hatred	Purging and cleansing Self-punishment
Despair	Comfort Relief
Fear	Escape
Anger	Release

These feelings and functions also intersect with the individual experiences, such as bullying, abuse and enforced medical treatments (see Chapter 3), which may also be linked to minority stress. The depth and complexity of all of these experiences, and the ways in which they intersect for each individual, require a response that is equally individual, complex and in-depth. This means focusing on the individual *within their context,* and supporting them to make changes that are both realistic and desirable for them. These might be real, practical changes – such as leaving home, coming out, or taking action against bullying and discrimination. However, in all cases it is likely that there will be negative consequences as well as benefits from tackling these issues – as described in relation to the benefits and disadvantages of coming out (above) – and individuals need to be prepared for and supported in this. Realistic expectations and a long-term perspective are essential. Neither self-injury nor the issues that underlie it can be 'fixed' overnight; for many people, this is a life-long process. Nonetheless, if people are supported in ways that are meaningful and appropriate for them, then these experiences can also become sources of strength and empowerment. For example, a stigmatised LGB identity may lead to the discovery of a new community and positive relationships.

The concept of minority stress highlights the ways in which society is an invalidating or abusive environment for many people. This is why a social model is essential to understanding and responding to self-injury. Much of the difficulty, distress and harm that underlies self-injury emerges as a direct result of social inequalities. Therefore:

> If we are going to work in progressive ways, we need a political approach that understands the impact of wider social structures [...] It is crucial to reintroduce issues of power, abuse, and oppression into discussions of self-harm. This is part of a principled approach to understanding self-harm. (Spandler & Warner, 2007: xx)

Learning into practice

Definition	Self-injury is social and contextual
Working principles	• Social issues, not individual pathology • Don't let the response mirror the context
Practice applications	• Awareness and self-awareness • Empowering identities

Definition: self-injury is social and contextual

Self-injury emerges from contexts in which people are marginalised, disempowered, stigmatised and mistreated. These experiences are integral to the structures of racism, homophobia, disability and disadvantage. The feminist slogan 'the personal is political' is particularly apt with regard to the individual experience of self-injury and the socially constructed minority stress that underpins it.

Working principles

1. Social issues, not individual pathology

Issues like racism, homophobia and social marginalisation have a significant relationship with self-injury, but these are clearly not pathologies of the person who hurts themself. They are powerful social structures that impact on identity and wellbeing. It is essential that helpers understand the impacts of minority stress, challenge stigma and prejudice, and promote positive identifications. This might include engaging with a range of identity-specific organisations. A supportive response, rather than focusing on 'what is wrong' with the individual and their way of coping, will enable them to deal with the very real impacts of social structures in positive and empowering ways. Clare described how it was precisely these kinds of contextual and political changes that had a significant impact on her wellbeing:

> I lived in a really, really helpful supported accommodation project for about six years, so I had a *nice* flat in a *good* area of town, I got *really good* benefits, so I was able to do the things I enjoyed. I had a really good housing support

worker, who was really active in Militant, so she had a real political edge and we *got on.*

2. Don't let the response mirror context!

An awareness of the ways in which social structures impact on individuals from marginalised identity groups is key to responding helpfully. It is essential that the responses do not reflect any of the damaging contexts that people who hurt themselves may have experienced. Helpers, especially formal services, must be sensitive to and challenge racism, homophobia and class and gender prejudice, as well as be inclusive of disabled service-users. Ongoing training is essential for staff, not only in order to 'equality proof' an organisation but also to reinforce understanding of minority stress and its impacts. At the same time, services cannot be expert at everything, and therefore partnerships with specialist organisations and the deployment of specialist workers (such as an LGB liaison person) can also be useful strategies.

Activity

- Investigate some of the key principles of social justice.
- How could you apply these principles to supporting someone who hurts themself? And what would be their impact?
- What might make it difficult for you to apply social justice principles?
- How could you overcome these challenges?

Practice applications

1. Awareness and self-awareness

Helpful responses are grounded in awareness and self-awareness. Awareness at the organisational/service level requires frequent training, input and feedback about self-injury and the related social factors. There also needs to be a genuinely egalitarian ethos and culture – it is of no use to have policies about equality and empowerment if workers (and thereby also, by implication, service-users) are treated in authoritarian ways (see Chapter 7). Self-awareness at the individual level is also essential. Everyone has their own specific beliefs, world-view and values, and we all need to be conscious of how these impact on the ways in which we respond to others. In services, good supervision and open discussion about clashes of beliefs and values are important. For example, is it appropriate for a member of staff with strong religious beliefs that homosexuality is wrong to work with a gay service-user (and vice versa)? In all contexts, awareness and self-awareness help to reduce the possibility of reinforcing minority stress.

2. Empowering identities

A response based in a social model is always strengths-based and empowering at both the individual and collective level. At the individual level, it looks beyond labels to the whole person. At the same time, it recognises the importance of identity and the impacts of marginalised identity experiences. It promotes identity awareness and supports the development of a positive identity, even in a marginalised context. Empowering identities also recognises that many of the experiences of minority stress, such as being from a BME group or a marginalised community, or being gay or disabled, have all been responded to through peer support, political action and community empowerment. Politicised peer/community responses can transform what was once a stigmatised or shamed aspect of one's identity into a source of connection with others, of self-empowerment and positive action (either in a political or support context). Empowering identities recognises the political aspects of identity as well as the individual impacts of social structures – such as minority stress – and responds to them in ways that promote transformation and wellbeing.

Activity

- What are your key values and beliefs?
- How do you practise them in your life?
- What do your attitudes and beliefs make easy and what do they make difficult when you are engaging with people who have different values and beliefs?
- How do you manage the difficulties?

5

Responding helpfully:
embodied and social interventions

This chapter moves forward from the main focus of the book so far – ie. understanding self-injury and how it functions in an individual's life – towards responding in supportive ways. However, the learning and the principles explored so far remain central here. For example, there is no one model that fits all and nor is there a 'quick fix' for self-injury. The ethos remains a holistic, person-centred and social-model response that is specific to each individual, their experiences, needs and desires.

This chapter explores some of the practices that have proved transformative for people who hurt themselves.[1] As in previous chapters, this is not an exhaustive account of all the possibilities; rather, it is an exploration of how holistic, embodied and social interventions connect with the functions of self-injury and the underlying experiences and allow the individual to make meaning and grow from them.

The most effective responses to self-injury always emerge from the individual themselves and draw on their needs, strengths and resources. An imposed response that is external to the individual will never be as strong or as effective as one that comes from within, because it is not authentic to that person. This is why working in collaboration with each individual, rather imposing top-down models, is the only meaningful way to respond. The need for responses at policy, institutional and practice levels to be guided by the

---

1. Some of these experiences were also explored in earlier publications: Inckle K (2010). At the Cutting Edge: creative and holistic responses to self-injury. Creative Nursing 16,4: 160–165, Springer Publishing; Inckle K (2011). Scarred for Life: women's creative self-journeys through stigmatised embodiment. *Somatechnics* 1(2): 314–333, Edinburgh University Press.

experiences of those who hurt themselves is increasingly recognised as the only way to develop effective services (Fortune, Sinclair & Hawton, 2005; Hadfield et al, 2009; McAllister, 2003; Simpson, 2006).

The practices that are highlighted in this chapter by people who hurt themselves include education, art, poetry and creative writing, meditation, alternative therapies and peer support. All of these practices help people to express, validate and make meaning from their experiences and build their own resources and potential. Before addressing these practices, it is important to highlight the core elements of responding helpfully. These are the quality of the relationship and a strengths-based ethos.

Responding helpfully: therapeutic relationships

Each person who hurts themself is a unique individual who requires an equally unique response. Nonetheless, there are some core guiding principles. First and foremost, there must be a purpose to the intervention – a clear rationale for whatever response is made. It can be helpful to think about this purpose in terms of exploring the functions of self-injury, working on the underlying issues from the inner world and outer context, or expressing the feelings that surround the self-injury. (Dealing with injuries and reducing the risks of them are dealt with in the next chapter, on harm-reduction.) User-centred services recognise that a helpful response starts with each individual, as described by this service-provider:

> The whole point really is to help people who self-harm to find out what it is
> that's going on with them in terms of feelings and problems that are making
> them feel so desperate that they need to harm themselves and to work
> with *that* rather than to kind of make the self-harm a *massive* issue, but
> obviously it does need to be responded to but in a kind of constructive way.

Focusing on the person requires a holistic approach based on listening, acceptance and having time and patience for the individual (Long & Jenkins, 2010). For Joseph, patience was integral to the support he received: 'My best friend and my wife at the time were a great help to me, they were very patient.' As such, a helpful response to self-injury emerges much more from the quality of the relationship with the helper than from any particular techniques or qualifications. Being accepting and non-judgmental and listening (to both what is said and unsaid) are essential qualities in a helpful response (Heslop

& Macaulay, 2009). Likewise, a service manager described how valuing and respecting the person who hurts themselves are also essential: 'If you are valued by the therapist you're going to feel valued and value yourself as well.' It is also important that the helper is sensitive and genuine, that they are trusting and trustworthy, and that they show solidarity and companionship with the person who hurts themself (Long & Jenkins, 2010; Simpson, 2006). For Emma, these qualities were embodied by a counsellor with whom she worked as a young adult:

> When I was 19 I got an appointment through my GP to see a person-centred counsellor. This woman was very patient and really seemed to care. She responded positively and truthfully to the questions I asked and really seemed to have faith that I could be ok and that I could feel positive about myself. She seemed to believe me and she seemed to respect me as a person… Her flexibility and her commitment to me helped me to feel safe enough to talk about, and draw, the things that I needed to.

These qualities form the basis of a therapeutic relationship, and this relationship is particularly important because, for many people who hurt themselves, their formative relationships, as well as previous encounters with helpers, are likely to have been negative and damaging. Thus, an extra level of sensitivity and trust, or 'being new', is required (Long & Jenkins, 2010: 197).

Overall, the key feature of any helpful response is the nature and quality of the relationship. Here, the term 'therapeutic relationship' is intended to refer to any support relationship between a person who hurts themself and a helper, regardless of the helper's role or status. It is possible for a relationship with a friend or family member, as well as any category of service-provider, to have therapeutic qualities and effects. Indeed, it is often those who have less professional status, such as social care workers and counsellors, who have much stronger, more positive relationships with service-users. These workers also tend to have a better understanding of self-injury (Warm, Murray & Fox, 2002), and to be rated most positively by service-users (Jeffery & Warm, 2002). The more high-status professionals, such as psychiatrists and nurses, often have only minimal relationships with people who hurt themselves and a limited understanding of self-injury (Jeffery & Warm, 2002). There is also wide variation within professions. Amanda experienced a radical contrast between psychiatrists:

The difference between her [current psychiatrist] and the doctors I would have been under at [psychiatric hospital] was that she just gives you a hundred per cent, she really listens, and she *believes* you, what's going on for you. In [psychiatric hospital] they *don't believe* what's going on for you, they label you as an attention-seeker.

Emma also contrasted professional attitudes towards her as a child user of psychiatric services and as an adult psychiatric inpatient:

I think what made people mostly more ok the first time I was in hospital was that the people who worked there were there because they wanted to 'help children' and not because they wanted to 'protect society from mad adults'. I think that because it was a ward for young people its general approach was more focused on trying to understand and not medicalise than I experienced on the adult ward later.

A genuine, respectful and equal relationship that is formed as a collaborative and supportive alliance is essential for supporting someone who hurts themself (Gallup, 2002; Long & Jenkins, 2010; Taylor et al, 2009). Moyer and Nelson describe this relationship in terms of 'core conditions for unconditional positive regard, empathic listening, genuineness and acceptance' (2007: 47). This was how Emma experienced support as a young person: 'I just believed that they cared that I felt awful, and that they didn't just judge me for feeling bad. They treated me as a person and not a patient. They didn't seem scared of my distress.'

Therapeutic/all relationships are damaged by attempts to control the person, to prevent self-injury (including checking for wounds), and breaches of confidentiality (Moyer & Nelson, 2007). Likewise, a response that is belittling (Taylor et al, 2009), or harsh and critical (Heslop & Macaulay, 2009) can also do irreversible damage. Unfortunately, the structures of many services mean that these responses are often enshrined in policy or become common protocol – especially for young people or in inpatient settings. Furthermore, the hierarchical nature of services and professionalisation mean the idea of an equal alliance between service-users and service-providers is antithetical to the very structures of 'care'. Therefore, many of the core elements that are essential to the kind of relationship that enables a helpful response to self-injury are at odds with the nature and structure of services. It is for these reasons that user-led services and peer support have often been the most effective in responding to self-injury, and, indeed, why it is suggested that user-led services and responses might be the only effective way forward (Simpson, 2006).

Responding helpfully: strengths-based approaches

The second core element of a helpful response is that it must be strengths-based. This means that the process of engaging with and working through self-injury and the related experiences draws on and reinforces the capacities and resources of the individual. In this way, the individual develops their own inner resources and outer skills to transform their life. Anyone who hurts themself has already demonstrated a huge amount of resilience and ability to cope, and these qualities need to be recognised and supported. Furthermore, self-injury is not the totality of any human being; each person is also contributing to life in a variety of ways, and has a range of talents and abilities. If these qualities are omitted from the support process, then the person is judged and pathologised solely on the basis of the most difficult aspect of their life, which will only further diminish and stigmatise them. Mark was emphatic that his self-injury did not take away from who he was overall:

> Even during times in my life when I was going through bad times and self-injuring, that wasn't all of who I was in my life either, I was doing other things, I was still evolving. Sometimes I was just clinging on, but that *wasn't all.* There were some times I would go through significant bouts of self-injury, then get up and go out and do some work, or get up and go out and *achieve* other things, or help somebody else, or just carry on with my daily life as normal – erm, [teasing] be a productive member of society!

The support process must focus on the individual's positive qualities and strengths, alongside their interests, goals and desires. The process should include joy and hope and it should validate the individual as they make sense of their experiences and their place in the world. Otherwise, the process will simply re-traumatise the person by solely focusing on the parts of their life where they have been hurt and powerless.

Overall then, it is essential that the process of working through self-injury is based on a genuine, supportive relationship that validates and develops the strengths, goals and desires of each person. It is an individual response that is made anew for each individual.

Embodied and social interventions

Embodied and social interventions are important for a number of reasons, including their connections to the functions of self-injury, their holistic and embodied ethos and their user-led origins. Self-injury is an embodied means of expressing and communicating thoughts, feelings and experiences that cannot be represented in any other way. It is therefore utterly counterproductive to expect people to express their difficulties in a neat, coherent, linear narrative – although this is very often what is demanded by services. Experiences can only be articulated in this way once they have been processed and made sense of; until then, other forms of expression are required.

> When events are truly 'unspeakable', speaking may not the logical or preferred way to process the past [...] Western emphasis on verbal testimony ignores other critical modes of remembering and disclosure [...] The talking cure [...] needs to be complemented by other means of understanding, expressing and processing the traumatic event. (Mallot, 2006: 165)

Unfortunately, 'western' culture in general,[2] and 'western' medicine in particular, remains enmeshed in the mind/body dualism that devalues embodied communication (Hadfield et al, 2009; Mallot, 2006). As such, embodied and social responses are often equally devalued, even when they have powerful impacts. For example, in a young people's group:

> The use of creative techniques resulted in some powerful and positive expressions of their issues, but the group would often see the use of these techniques as play and talking as the 'real' work. However, as the group progressed they embraced 'playing' far more and it began to become part of their collective voice. (Green, 2007: 57)

---

2. Using the term 'western' is politically contentious as it is based on an ethnocentric world view that divides the world into a hierarchy of western/norm and non-western/Other. However, 'western' values and perspectives have had a major impact on approaches to health and illness – many of which are particularly counterproductive for understanding and responding to self-injury. Therefore, the 'western' origin of a number of ideas, beliefs and perspectives needs to be acknowledged without legitimating uncritical use of the term. Wherever the term 'western' is used in this book, I intend a critical use of it and I place it in inverted commas and do not use a capital letter to highlight this critical use.

In recent years, some statutory services have begun to adopt a broader range of approaches to working with people who hurt themselves.[3] For example, the self-harm service at the Royal Edinburgh Hospital supports a wide range of responses to self-injury, including women-only swimming, art therapy and peer support.[4]

The Self-harm Service at the Maudsley Hospital in South London includes movement and creative therapies, cookery, creative writing, projective art and a patient-led group (Crowe & Bunclark, 2000; South London & Maudsley NHS Foundation Trust (SLaM), 2010). Zest, a community-based service in Derry/ Londonderry, which is integrated into the statutory services referral pathway, offers alternative therapies as an integral part of the support programme,[5] and therapists working in a variety of settings have found that journaling and painting are very effective forms of expression for people who hurt themselves (Long & Jenkins, 2010). There is, therefore, some evidence of more diverse and user-led approaches being incorporated into mainstream responses to self-injury – and this is also true for harm-reduction (see Chapter 6). The remainder of this chapter explores some of the embodied and social interventions that have been transformative for people who hurt themselves. These are education, art, poetry and creative writing, meditation and mindfulness, alternative therapies and peer groups.

Education

In my research I always asked participants what had helped them in their journey with self-injury, and a significant number spoke about the transformative and empowering impact of education. Initially this surprised me. However, on reflection, I realised that education addresses many of the functions and underlying experiences of self-injury. A good educational experience[6] provides learning, knowledge and skills that can increase critical awareness about the world and the way it functions. Learning can be a source of empowerment, and educational achievement can increase self-esteem and the

---

3. Creative practices have also been incorporated into the curriculum for medical students, to enable them to develop empathy, emotional awareness and interpersonal skills (see Thompson, Lamont-Robinson & Younie, 2010; Thompson et al, 2011).

4. See www.mwcscot.org.uk/media/176971/royal_edinburgh_hospital_self.pdf (accessed 18 August, 2016).

5. See www.zestni.org/complementary-therapies.html (accessed 18 August, 2016).

6. Education can also be a damaging and alienating experience, particularly where there is bullying and marginalisation. Likewise, the increasing marketisation of higher education diminishes much of the critical and creative potential education once offered.

range of possible life choices and chances, and social mobility. As such, it can lead to autonomy and independence in material and social terms. Education can also improve communication skills, and can validate an individual's perspective and experiences. In Clare's experience, even post-modernism – a much maligned area of social theory – had an important impact:

> For me that's where things like deconstructionism and post-modernism *really* made sense – is that, you know, there is more than one reality, and the *one reality* that I had been presented with wasn't necessarily the be-all and end-all. So the kind of academia or information-based resources had, I think, as much impact on me as, for example, therapy.

Education that encourages the questioning of conventional structures of power and knowledge can also have transformative effects. People who hurt themselves are usually defined by medical authorities in ways that do little to reflect their actual experiences, and more often disempower and stigmatise them – as highlighted in earlier chapters. Thus, critically-based education can impact on this power imbalance in a number of ways. Clare described how:

> I just *love* that question *why?* and that's kind of at the *root* of the *best* kind of academia, isn't it? Why? What? Is there a different way of looking at this? *Why* would you look at it in a particular way? What are the consequences? And they have just become the most *central* questions in my life.

Emma also identified education as significant in transforming her life. Her academic learning helped her to understand her experiences in a politicised and empowering framework:

> I did a social sciences degree, which helped me understand my experiences in a wider context. I learnt about the feminist idea that the personal is the political, which really helped me, and I ended up writing my dissertation on the medicalisation and depoliticalisation of people's experiences.

Emma also described how educational opportunities outside academia continue to play an important role for her:

> I spent some time doing counselling skills courses, which helped me identify my boundaries and learn that it was ok to expect people to respect

these. I had taken on board some belief that I was mad, and these courses helped me learn that lots of people have lots of experiences and respond in lots of different ways and that this doesn't mean that they are mad. It made this knowledge and belief more than just theoretical. I'm doing an art course now about identity and family so we'll see how that is helpful!

Information-based learning is also an important resource for service-users and service-providers. Clare explained that new information was just as important as her academic learning experience:

Even just coming across things like the Bristol Crisis Service for Women who were looking at self-injury in a *completely different* way to psychiatry, or just thinking that – there are *different* ways of looking at this and, actually, I *like* them better, and that's good enough!

Likewise, information-based education is also important within services to ensure that responses to self-injury are based on knowledge and resources, rather than fear and prejudices (Jeffery & Warm, 2002). Indeed, from a service-provider perspective, information, education and training, rather than more research about self-injury, are the most pressing current need: 'Information and training as well, is what is needed… There is still some *really* difficult stuff that goes on in A&E and GP surgeries and things like that, and it just seems like education is needed.'

Education, or an educative approach, can also play an important role in the therapeutic relationship and process. One service-provider described how education, with the attendant benefits of empowerment, choice and control, was integral to his therapeutic work:

They're surviving, they're coping, they're doing their very best, they're struggling, they're showing *amazing* amounts of courage and huge amounts of character. So my job is educational, it's facilitative, and it's bringing it down to a sense where we can *collaborate* on them looking after themselves… It's an educational approach from where an individual is at, at any given moment in time.

The breadth of educational possibilities within and beyond therapy offers countless opportunities to directly and indirectly impact on people's lives. For Rachel (below), art school and creative practices became a catalyst for transforming her relationship with her experiences and self-injury.

Arts-based practices

Visual arts

Visual arts, such as painting, drawing and collage, have a formal role in art therapy, which provides a safe space for people to 'let go' and express experiences in ways that can bring insight and transformation (McNiff, 2004: 29). But creative and arts-based practices can also have a powerful impact outside of therapy, as a means to express and integrate experiences. Rachel, who has worked with painting, performance art and costume design, found that all of these practices had an important and positive relationship with her self-injury, even though she was pursuing them for professional rather than personal/therapeutic reasons. As a young woman, Rachel had to overcome significant obstacles to attend art college, but when she did, it had a powerful impact on her life:

> I think as soon as I discovered art school everything kind of got better, you know, it all sort of sorted itself out. I had a direction then… and so my art work became really organic. I mean that's not what I do *now,* but I think that the reason that I painted and the reason that I worked like that was because it gave me an outlet that was really non-stressful that I could use in a therapeutic way.

Rachel's art education also enabled her to be geographically mobile and to move to a more diverse and accepting locale than where she had grown up. 'I felt very separate… but when I came to [city] I found all of these people, *crazy* people, who do these *crazy* things, and I was like: "Oh they're normal! Fabulous!"' In later years Rachel produced costume work, which included designs that integrated her experience of self-injury and her desire to challenge conventions of beauty. This work not only validated her own embodied experience; it also led to her becoming very successful in her own field:

> There was a little black jacket that was used in *The Clothes Show* [...] and they were like, 'Oh we love it! It's so beautiful, it's so beautiful, it's really rock and roll.' It's like this little jacket with lots of tassely fringing and all the arms are embroidered as cuts, and I just don't think they clicked on to what it was, but they had never seen my arms...

Rachel's art work, then, enabled her to integrate and express her relationship with self-injury. It also provided a validation of her (scarred) embodiment and enabled her to integrate her life experiences in her work in productive and effective ways.

Emma also explored a range of artistic practices for both therapeutic and aesthetic reasons. She worked with a therapist who supported her in drawing experiences that she did not feel able to speak about (see page 123). This experience inspired her to use art and print-making outside of therapy to explore her relationship with her self-injury and her scars. She initially began to work artistically with her scars in response to other people's reactions to them:

> To be honest I think I started doing photocopies and prints of my scars
> to try and get an understanding of how they look to other people. People
> would react to them and I wanted to see what it was they were reacting to.

However, the wider perception of self-injury as something shocking or strange affected Emma's creative expression in a number of ways:

> Later, people around me were trying to encourage me to do work around
> self-harm – I think partly because they think it is different/dramatic and
> so would make interesting/shocking art. I didn't want to do this because I
> don't like the way that it is represented as an extreme/shocking thing and
> so I wanted to create some images where the scars from self-harm were
> obviously old and incidental or where the scars were just like a pattern
> which was part of the texture of the skin. Print seemed like a good way of
> doing this and reproducing texture.

Overall, then, these visual, arts-based practices have a range of impacts on self-injury and enable people to explore and express the experiences that underlie it. Art may also be used as a way to challenge perceptions and stigma about self-injury, in both direct and indirect ways. Art can also be validating and empowering in material, symbolic and psychological terms. Art is not restricted to visual forms either; there are a range of physical art forms, such as performance, dance and drama, that can be useful interventions for people who hurt themselves.

Physical arts

Physical art forms, such as performance, dance and drama, can be powerful means to explore and express self-injury and the experiences that underlie it. The embodied nature of the physical arts, and their increasing accessibility through community-led groups, mean that they can provide an easily available resource for people who hurt themselves.

When Rachel moved to a large city to undertake her art degree, she had access to a wide variety of social and cultural spaces. For a while she used physical performance art as a form of personal expression that briefly became a substitute for her self-injury: 'For a while I found it in *these things* that I was doing.' Her performance art included physically painful processes, such as branding and having her back pierced with meat hooks and ornamental wings hung from her flesh. These art forms provided both a substitute for and an expression of her self-injury, and her performances had important emotional and psychological impacts for her:

> When you cut yourself it's like, sort of, like panicked; it's like whether you want to do it, it's such an intense *moment,* that to have that moment become… really gentle… like, the property of a room, instead of it being absolutely of your control… [It was] just this amazing experience, and it just felt like everything was really soft, and I just felt like I let everything go.

Her performances also challenged the secrecy and stigma she had experienced about self-injury, and provided validation for her self-expression:

> The response that I got from it was *amazing,* and the way that it made *me feel,* and then the response, was for me the most amazing experience. Because, you know, suddenly it was *okay,* people were really freaked out by it, but suddenly it was ok for me to have this *thing.*

Louise Pembroke, who has been one of the pioneers of the user-led, harm-reduction approach to self-injury, has also made significant use of physical art forms. Originally trained in classical dance, Louise has used contemporary dance to explore a number of her experiences as a mental health service-user. She has even performed her piece about hearing voices, *Dedication to the Seven,* for the Royal College of Psychiatrists, to help them to develop a deeper and more holistic understanding of the experiences of voice-hearers. Louise hopes that her work will reinforce the importance of the use of the arts in general, and dance in particular, as key to mental health practices:

> As a mental health activist I've been inspired by others who have put their experience of mental distress into different art forms. Art, drama

and poetry are mediums which have been used to explain and celebrate the differences that some of us live with [...] It is my hope that this dance might encourage others to explore the subject of mental distress in dance for both educational and creative entertainment purposes. (Pembroke, 2007b: 5)

These forms of physical art exemplified by Rachel and Louise may be exceptional, and may seem beyond the reach of many. However, there are much more accessible forms of physical arts that have been used by people who hurt themselves, and have been reported as powerful and transformative creative practices. For example, Clare described how one of the women's self-injury support groups in which she participated used physical arts as a form of creativity and communication: 'Communicating *creatively* was important for quite a lot of the women in the group... like dancing and performance art and music and *loads and loads of writing*, tons of writing.' Another group put on a cabaret as a way to publicly explore and critique their experiences as mental health service-users (see also below). Simple forms of physical arts have also been incorporated into inpatient self-injury services. The Self-harm Service at the Maudsley Hospital in South London uses both movement and drama in its recovery programme (SLaM, 2010).

In the community, there is a range of physical arts-based groups that can be useful in helping people who hurt themselves to explore their embodiment or the feelings and experiences related to self-injury. For example, authentic movement, which is part of the Feldenkrais method, can be a safe and simple way for people to connect with their bodies. Likewise, theatre groups such as Theatre of the Oppressed and Playback Theatre can be powerful vehicles through which people re-articulate their experiences in ways that highlight the political and social dimensions of what once seemed like individual problems. Theatre can also be a powerful way to forge community across identities and inequalities – see, for example, the Misfits Theatre Company, who co-produced a DVD dramatisation of Heslop and Macaulay's (2009) research about people with learning disabilities who self-injure.

Overall, then, arts-based practices, whether they are visual or physical, can offer important interventions for people who hurt themselves. They offer visible and/or physical forms of expression that do not require a linear, verbal narrative to communicate and express meaning. These practices can therefore connect with and externalise experiences and feelings in powerfully transformative ways.

Creative writing that also eschews the need to express the 'truth' in a linear and coherent narrative can also be an important vehicle for communicating complex and traumatic experiences.

Creative writing and poetry

Creative writing and poetry are also practices through which feelings and experiences can be expressed. Creative writing does not have to be logical, 'add up' or make sense in the same way as 'telling the truth', which means it can allow the expression of partial and confused understandings when there is not yet a coherent story to tell. Creative writing allows these stories to unfold, and the author to make meaning from them in ways that feel less threatening and rigid. This can be liberating, as are the possibilities for expression through metaphor, exaggeration and under- or over-playing 'facts', or telling stories about 'someone else'. Creative writing also enables experimentation with outcomes and retelling stories, which can allow for therapeutic resolutions to be explored.

For Clare, creative writing was a key element of her journey with self-injury, as it enabled her to express in words what she had previously communicated through her body. She described creative writing as 'moving the metaphor from the body onto the page':

> When I look back at my own self-harm, and *why I did it* and what functions it served, I *really* think that *communication* was up there at the top. So I think that moving forward for me, from that point of intense distress and intense need, *has* been about different ways of thinking, and different ways of communicating, basically, which creative writing does *both* doesn't it? Different ways of looking at the world, and different ways of expressing those different ways of looking at the world. And expressing them as impactfully and articulately as you *can*.

Creative writing, especially poetry, features strongly in survivor-led resources and publications (see, for example, The Survivor's Art Foundation[7] and various authors in Grant, Biley and Walker (2011) and Harrison (in Pembroke, 1996)). For survivors, this kind of writing enables a fuller expression and communication of experiences than is possible in 'factual' accounts. It also

---

7. See www.survivorsartfoundation.org/gallery/poetry1.html (accessed 18 August, 2016).

directly contrasts with the representation of experiences in case notes and diagnosis: 'Relying exclusively on scientific or realist tales risks misrepresenting participants' sometimes "messy" stories' (Carless & Douglas, 2009: 1547). As such, creative writing challenges not only linear and one-dimensional accounts of experience, but also the power structures that validate only certain representations and perspectives.

It is increasingly common for services to integrate creative writing into their work with their clients. For example, one service-provider described how writing poems or letters can be useful ways for clients to bring difficult experiences into their therapy sessions. Here, writing allows the clients to maintain a sense of safety, choice and control over their disclosure:

> They are making an informed choice of whether to talk about it or not. And then *how* we talk about [it], how we move forward... There are people who *write*, who have written stuff out. So if somebody writes it to me, or writes out whatever they want to bring up, then we get into a choice of: do you want to read it out, do you want me to read it out? Do you want me to read it quietly and come back? Do you want me to ask questions on it, do you *not* want me to ask questions on it? So even with that you have choices.

Zest, in Derry/Londonderry, supports service-users' creative explorations of their experiences and has published a service-user's collection of poetry and drawings (Harkin, 2000). Likewise, Self-injury Support in Bristol has produced *Ride On*, a collection of poetry by young women with experience of self-injury.[8] Creative writing, like all arts-based interventions, not only allows for the expression of complex and difficult experiences but also validates and makes meaning from them. Validating the self and finding meaning in a range of experiences are also integral to holistic practices such as meditation and mindfulness.

Meditation and mindfulness

Mindfulness, which originates in the Buddhist tradition as part of a wider spiritual practice, has been adopted into a range of conventional social and medical services in recent years, including social work (Hamer, 2006), cognitive behavioural therapy (Hayes, Follette & Linehan, 2004),

---

8. See www.selfinjurysupport.org.uk/files/docs/Ride%20On_0.pdf (accessed 18 August, 2016).

psychotherapy (Germer, Siegel & Fulton, 2005) and clinical treatment (Baer, 2006).[9] Mindfulness and other forms of meditation have been found to be effective in 'treating' a whole range of issues, including depression (Vohra-Gupta, Russell & Lo, 2007), addiction (Bowen, Chalwa & Marlatt, 2011) and anxiety (Greenson & Brantley, 2009).

Meditation and mindfulness are based on a practice of conscious presence and non-judgmental attention. In this way, rather than attempting to eradicate difficult aspects of the self, these aspects are observed and accepted as a path to learning. Focusing on the breath is a common method to ground and focus the meditation practice in the present moment. Thus it becomes possible to stay present with, observe and learn from elements of the inner self that are usually denied, distorted or neglected (see Chödrön, 2001). Meditation 'allows the meditator to control inner conflict and discover the element of choice within a perceived problem. [It] aims at expanding self-awareness with an increased sense of integration and cohesiveness' (Vohra-Gupta, Russell & Lo, 2007: 58). It is not, however, easy: learning meditation and mindfulness is not something that is quickly achieved once and for all; it is a lifelong process. This permanent state of learning also teaches patience and self-acceptance, rather than striving for immediate and unattainable perfection.

Meditation practice can also have a specific focus. Colm used body-focused meditation as part of his recovery journey. His formative experiences led him to have a very difficult relationship with his body, and, as well as self-injuring, he also hurt himself with drugs, alcohol and food. He said, 'Honestly, I don't think there has been a single part of my body that I haven't fucked up.' Colm discovered meditation while working through the stages of a 12-step recovery programme in which he was encouraged to make amends to his body as a way of making peace with himself.

> *Now* I use [meditation] techniques. The first time [I did so] was coming up
> to what we call step nine, which would be making amends. I started this
> meditation of making amends to your body, starting with your toes, and
> you think about your toes, and then your feet, and then your ankles, and
> you start moving all the way up through your body, and you think about
> the damage and the hurt that you've done to it, and you send love and

9. Mindfulness and meditation originate from a very different ethos and tradition to 'western' medicine, but in recent years they have been increasingly integrated into it. There are some questions regarding the efficacy of a version of meditation or mindfulness when it is stripped of its wider ethos and transplanted into 'western' medical culture.

peace and serenity. And you talk to your body like, 'I'm now going to look after you, and I'm not going to hurt you anymore, and I'll make amends.'

Meditation techniques (and alternative therapies – see below) are not magic cures. They do not provide an instant or easy fix, but they can create a sense of acceptance, choice and control. These qualities are often alien to the formative experiences of people who hurt themselves, and are therefore important on a number of levels. Colm still sometimes encountered the difficulties and distress at the root of his self-injury but his meditation practice helped him to cope in more empowered ways:

> At times when I still have *extreme* frustration and stress, I can still have moments of thoughts about hitting or hurting myself, but I usually try and go back into that meditation of, 'I'm *not* going to harm you, I'm going to make *amends* to you.' I *talk* to my body. My body is my oldest, loyalest most trustworthy friend; it's always been with me and it'll always try and help me, so I am going to try and help *it*, and try and not hurt it, and try and be loving and caring and nurturing to it. So I find when I go into that and say that to myself, it slows it down.

User-centred services are also often supportive of mindfulness and/or meditation practices in the wider community.

> There's mindfulness, mindfulness and breathing [in the local community]. So that's great to see actually, and you don't *have* to have experienced self-injury to go there but it's promoted to people that might have. [It helps you to] really creatively channel your experience… And you get deeper meanings of it, and you get a deeper understanding of what it has meant to you.

Overall then, mindfulness and meditation have been found to be useful resources for people who hurt themselves, as well as for wider forms of distress. Other alternative therapies may be equally beneficial, although they are less widely endorsed in conventional services.

Alternative therapies: healing not cure

Alternative therapies have been less readily integrated into mainstream mental health services, despite being shown to have an important role in addressing issues related to self-injury.[10] This is perhaps because alternative therapies are often based on a radically different perception of human health and wellbeing than conventional medicine (McNiff, 2004; see also Chapter 2). Rather than focusing on 'cure', which is the eradication of 'pathological' traits, alternative therapies focus on integrating, learning and growing from difficulty and disease. This is often expressed in terms of the contrast between healing and cure. 'Healing is not the elimination of a thing (an illness, a problem, a symptom, a disorder), but a transformation of a person, a self, that is a bodily being' (Csordas, 2002: 3). Cure, in contrast, is the attempt to restore a person to their prior state of being. Healing does not attempt to restore someone to their former self, or offer a pre-defined outcome; rather, it embarks on a process of working with the experience in transformative ways: 'Like planting a seed, or like nudging a rolling ball to slightly change its trajectory so that it ends up in a different place' (Csordas, 2002: 5).

An ethos of healing is particularly important when medical resolution is not possible, such as in the case of spinal cord injuries (see Smith & Sparkes, 2005): 'There can be healing when curing is impossible' (McNiff, 2004: 4). The ethos of healing offers a range of possible interventions, all of which are based on the acceptance of the individual and the belief in the value and purpose of their life, regardless of medical labels. There is no single healing practice or alternative therapy that will help everyone, but a range of options is increasingly advocated by user-centred services:

> A lot of people have talked about different things that helped them in ways that they've helped themselves, and ways that they have found helpful outside of the conventional kind of mental health system. But they've varied a lot. Some people have found things like massage or homeopathy or aromatherapy and things *really* helpful and then other people wouldn't have found those same things helpful. So I wouldn't say that there's one particular thing that stands out as that's been a really helpful thing, but lots of people have found different things helpful.

Another service-provider described the benefits of 'things like drawing, drama, aromatherapy… I know somebody that taught emotional freedom technique very recently'. As noted above, Zest, the Derry/Londonderry-based self-injury and suicide service, has integrated alternative therapies into their service.

---

10. See http://zestni.org/complementary-therapies.html (accessed 18 August, 2016).

Options include Indian head massage, hot stones massage, aromatherapy, reflexology and Swedish body massage. These alternative therapies are rooted in Zest's holistic approach, and are seen to offer a range of potential benefits: to 'boost the immune system, help eliminate toxins, help relieve pain, improve circulation, improve sleep patterns, increase energy levels, induce deep relaxation, reduce stress and tension and restore balance to body systems'.[11]

The experience of healing touch – through massage, for example – can also be very powerful for people who have often experienced negative physical contact from themselves and from others. A service manager described the importance of therapeutic touch:

> Any alternative therapy that makes a person feel even a *tiny* bit better
> is *terrific*... Massage, if you think about it, it's about self-care isn't it? If
> someone is upset you rub them, and massage is the perfect rub isn't it?

Fundamental to all alternative therapies is an ethos of acceptance and non-judgment. This in itself can be hugely transformative for people who are used to being diagnosed and worked *on*, rather than accepted and worked *with*. Amanda had a positive – and unusual – experience of working simultaneously with a psychiatrist and a spiritual healer, both of whom were supportive of her work with the other. The ethos through which the spiritual healer worked was particularly important for her:

> [Name of healer] just really accepted me for who I am. She never
> interfered with the medical side; she always said, 'If you need help, go for
> it.' She's very unconditionally loving and accepting, and she helps you find
> your own path in life, your own journey, a sort of wholeness, that gives
> you back to yourself.

The relationship with the healer as well as the therapy itself was empowering and validating for Amanda. The therapy used visualisation techniques that were not problem-focused but instead worked to integrate Amanda's experiences into her sense of self and life trajectory:

> [The visualisations were] for my whole life, like whatever was going on
> in my life. The visualisations would kind of take you on a journey. The

---

11. See http://zestni.org/complementary-therapies.html (accessed 18 August, 2016).

visualisations that [name of healer] would have done were to take you on a journey of self-discovery, and being able to heal your life and heal yourself.

The healing work empowered Amanda in a number of ways, including developing the confidence to articulate her experiences and also to begin to move away from hurting herself.

> The spiritual healer gave me voice to kind of like, to be able to speak what was going on… Every now and then I get a feeling to kind of self-harm, but it *won't* happen, *I won't* go through with it. I think the whole spiritual side of things helped me to cope with not wanting to hurt myself.

Amanda's experiences were so transformative for her that she hoped alternative therapies/spiritual healing would become much more widely accepted and integrated into treatment teams:

> I really believe the spiritual side of the person is just as important as the biological side of the person. I really believe that… and I really believe that if *they* [spiritual healers] became part of a multidisciplinary team that would make so much difference.

Alternative therapies that promote healing rather than cure can have a powerful impact on individuals. Because they are based on acceptance, non-judgment and the belief in the value and worth of all lives and experiences, they contrast significantly with the conventional medical approaches of 'normalisation' and 'cure'. Healing interventions can be seen as 'a kind of ripening' (Sutherland, 1997: 3) that integrates and makes meaning from difficult experiences, rather than pathologising and attempting to eradicate them. Some of these features of healing relationships may also be found in peer support, since the peer ethos is also based on acceptance and making meaning from experiences.

Peer groups

Peer support for people who hurt themselves is often regarded negatively by mainstream service-providers, with emotions ranging from discomfort to outright fear and rejection. This reaction is largely based on misperceptions about self-injury and stereotypes about people who hurt themselves. For example, if self-injury is assumed to be a learnt or copycat behaviour, and people who hurt themselves are viewed as attention-seeking, then a peer support group will be seen as a place where individuals teach each other new ways to self-injure and encourage one another to do so (Green, 2007) (see also Chapter 2). However, this is the opposite of their role, purpose and function.

One of the core features of peer support is breaking down isolation and alienation. 'Sharing self-injury experiences apparently reduces its associated secrecy, isolation, guilt, shame and perhaps consequently the need to self-injure' (Corcoran, Mewse & Babiker, 2007: 49). Indeed, rather than peer groups focusing entirely on acts of self-injury, peer support groups have a much wider and more holistic focus, which often includes political and social action. In peer groups, members are able to explore a range of issues and experiences, to support and validate one another as whole human beings, and to take collective action in response to injustice. Moreover, the act of being able to give support can be just as validating as receiving it. Peer groups also empower members by allowing autonomy and control over the group's purpose, function and activities, again challenging many of the underlying experiences its members may have.

There are two main types of peer support group: face-to-face and distance. Both of these may be peer run and led, or they may have a professional facilitator.

Face-to-face peer groups

Professionally facilitated face-to-face peer groups have the advantage of easy access to resources such as meeting spaces, because they are usually run as part of a wider, funded service. For example, The Basement Project[12] and 42nd Street in Manchester[13] are both self-injury services that facilitate peer support groups. Facilitated peer support groups tend to focus on a particular demographic of service-users: The Basement Project runs groups for adult women, and 42nd Street runs groups for young people. The focus on a particular demographic is important when people are from marginalised social groups and may have experienced specific identity-related stigma and isolation (see Chapter 4).

The Basement Project women's support group provides a wide range of benefits for participants:

---

12. See https://basementprojectbooks.wordpress.com/ (accessed 18 August, 2016).

13. See http://42ndstreet.org.uk/ (accessed 18 August, 2016).

A *lot* of women have felt that it was *fantastic* to feel kind of the support and friendship of other women, and to feel like you're not alone with this, and you can share stuff and not feel different and crazy and feel kind of like you can offer something *back* to other people *as well*. You're not just this messy wreck of a person that's useless, as well as getting support from other people, you can help *them*.

Professionally facilitated peer support groups should allow participants to have control of the key aspects of the group structure and process. This is particularly important in redressing many of the experiences that underlie self-injury, such as lack of control, safety and self-determination, as well as counterbalancing many of the experiences members may have had in conventional services. As such, the focus of the women's self-injury support group was on 'people coming together':

I mean we [the professional facilitators] would facilitate them, but the people who come would set the agenda of what they want to talk about and we would feed in ideas, of things that we could do, or ways that it might be helpful to look at things, or talk about, but, you know, [the main focus was] encouraging people to support each other.

This group was often women's first experience of ownership and self-determination around their distress and self-injury, and that was a hugely empowering feature:

People have felt like the group was *theirs, their* space, and it might feel like a kind of unusual [experience] to have a space that they could determine what happened there, and make their wishes known and be listened to and that kind of stuff is really important. I mean the actual work that people *did* in understanding what had happened to them and expressing stuff about it was really, really important, but also the whole kind of *group* nature of it and the respecting and listening to each other and being respected and listened to by each other and that kind of stuff is what people have often said.

Peer groups, then, function to redress issues around self-injury on a number of levels, which include the focus of the group-work, as well as the nature of the group itself.

The young people's group, 42ⁿᵈ Street in Manchester, was formed on a 'social action' model, which means that the professional's role is as an ally to service-users, rather than the 'expert' in charge (Green, 2007).[14] The group evolved specifically to meet the stated needs of the group members and operated on principles of equality and collectivity, with an emphasis on the social and contextual nature of experiences, rather than individual pathology or labels. The group set the ground rules and goals of the groupwork, and Green (2007) reports that this included complex negotiations around how self-injury was to be managed during the group meetings and on the premises where the group took place. These discussions were empowering and challenged the control, stigma and labelling that the young people commonly experienced. Allowing the group autonomy was an equally important experience:

> Leaving the group to work alone provided a powerful message to the
> young people that they could be left alone, as they had often experienced
> attitudes that they weren't responsible enough, or wouldn't be able to cope
> on their own. (Green, 2007: 59)

Once established, the group continued to develop its goals and processes and moved towards political actions, as well as providing support to group members. The multi-faceted work of the group highlights the ways in which the complexity of self-injury needs to be addressed in a multi-layered approach:

> Significantly, the group began to express a desire to move from an
> individual perspective to more politically motivated action and awareness-
> raising outside of the group themselves. This included making demands
> of psychiatrists, petitioning, producing leaflets, protesting, contacting the
> media, organising conferences, and even just yelling. (Green, 2007: 55)

Peer groups function, then, not just through the content of the group process and activities but also in allowing people who hurt themselves choice, control and autonomy over their lives and bodies – experiences that have often been absent from their lives and conventional services. Professionally facilitated peer groups can be a powerful resource for people, but they do pose challenges to professionals. They run counter to ingrained attitudes and misperceptions

---

14. See Dale Hunter's (2007) *The Art of Facilitation* for an excellent guide to person-centred group facilitation.

about self-injury. They also demand that the group is trusted to deal with difficult issues, and require professionals not to reassert control when challenges arise. For the group to be effective, it needs to be allowed to deal with even the most difficult issues. In 42nd Street this occurred when a member of the group disclosed that she hoped it was an opportunity to form a suicide pact:

> At the beginning of the group, one young woman said that she liked our idea of collectivity. However, what she liked about it was that it presented the possibility that it could collectivise her (and potentially other members') desire to kill themselves – a chance to form a suicide pact. This obviously shocked us as workers. We worked with this very carefully. We ensured that we took the distress very seriously, whilst not overreacting. We emphasised the aims of the group and the possibility of using the group to achieve change in some other way. We had to work hard in the early stage of the group to help the young people turn these very negative and self-damaging ideas around, and to use this energy for other purposes. (Green, 2007: 58)

Overall, then, professionally facilitated peer groups offer an important vehicle to support people who hurt themselves in multifaceted ways. The variety of group activities and goals reflect the individual and contextual nature of self-injury, as well as connecting directly with a number of its functions. These groups can also offer service-users a radically different experience of themselves. By allowing members to control the group function and process, they provide empowering and validating forums for personal and collective transformation. This is also true of peer-facilitated support groups.

Peer-run groups

Peer-facilitated groups share many of the benefits of professionally facilitated groups, but also have additional advantages and difficulties. It can be harder for peer-facilitated groups to access regular meeting spaces and, because they are voluntary, peer-run groups rely on the availability of members to undertake all of the work, which can be onerous and demanding. On the other hand, peer groups have the advantages of being completely autonomous and of not being restricted by professional policies or fears. Peer-facilitated groups can also be particularly empowering, as service-users take control of redressing deficits in conventional services. Clare described a number of features of STEPS, a women's self-injury support group:

We set up STEPS just to have a halfway decent place that we could go to on a regular basis. So what made that unique was the fact that it *was* halfway decent! That it was women only, but I think the fact as well that it was non-hierarchical, was really, really important, and that everybody that came to the group was somebody who *did* self-harm and actively identified as having personal experience of self-harm, and that was kind of part of the whole point really, that you kind of went to the group to receive support and to offer it at the same time, and recognition of the fact that you were able to do *that* [ie. give support], even at times of kind of really extreme distress you could still play a role in supporting other people.

As such, the group validated members in a number of ways. It also provided a space that broke through the isolation and stigma that members had experienced. This was important for Rachel, who also attended STEPS:

I think with STEPS it was just the idea that there were *other people*; it was more like I just needed to know that I wasn't on my own – and those girls were *great*. We used to, it was so *normal*, we used to do amazing stuff, but it was just so normal. It was just having a cup of tea and spending time with people, and being able to be *honest* about those things was just, like, *unbelievable*. You know, it was like this little revolution in my head where I was like, 'Okay, I think I'm fine,' you know.

Emma highlighted that useful information was often shared in peer groups – which contrasts starkly with professionals' fear about group members using the forum to promote methods of self-injury:

People just talked about what they wanted, whether that was how they felt about their childhood/their therapist/their pet dog. I think we were just really respectful of each other and got a lot from realising that we were not the only person that self-harmed/that had experienced trauma/ had been abused/was pissed off at the psychiatric system. [It] was also useful to share positive experiences of counselling, therapy, creativity and life.

The groups also supported creative forms of expression as positive and powerful ways of working with self-injury (see above).

Furthermore, like the young people's group at 42nd Street, engagement with the wider social and political issues also became important to members of STEPS. This led to the formation of another peer group, called Mad Women. Mad Women was set up to tackle the wider social and political issues related to members' experiences of self-injury and mental health services. Members undertook a variety of activities, ranging from speaking on local radio to putting on a cabaret:

> Mad Women was born out of frustration with the women's groups that we
> had been involved in that didn't seem so political, and just the fact that
> we believed that women's mental health was an inherently political issue.
> We just wanted to be able to relate *women's mental distress* to *poverty* or
> *patriarchy* or any of the myriad political things that impact on women's
> mental health, and we wanted to be able to do something about it rather
> than sitting around having cups of tea or offering each other support –
> which is *really, really important* but ultimately frustrating if you don't feel
> that you're playing an active role in doing something about what causes
> the need for support in the first place.

Peer support groups, then, allow members to address the full range of issues related to their self-injury and often do so using best practice approaches, such as holistic and creative interventions.

In recent years research has begun to explore the benefits of peer support groups for people who hurt themselves. Corcoran, Mewse and Babiker (2007) conducted research with members of three women's self-injury support groups and found they had significant impacts in addressing the needs and issues that members faced. The groups were particularly effective because they didn't separate the self-injury from the rest of the person's life but approached it in an interconnected, holistic way. At the centre of the group process was the empowerment of the members, and this promoted experiences of belonging, sharing and autonomy. The environment was safe, accepting and inspiring, and this led to positive feelings, and enabled change.

Melanie Boyce (2012) also found that peer support groups (women-only and mixed-sex) had a range of similar positive impacts for participants. However, they often struggled to survive for any length of time because they depended on volunteer organisers and lacked access to resources. This, and other research (Boyce, 2012; Corcoran, Mewse and Babiker, 2007; Green, 2007; Jones et al, 2010; Simpson, 2006; Warm, Murray & Fox, 2002), report that peer support groups have overwhelmingly positive impacts and recommend that groups are supported by services, particularly in terms of providing resources for meeting spaces and changing attitudes towards them.

Overall then, face-to-face peer groups, whether they are peer run or professionally facilitated, have a range of powerful benefits for people who hurt themselves, by redressing some of the underlying needs, experiences and functions of self-injury. Peer-run groups have also been integral to developing some of the most effective responses to self-injury, including harm-reduction, which is explored in the next chapter. Face-to-face groups are not the only kind of peer support available, and in the digital age there is an increasing number of distance, online peer groups, networks and resources.

Distance peer groups

Distance peer support groups did not emerge only with the advent of internet forums; they actually pre-dated them. Pen-friend networks and newsletters such as SASH (Survivors of Sexual Abuse and Self-Harm) existed for a significant period of time in the UK. SASH produced a quarterly newsletter made up largely from submissions by group members, which addressed a range of self-injury-related issues, as well as providing space for poetry and creative work. SASH also facilitated a pen-friend network, where members could write to one another and build community and support. It folded in the early 2000s, largely due to the difficulties in maintaining the publication and distribution of a newsletter on a voluntary basis.

As a young man, Joseph participated in a pen-friend network that helped him to overcome some of his sense of isolation and provided him with a forum that felt safe and manageable.

> [It was] a connection. It was great to share with people that you knew you didn't have to meet face to face, because I would be hopeless at that kind of thing, which would be something else in my life. And of course the letters wouldn't really be about you, they'd be about your cutting. Which really – it was *you* but it *wasn't* you... Just having something in common with people, not people, strangers.

Distance groups afford an extra level of safety and anonymity that isn't possible in face-to-face groups, and that can be an important safety mechanism for people like Joseph, who was clear that, 'I never wanted to meet them, no way.'

147

Nonetheless, Joseph generally felt his experience in this group was positive and supportive, even though he experienced some sense of difference as the only male in a group: 'It was all just a name, they were always women I remember, and they were always about between 20 and 40 and married and all living usually around the London area.'

Today, a huge amount of work, social activity and connection takes places over the internet, and this is also true of self-injury peer support groups. Nonetheless, the fears around peer support groups are often intensified with regard to online groups, because of the unregulated nature of the internet. However, major search engines such as Google have policies (available online) in which they commit to removing any material that 'promotes' self-injury, suicide, anorexia or direct harm to others. Moreover, there is as yet no research that indicates that online groups are having a detrimental impact on people who hurt themselves. Indeed, there is evidence to the contrary, demonstrating that online self-injury support groups can be positive and supportive. For example, Murray and Fox (2006) found that internet support groups had many positive impacts, including being continuously available and providing a depth of intimacy, bonding and support that members appreciated. There were also some indications that the support contributed to a reduction in self-injury among members. Likewise, Warm, Murray and Fox (2002) found that internet support forums have a range of benefits, including their 24-hour-a-day availability, which is especially important at times when conventional services are closed. This research also found that online forums were rated more highly by service-users than were medical services, including psychiatry.

The internet can also provide a range of resources for helpers (Moyer & Marbach, 2008), and is increasingly used to conduct research about self-injury, with no apparent negative impacts on participants (eg. Adams, Rodham & Gavin, 2005; Jeffery & Warm, 2002; Murray, Warm & Fox, 2005; Warm, Murray & Fox, 2002). Recent years have also seen the development of online, user-led support groups, such as LifeSIGNS,[15] and recovery programmes, such as the Alumina programme run by selfharm.co.uk,[16] which are proving popular and effective. Indeed, these peer-run, web-based organisations are increasingly being called upon to develop and provide training for mainstream services.

However, some caution is needed with all responses to self-injury. It is advisable to do some research into any service, practitioner or group before

---

15. See www.lifesigns.org.uk (accessed 18 August, 2016).

16. See www.selfharm.co.uk (accessed 18 August, 2016).

committing to it, to make sure it is a safe and accountable space. Alternative practitioners should belong to a professional regulatory body (whatever their service), and groups and organisations should have clear ground rules, values and codes of conduct. The Bristol-based organisation Self-injury Support has an online directory of reliable face-to-face and internet support groups and resources.[17]

• Chapter summary

This chapter has explored a range of embodied and social interventions that people who hurt themselves have found useful. These include education, arts-based practices, creative writing, peer groups, meditation and alternative therapies. This is not an exhaustive list, but it is intended to illustrate how embodied and social practices that focus on the whole person, rather than just their self-injury or difficulties, can have powerfully transformative effects. Embodied and social interventions for people who hurt themselves have a strong basis in user-led and non-mainstream services but are also increasingly being recognised in statutory and conventional provision.

Embodied and social interventions are particularly significant because they address a number of the functions of self-injury. This is especially true in terms of providing a visible and physical expression of feelings and experiences that cannot be put into words, as well as validating a person and their experiences. The table below sets out the ways in which the creative practices explored in this chapter address some of the meanings and functions of self-injury.

Practice	Impacts
Education	Autonomy, empowerment, communication, validation, self-esteem, choices
Arts-based practices	Expression, communication, validation, symbolic representation
Peer groups	Identity, strengths, de-stigmatising, support, communication, validation, control

17. See www.selfinjurysupport.org.uk/resources (accessed 18 August, 2016).

Meditation	Holistic, time, acceptance, symbolic representation, control, strengths
Alternative therapies	Holistic, acceptance, symbolic representation, strengths, validation, choice

All of these approaches are also significant because they allow each individual to express and make meaning from their experiences on their own terms and within their own frame of reference. In doing so, they enable the acceptance and integration of difficult experiences in empowering and transformative ways.

Finally, it is important to remember that many people are quite intimidated by the idea of arts-based or creative practices, and describe themselves as 'not creative'. Creative practices are not about producing works of fine art (although some people may well do this); they are simply about being open to exploration, using a range of different media. There is no right or wrong in creativity, no good or bad. Every expression is authentic, valid and meaningful. There is no goal or rules to follow: simply a space and an opportunity for a person to be themselves (see McNiff, 2004). This in itself can be a significant experience for people, even if difficult at first. Ultimately, creative practices are about trusting the process of exploration and the value of an agendaless, goalless opportunity. As such, embodied and social interventions require helpers who can tolerate uncertainty and who are open to collaborative, and often creative, explorations.

Learning into practice

Definition	Self-injury is symbolic and expressive
Working principles	• Collaboration and creativity • Strengths not sickness
Practice applications	• Openness • Creativity has no goals, agenda or wrong

Definition: self-injury is symbolic and expressive

Self-injury is a visible and/or physical expression of an individual's inner world that has significant symbolism for that person. Like self-injury, embodied and social interventions are also physical, visible and expressive, and therefore reflect many of the functions of self-injury. Embodied and social interventions can fill the void of the unspeakable and powerfully engage with the complexities of human experience in accessible and non-threatening ways.

Working principles

1. Collaboration and creativity

Creativity, in the broadest sense, is essential in all dimensions of understanding and responding to self-injury, but especially embodied and social interventions. A creative response is a collaborative one; no one has authority over creativity. Fixed models and agendas are redundant when there is an equal relationship between the helper and the individual they are supporting. Instead, an approach emerges that is creative in both form and content. Here, creativity in responding to self-injury is not just about the range of embodied and social practices that might be useful; it is also about openness and creativity in response. Many service-providers recognise the need for collaborative, strengths-based and creative responses that 'build up ways of coping, and expressing feelings, working on using art or writing or stuff like that to help them have other outlets for feelings and so on'.

2. Strengths not sickness

Embodied and creative interventions are based on the principle that all human beings – even in times of great difficulty and distress – are valuable people with unique skills and abilities. As such, in times of difficulty it is just as important to spend time exploring and reinforcing strengths as it is to focus on difficulties. Far too many people are labelled and processed through services based only on information about the worst elements of their life and experiences. Not only does this potentially re-traumatise people and damage them further, it also totally fails to acknowledge and respond to the whole of their humanity – which in itself is an abuse of personhood. A helpful and meaningful response to someone who hurts themselves must be rooted in, and reinforce, their strengths and abilities, otherwise it will become debilitating, as one service-provider pointed out: 'The whole thing of what do you like and what makes you feel better, those things are very important.'

Activity

- Think of a person that you know who you find difficult, reflect on what it is that you find difficult about them.
- Now think about that person again, but this time make a list of all their strengths and good qualities.
- What do you think would happen if every time you thought about or interacted with that person you prioritised their strengths and positive qualities? Try it out and see what the results are!

Practice applications

1. Openness

Embodied and social interventions require helpers who are open and comfortable with complexity, ambiguity and uncertainty. They also require a sensitivity to the symbolic and abstract ways in which experience is expressed, rather than always searching for 'literal' truth. It is also essential that any creative expression is not seen as a vehicle for revealing and diagnosing pathology – as has been traditionally the case in mental health services (McNiff, 2004). The *process* of creative and embodied expression is just as important as the product, and even the opportunity to explore materials or movement can have powerful effects (see below). Supporting embodied and creative practices not only provides an opportunity for an individual to begin to express their feelings and experiences, it also offers the acceptance and validation that are integral to responding helpfully. One service-provider emphasised the importance of 'being able to just accept the person for the way they are and what they are going through'.

2. Creativity has no goals, no agenda, no right or wrong

Creativity is not a test and it is not a diagnostic tool. It is a holistic practice that has no right and wrong, and no agenda or goal. Therefore, while the idea of 'being creative' may be intimidating for some people, or conjure up ideas of fine art and complex sculptures, in essence creativity is simply an expression of humanity. It is therefore something that everyone has their own way of exploring and there needs to be a breadth of ways to engage with creativity. Rap, dance, painting, collage, physical theatre, poetry and songwriting are all valuable creative practices. Indeed, many researchers have found that, when people are just left with materials, they engage with them in ways that connect with memories and experiences that no amount of task-setting or questioning could elicit (Frimberger, 2013; McNiff, 2004; van Son, 2000). As noted above, creative interventions require creative thinking, and this is also an essential element of effective policy (discussed in detail in Chapter 7).

Activity

- Think about something that is artistic, embodied or social that has really moved you and/or changed your understanding about something. This might be, for example, a protest about the treatment of refugees, a song, an autobiography or a piece of visual art or theatre.
- What did you learn from this, and why do you think it had such an impact?
- Do you think that a simple 'factual' account of the issue would have been as evocative in conveying the experience?
- Now reflect on the implications of this in terms of the use of diagnostic questionnaires and case notes for people in health and social care services and the difference in understanding that might be achieved through creative, embodied and social forms of expression.

6

Staying safe:
harm-reduction

In the previous chapters, I set out an approach to self-injury that addresses the meaning, purpose and functions of injuries, as well as the distress that underlies them. Chapter 5 explored ways of working creatively with the issues that surround self-injury, within a holistic and person-centred framework. This chapter focuses on interventions that deal directly with injuries – namely, harm-reduction.[1] Harm-reduction reduces the physical risks and emotional harms of self-injury – and the responses to it – and promotes self-care. It creates a context where people are safe (physically and emotionally), and are supported to explore the immediate and long-term issues related to their self-injury. In doing so, despite not focusing directly on stopping self-injury, harm-reduction nonetheless reduces both the lethality and extent of injuries and promotes individual choice and control.

This chapter will begin by defining harm-reduction, exploring its origins and highlighting why it is so important for self-injury. It will then outline a number of key harm-reduction interventions, including aftercare and self-care; high-risk injuries; clean kit, safe kit, and alternatives to self-injury; slowing it down; emotional harm-reduction; crisis cards, and a safer context. All harm-reduction interventions are founded on principles of acceptance and non-judgment and aim to reduce physical risk and emotional harm and to promote

---

1. Some of the material from this chapter has been previously published in: Inckle K (2010). *Flesh Wounds: new ways of understanding self-injury.* Ross-on-Wye: PCCS Books; Inckle K (2010). At the Cutting Edge: creative and holistic responses to self-injury. *Creative Nursing,16,* 4: 160–165, Springer Publishing; Inckle K (2011). The First Cut is the Deepest: exploring a harm-reduction approach to self-injury. *Social Work in Mental Health* 9(5): 364–378, Taylor and Francis Publishing.

self-care. This requires authentic and trusting relationships between people who hurt themselves and helpers, and a robust rationale and policy context in services (see Chapter 7).

What is harm-reduction?

Harm-reduction (sometimes called harm-minimisation) is a user-led intervention for self-injury that was developed in direct response to the failures of mainstream services to respond in a meaningful or helpful way to people who hurt themselves (see Pembroke, 1996; 2007a). Harm-reduction is based on the recognition that self-injury is a coping mechanism that has deep meaning and purpose for an individual, but that nonetheless poses physical risks. The purpose of harm-reduction is to reduce these risks so that an individual can stay safe and avoid irreversible, unwanted or fatal damage to themself.

> Harm-minimisation is an alternative to preventative approaches that aim to prevent people from self-harming. Harm-minimisation approaches accept that someone may need to self-harm at a given point and focus, instead, on supporting that person to reduce the risk and the damage inherent in their self-harm. (Shaw & Shaw, 2009: 6)

Harm-reduction acknowledges that self-injury may be someone's best option at a given point and their only means of coping and surviving. For Mark, self-injury '*was* a way of dealing with stuff and that's just it... sometimes it's the very, very best one you can possibly do'. Elaine, likewise, highlighted the survival functions of self-injury:

> I did that at the time because that was right for me at the time, and it wasn't *healthy*, but I didn't have the tools to do anything else... If I'd been able to do something different then I would have done something different.

The understanding that self-injury is a coping mechanism that is fundamentally different to a suicide attempt (Chapter 1) is integral to a harm-reduction approach to self-injury. 'Harm-minimisation is about accepting the need to self-harm as a valid method of survival until survival is possible by other means' (Pembroke, 2007a: 166). As such, harm-reduction prioritises making the coping mechanism as safe as possible rather than trying to prevent the individual from using their means of coping. It also recognises the potentially lethal implications of attempting to remove an individual's coping mechanism from them: 'Removing the only effective coping strategy may lead to more serious self-harm behaviour or suicide' (Gallup, 2002: 25).

Harm-reduction offers practical ways to reduce the risks of injuries and provides a context for holistic work with the individual. It has been described as a 'non-judgemental, non-discriminatory and needs-led approach' (Cadman & Hoy, 2009: 55).

The origins of harm-reduction

Harm-reduction, which is also sometimes referred to as risk-minimisation, risk-reduction and, less frequently, risk-management or secondary prevention (Riley & O'Hare, 2000: 7), originated in policy around sexual health and drug use.[2] It became prevalent internationally following the outbreak and spread of HIV/AIDs in the late 1980s (Inciardi & Harrison, 2000). Prior to this, drug and sexual health policy and services had followed a 'zero tolerance' or abstinence-based ethos, where the primary goal was behaviour cessation (Riley & O'Hare, 2000; Riley & Pates, 2012). However, it became apparent that telling people simply to stop having sex – especially, for example, if they were supporting their family through sex work – or to quit using drugs (including those that are physically and/or psychologically addictive) was neither a realistic nor helpful response (Inciardi & Harrison, 2000; Vuylsteke et al, 2009). It was also clear that prevention-based policies failed to meet the basic health and care needs of service-users and were counterproductive, often exacerbating the risks and harms that service-users faced (Riley & O'Hare, 2000; Riley et al, 2012).

Harm-reduction was developed to directly address the failings of zero tolerance policies and to support the health and wellbeing of service-users. There is no single definition of harm-reduction (Inciardi & Harrison, 2000), but there is some consensus about the ethos and values on which it is based. These include a pragmatic view of human behaviour (eg. acceptance), a non-judgmental and respectful attitude, and an understanding that effective interventions are individually-focused and contain a range of goals, rather than one single outcome (Riley & O'Hare, 2000; Riley et al, 2012; Vuylsteke et al, 2009). Harm-reduction encourages peer organisation and education and seeks

---

2. More recently, harm-reduction has been also applied to alcohol and smoking (Inciardi & Harrison, 2000; McNeill, 2004).

to challenge stigma (Healy, Bennachie & Marshall, 2012; Gowan, Whetstone & Andic, 2012; Vuylsteke et al, 2009). It also draws critical attention to the effects of wider structural and contextual factors, such as social and material deprivation, inequalities and marginalisation (Inciardi & Harrison, 2000; Vuylsteke et al, 2009) (see Chapter 4).

The first priority of harm-reduction is a 'decrease in negative consequences' for the individual (Riley et al, 2012: 10). This is based on acceptance that the person engages in the activity, and then providing support to reduce the risks. In sexual health services, this involves education around safer sex and the provision of condoms, dental dams, latex gloves etc, so that the individual has both the knowledge and the resources to keep themself safe (Sylla, Harawa & Grinstead Reznick, 2010; Vuylsteke et al, 2009). In services for drug users, harm-reduction includes education about risks, such as sharing needles and injecting into vulnerable parts of the body, and the provision of clean equipment, such as needles, swabs and distilled water (Riley & O'Hare, 2000; Stancliff et al, 2015).

In summary, then, a harm-reduction approach accepts that the person engages in a risky activity and prioritises enabling them to stay safe and avoid unwanted, irreversible or fatal damage. Harm-reduction also acknowledges the context of the person's actions, and recognises that a meaningful response is going to be long term and multifaceted. This underlying ethos of acceptance, education and acknowledgement of the individual's context is integral to a harm-reduction approach to self-injury.

However, harm-reduction for self-injury has one essential difference to harm-reduction for other issues. While all forms of harm-reduction include education about specific ways to reduce harm, harm-reduction for self-injury *does not* include giving out tools of injury. An urban myth about harm-reduction for self-injury is that practitioners simply hand out fresh razor blades to service-users *en masse* and leave them to slice up their bodies.[3] Obviously this practice would violate the first aim of harm-reduction, in that it promotes some forms of self-injury, rather than reduces risks. It is also hard to see how this

---

3. Urban myths can have a great impact on the collective consciousness. Thus, whenever I do harm-reduction training, I insist the group learns and repeats the following mantra: 'Harm-reduction is NOT about giving people blades and telling them to go and cut themselves.' Trainees have subsequently reported back, with some surprise, that they have found themselves using the mantra on different occasions. This might be during in-service discussion or training where harm-reduction and other non-preventative approaches to self-injury are being dismissed, or in more general conversation. (Gutridge (2010) refers to giving out implements of injury as 'assisted self-harm' , which is distinct from harm-reduction.)

would reduce physical and emotional harm for many service-users or, indeed, service-providers. Actual risk-reduction will vary for each individual and depend on the type and method of self-injury each individual has developed. So that while, for example, Clare described how using a clean blade reduced the risks of her injuries – 'I learnt how to minimise the risk of infection, by using a clean blade' – this same intervention would *increase* risk for Joseph, who said:

> I much preferred to cut myself with glass. I used to cut myself with razor blades, but I was afraid of blades, but I had no fear with glass, I felt much more in control with glass. Because you have to *force* glass to go deeper, but with a *blade* you just cut and that was it, and you didn't know how deep it was, but if you cut with the glass you could *feel* [the depth] as you were cutting yourself.

Likewise, for Colm, who punched himself, banged his head, burned himself with cigarettes and would 'stick myself with a compass', cutting with blades would create additional risks, rather than minimise current harm. Therefore, to reiterate, harm-reduction for self-injury is not about giving out razor blades (or other means of injury) to service-users (see also Arnold & Magill, 2007). It is about understanding the ways in which each individual hurts themself, the risks involved for that person, and how they can be supported in reducing those risks.

As noted above, harm-reduction for self-injury is a user-led approach that developed in the UK during the 1990s. It emerged from the efforts of service-users who were struggling to survive conventional responses to self-injury in both psychiatry and mainstream medical services, such as A&E departments (see Pembroke, 1996; 2007a). These survivors established organisations such as the National Self-Harm Network (NSHN) and Survivors Speak Out, which produced harm-reduction information and resources (eg. Dace et al, 1998; National Self-Harm Network, 2000; Pembroke, 1996). The subsequent decades saw harm-reduction recognised by NICE (the National Institute for Health and Care Excellence), the UK body responsible for drawing up guidelines for best practice in medical, health and social care. In 2004, NICE produced specific guidelines on the short-term physical and psychological management of self-harm. The document recommends that professionals 'consider giving advice and instruction on self-management of superficial injuries, including providing tissue adhesive [and] harm-minimisation issues and techniques' (2004: 18). The official endorsement of harm-reduction approaches to self-injury is reiterated in the 2011 NICE guidelines on the long-term management of self-harm. This document not only endorses harm-reduction practices but also stresses the need for more research and a better understanding of harm-reduction (NICE, 2011).

In recent years, a number of UK statutory services have adopted a harm-reduction approach to self-injury. It was pioneered at the Bethlem and Maudsley Hospital during the late 1990s (Crowe & Bunclark, 2000). More recently, harm-reduction has been adopted in Selby and York primary care services (Pengelly et al, 2008) and South Staffordshire and Shropshire NHS Foundation Trust (Holley et al, 2012), and in some community and secure facilities (Birch et al, 2011). There is also evidence of a changing approach across a range of services that, according to one provider:

> … are *very good* and very realistic, and have really thought it all through and have looked at, realistically, how much can we be expected to prevent every single incident of self-harm that might ever happen, and have realised that they *can't*, and that they have to work within a framework of some sort of risk [and risk-reduction].

However, harm-reduction for self-injury is not yet fully mainstreamed and remains a contentious issue. This seems to result largely from fear and confusion about both self-injury and harm-reduction. It is therefore important to set out the evidence that underpins a harm-reduction approach to self-injury.

Why harm-reduction for self-injury?

The very simple answer to 'why harm-reduction?' is that prevention and control do not work. They meet neither the immediate nor long-term needs of the individual, and nor do they reduce the severity or incidence of injury. In fact, highly punitive, controlling and preventative regimes tend to increase both the frequency and intensity of self-injury and also the emotional and psychological harm experienced by service-users – mirroring precisely the contexts and experiences that underlie self-injury (see Chapters 2 and 3).

The failure of approaches based on prevention, punishment and control to effectively address self-injury is evident from a spectrum of research. This research indicates that settings where people are rigidly controlled and where self-injury is strictly prohibited – such as prisons (Groves, 2004; Lord, 2008), psychiatric and special hospitals (Clarke & Whittaker, 1998; Liebling, Chipchase & Velangi, 1997; Gallup, 2002), facilities for people with intellectual disabilities (Heslop & Macaulay, 2009), care facilities for young people (Spandler, 1996;

Storey et al, 2005; Swannell et al, 2008) and services for homeless and vulnerable persons (Tyler et al, 2003) – are those that have the highest rates of self-injury. Moreover, incarceration is itself a strong determinant of self-injury, as are traumatic experiences such as being strip-searched or placed in seclusion. From her advocacy work, Clare reported that:

> What consistently comes out of their stories is the harm that's about being controlled, about being restrained, about not being listened to, not being acknowledged, about being detained, about being abused within services, about being medicated in ways that cause all sorts of problems (see also Gallup, 2002).

Indeed, these kinds of preventative approaches to self-injury appear to be much more focused on allaying service-provider anxieties around self-injury, suicide risk and legal accountability than addressing the needs of service-users.[4]

Controlling, prevention-based approaches not only fail to meet the needs of people who hurt themselves, they also actually increase emotional distress and physical harm. Research demonstrates that short-term, prevention-based interventions are both ineffective and potentially lethal (Clarke & Whittaker, 1998; Gallup, 2002; Inckle, 2010b; Lord, 2008; Mental Health Foundation, 2006; Shaw & Shaw, 2009). Gallup found that 'attempting to stop [self-injurious] behaviour [...] will only escalate self-harm efforts' (2002: 25), and Clare and Elaine both highlighted how their self-injury worsened once they were detained in prevention-based settings.

Clare described the adult psychiatric unit where she was an inpatient as 'a frightening, bewildering, upsetting place, where harassment and threat were a daily reality and supportive conversations with staff were few and far between'. She continued:

> It's no surprise then that my need to self-harm increased. I became desperate to hurt myself – the only coping strategy that had consistently worked for me over the last 10 years. But self-harm wasn't allowed. So what did I do?
>
> I made it my goal. I used all the time and energy I had on my hands to pit my wits against the staff and I found new and ingenuous ways of self-

---

4. In some services, staff are compelled to intervene in this way; in other instances service-providers may do so as a result of misinformed beliefs or practices about self-injury.

harming. I did it in secret; I seized the opportunities when they arose; and I did it as quickly and severely as possible, before I was found and stopped.

During my months on different inpatient units, I cut myself with razors, I re-opened sutures, I inserted objects and rubbed dirt into wounds, I injured myself with broken glass and crockery, I gouged myself with a fork, I cut myself with a ripped-up can, I punched myself repeatedly, I banged my head on the wall, I overdosed, I hung myself from the back of the bathroom door until I lost consciousness, and every day I binged and vomited and starved. These were all units that did not allow self-harm. (In Shaw & Shaw, 2009: 7; 2007: 28–29)

Elaine spent time in an adolescent unit that had a very contradictory approach to self-injury, in that it was both an everyday occurrence but also strictly taboo: 'They [the inpatients/residents] are told they can't do it, they're not allowed to do it, they're treated like they're *mentally ill*.' Yet at the same time she described an 'environment where the social acceptability of doing it is very high. So they'll only come out however long later really a lot more messed up'. Paradoxically, in that environment, self-injury was one of the few ways for Elaine to access what felt like love and care (reported also in Chapter 2).

Like, when you're a self-harmer, and especially if you're a self-harmer in an adolescent unit… you're very cut off from the outside world, self-harm is really a form of communication. I mean I'm *not* saying that people do it to *get* attention, but when you're in that environment, you know, quite often the only time that anyone has got time for you is when you need a bandage. Quite often, for me, the only time I got care was when I was having my [part of body] stitched up. So that, you know, *care* came for me, as someone without a family, in the form of a nurse *having* to give me *medical* care. And that was the closest I got to, to I guess what felt like parental care, you know. And, kind of, in that way at the *time*, when you're self-harming, *for me*, the bigger scar the better.

As a result, Elaine's self-injury worsened in the very environment that was supposed to be improving her wellbeing.

I had all kinds of sets of rules: it was only self-harm if it was over 10 stitches. I upped it, and I upped it, and I upped it. It was only self-harm if I was stitched, or it was only self-harm, you know, to the point where at the *end* it was only self-harm if, it only mattered, it was only *worthy*, it was only important if it was *big* injury… Or, you know, a *small* scar that didn't require a skin graft wasn't good enough… That shows how *quickly* – like I started off doing scratches on my [part of body] – how in a period of three years you can go from very minor to very severe. And that's why I think that it didn't help that I was in an adolescent unit, cut off from reality.

It is clear from Elaine's and Clare's experiences that preventative approaches to self-injury create environments that are confusing and emotionally damaging and that increase rather than decrease self-injury. This is echoed across research with people who hurt themselves, who express an 'overwhelming view that people who self-harm should not be made to stop' (Warm, Murray & Fox, 2002: 77; see also Inckle, 2010b; Pembroke, 1996; Shaw & Shaw, 2009).

Furthermore, the notion that someone could, or should, simply cease to hurt themself because rules prohibit it is absurd. As Elaine pointed out: 'People don't self-harm cos it's *fun*… "Stopping" people self-harming isn't going to stop them doing it. I don't believe it's a behaviour that people just stop… they *can't* as they wouldn't be doing it in the first place.' Likewise, Clare emphasised that: 'Being told to stop is really not a constructive or meaningful response, it makes you feel worse, and you do it anyway.' Mark similarly explained:

> That was a period of time when I actually couldn't stop injuring even though I wanted to. I mean I never wanted to injure, that's the strange thing, and I hated the fact that I did, *but* I also recognise that it was nothing I could actually control at certain times.

Preventative and punitive approaches are utterly counterproductive because self-injury is a means of coping with deep distress, and prevention-based responses only intensify that distress. Prevention makes the situation – ie. someone's level of distress and the subsequent extent of their injuries – far worse. It creates an invalidating, punitive, controlling and potentially traumatising environment that often mirrors the experiences to which self-injury is a coping response. Emma's experiences of preventative interventions highlight how damaging and abusive these approaches can be.

> One time while I was in hospital I had some bad news over the phone and I started pulling my hair because I was frustrated and the nursing staff decided to restrain me. Being restrained involved having one nurse hold

each of my legs, one nurse sitting on my chest and another nurse pulling my arms up behind me – this was really not good and it completely freaked me out and made me feel really powerless. My reaction to being restrained at the time was very similar to that when I was raped and abused. This felt really difficult as I didn't feel able to tell anyone this. In fact what I think this did was remind me how effectively I could switch off and meant that I made even more use of this coping mechanism. After they had restrained me, the hospital staff insisted that I take off my clothes because they wanted to check that they hadn't broken any of my ribs whilst they were restraining me – I think that this was wrong and completely unnecessary and unhelpful.

Overall, then, because self-injury is a coping mechanism, interventions that prevent a person accessing their means of coping are illogical and dangerous. They fail to address the underlying cause of the distress, and often exacerbate it. Preventative regimes also fail in their intention to prevent self-injury and often result in higher incidence. Furthermore, negative experiences of prevention-based services often lead people to avoid seeking help, even when significant medical attention is required: 'Even if my life was in danger, I'd rather sit at home and sit it out and see whether I survived than risk the humiliation' (in Simpson, 2006; see also Cadman & Hoy, 2009).

As previously noted, harm-reduction has been trialled and implemented in a number of statutory services, including psychiatric hospitals (Crowe & Bunclark, 2000), primary care services (Holley et al, 2012; Pengelly et al, 2008) and secure facilities (Birch et al, 2011). Substantial clinical and legal investigation, clear policy guidelines and training underpinned these shifts in practice from prevention to harm-reduction (Crowe & Bunclark, 2000; Holley, et al, 2012; Pengelly et al, 2008) – and this is why the next chapter of this book focuses on developing a robust policy framework.[5] With clear policy and practice guidance in place, harm-reduction has been effective not only in reducing the incidence and gravity of injuries over the long term, but also in providing a more positive and effective therapeutic environment for service-users and service-providers alike (Crowe & Bunclark, 2000; Birch et al, 2011; Holley et al, 2012; Pengelly et al, 2008). Paradoxically, then, by shifting the

---

5. Helpers who are not formal service-providers do not have the constraints of organisational policy to deal with, but they may still be challenged about harm-reduction by those around them or, indeed, by services connected to the person who hurts themself. It is therefore useful to have a clear understanding of policy and practice around harm-reduction in existing services.

focus away from the prevention of injuries, harm-reduction achieves what mainstream prevention policies allegedly strive for: namely, the reduction in incidence and severity of self-injury and positive and meaningful support work.

Harm-reduction in practice

As noted above, harm-reduction is a user-led intervention that is increasingly moving into mainstream services and policy. As such, it is continually evolving, with new approaches, practices and resources continually being developed (eg. Cadman & Hoy, 2009). This section outlines some key harm-reduction practices: aftercare and self-care; high-risk injuries; clean kit, safe kit and alternatives to self-injury; slowing it down; emotional harm-reduction; crisis cards, and a safer context. However, these practices should not, on the whole, be taken as rigid protocols – the only area where there needs to be a single, rigid protocol is with regard to injuries that can never be made safe. Otherwise, the information provided here is a snapshot of interventions that are currently practised and that will continue to develop over time. The ongoing development of harm-reduction practices is essential as harm-reduction becomes more widely understood and applied to a wider range of individuals and contexts. In this evolving context, collaboration between helpers, the people who hurt themselves and supportive medical practitioners offers a route to understanding the risks of injuries and how to stay safe.

Aftercare and self-care

One of the first, and least contentious, elements of a harm-reduction approach to self-injury is supporting the care of injuries after they have occurred. Everyone who hurts themself can have their own first-aid kit, with everything they need to take care of their injuries. The contents of this kit must be specific to the ways in which each individual hurts themself, not a generic set of supplies. For example, wound treatment for burns is very different to the treatments needed for cuts or bruises. Likewise, a burn made with a chemical substance will need to be treated very differently to a burn made with flame – and water may exacerbate rather than soothe a chemical injury. A supportive medical practitioner such as a nurse, GP or pharmacist can offer useful advice on appropriate aftercare, and user-led groups also provide accessible information about how to treat injuries (eg. LifeSIGNS, 2004; National Self-Harm Network, 2000; Pembroke, 2007a).

Aftercare for self-injury has two key functions in risk-reduction. The first is the straightforward physical benefits of aftercare. Wounds that are correctly cared for will heal better, and are less likely to become infected and cause long-term problems. Second, aftercare has important emotional and psychological effects that are connected with the positive or healing motivations behind self-injury (Chapter 2). Aftercare builds on this positive intention and allows it to be fully realised through providing actual physical care for injuries. As such, aftercare works positively with the underlying functions of self-injury.

Aftercare also works against some of the stigma and shame that many people feel about the wounds and injuries they create. This stigma is often reinforced in prevention-based practices where people who hurt themselves are not seen as deserving care (Chapter 3). Practising self-care can therefore have significant effects on a person's sense of worth and entitlement to care, even when they are feeling bad. This was true for Emma, who described how harm-reduction 'gave me the option/permission to look after myself after I had cut myself'. For Rachel, aftercare was crucial to maintaining control and promoting her wellbeing. Nonetheless, this was still difficult for her to express in a positive way: 'I have always been able to look after my own cuts pretty well. I have *stitched* my own cuts, which is quite a mental thing to do yourself, but I have done it.' That Rachel describes her aftercare as 'mental' rather than, for example, courageous and resourceful, highlights the need for validation and support for aftercare.

Finally, aftercare is also important in that it can provide a non-threatening opportunity for helpers to engage in a practical and meaningful way with someone who hurts themself. It is an opportunity to establish a positive engagement around self-injury without the need for deep personal disclosure. It also makes self-care (rather than self-injury or the prevention of it) the priority, which transforms the focus of the engagement and the individual's self-experience. Aftercare, then, has significant physical and emotional benefits for people who hurt themselves, and offers straightforward, practical and positive interventions.

Risks, high risks and reducing risks

All forms of self-injury involve some degree of risk, because self-injury is by nature harmful. However, some forms of injury are very risky and cannot be made safe (see below), while other injuries can be managed in such a way as to avoid unwanted, irreversible or fatal damage.

The primary means of reducing risk is through provision of clear, accurate information about different injuries (see next section) and the human body. A basic understanding of human physiology is essential if people are to avoid causing irreversible and unwanted damage to themselves. Physiological knowledge also ensures clarity about which injuries require urgent medical attention. For example, cutting can risk fatal injuries if an artery is severed. Here, blood loss is rapid, difficult to stem, and will quickly cause loss of consciousness. If a tendon is severed – for example, in the wrist or ankle – it can cause irreversible damage, resulting in the permanent loss of function of the hand or foot. Cutting can also cause permanent nerve damage and deplete feeling and function in affected parts of the body. Therefore, basic anatomical knowledge about the location of arteries, tendons and nerves in the body is an essential resource for staying safe. Likewise, awareness of the symptoms of damage to any of these vulnerable areas – for example, that blood spurts from an artery but oozes from a vein – can provide a solid basis for staying safe. The survivor publication *Cutting the Risk* (National Self-harm Network, 2000) includes basic maps of the body and high-risk areas, presented in a user-friendly, self-injury-specific format. Basic anatomy and physiology text books, or a helpful medical practitioner, can also provide relevant information (however, caution is needed with internet resources as not everything online is reliable or correct).

Many people who hurt themselves develop their own techniques for attempting to reduce the risks of their injuries, using what anatomical/medical knowledge they have available to them – although this might not always be accurate. For example, Joseph described how he attempted to reduce the risks of his injuries by being careful about both which part of his body he cut and the implement he used to do so: 'Those people who didn't know what I was doing thought I was trying to commit suicide, but there was *no* way I was going to cut my neck, there was *no* way I was going to cut my wrist.' As described above, for Joseph, cutting with glass was much safer than cutting with blades, because he could feel and monitor the extent of the cuts he was making. He was also careful not to damage particularly vulnerable or visible parts of his body: 'I wouldn't cut my face, I wouldn't cut my hands, but I would cut my arms, my chest, my legs, anything that wouldn't be seen in public.' And, while not all of his assessments of high-risk locations were accurate (there are arteries and tendons in the legs, for example, and the stomach is relatively safe), Joseph nonetheless used his own strategies to reduce harm:

This was a great place to cut yourself [gesturing to backs of arms]. This isn't such a good place to cut yourself [palms of hands and undersides of arms] but here [back of arms] is a very good place to cut yourself, because, I don't know, it's a nice space. I don't know what I mean by that, but I wouldn't cut myself *here* [front of wrists] because I might do damage or whatever, and I would always cut myself *here* [back of arms] because it seems stronger, whereas *here* [undersides of arms] I actually wouldn't cut myself. And I'd cut myself on my chest but not around my nipples, and I would *never* touch my stomach. And your legs were an open area, you could cut yourself anywhere, it doesn't matter, but your neck and your wrists would be out.

Joseph's experience not only highlights the strong survival functions of self-injury and the related strategies he employed to avoid irreversible or fatal damage, but also how essential it is that people have access to accurate information. Clare and Emma discovered harm-reduction resources that were produced by other service-users, and described their powerful impacts. For Emma:

The first time I came across the idea of harm-reduction was when I went to a conference in Manchester by the National Self-Harm Network. Someone there was talking about it – possibly Louise Pembroke – and they published a leaflet/booklet from a previous conference they had done, and it had hand-drawn diagrams in it showing where arteries and veins were in the body and information about where they were more close to the surface. There was something about clean blades and aftercare, and also something about how if you cut your arm lengthways you are less likely to damage your nerves badly. It was really basic and not very medical but it was all I had at the time so I did often use this to try and minimise my chances of damage I might later regret. I felt like it gave me the option/ permission to look after myself after I had cut myself and it meant that I only did the damage I meant to do, which I am very glad of.

Clare also described how the discovery of harm-reduction practices was equally life preserving for her:

It was only after I'd accidentally severed the tendons in my wrist that I first came across the work of Lou Pembroke and the Self-Harm Network. It was a revelation to me [...] that there were organisations who accepted that I might need to continue to self-harm, but who recognised that I still had choices; and that there were practical strategies by which I could take care of myself and keep myself as safe as possible.

So I learnt about my own body, and about how to minimise the chances of damaging bodily structures like arteries and tendons. I learnt how to care for my wounds, and when to seek medical attention. I learnt how to minimise the risk of infection, by using a clean blade. I learnt the consequences of taking overdoses, and the importance of seeking help. (In Shaw & Shaw, 2009: 8)

These experiences highlight that many people who hurt themselves are already attempting to minimise risks. It is crucial that this positive, life-saving and self-caring intention is validated and supported. This means supporting someone in developing an accurate understanding of the anatomical issues and physical risks that are relevant to their injuries, so they can further reduce them. The failure to provide accurate and reliable information will not prevent someone from hurting themself, but it will reduce the effectiveness of their attempts to reduce risks and may make them vulnerable to irreversible or fatal damage.

For injuries such as burns, reopened wounds, self-hitting or head-banging, similar knowledge about safe limits and reducing risks can also be really useful. For example, it is often recommended that a burn that is larger than the size of a UK 50p coin should be medically checked (Arnold & Magill, 1997). A burn or wound that is infected (that is, oozing clear or yellow fluid or blood) should also have medical attention. If someone bangs their head, it is important that they are alert to the symptoms of concussion – memory loss, blackouts – and that these might occur some time after the injury. They should also consider the risks of driving, using machinery or engaging in some sports activities after they have hurt themselves in this way. It might also be useful to try to reduce the severity of the impact by placing a cushion, pillow, folded towel or item of clothing over the surface, or experiment with hitting against softer surfaces, such as a mattress or an upholstered chair.

Where injury is caused by scratching or picking, the damage can be reduced by attempting to diffuse the focus of the injury. Even if someone repeatedly scratches or picks at a particular area, harm-reduction is possible. For example, attempting to divert the scratching or picking to unbroken skin in the proximity of the wound, rather than the wound itself, can allow it some respite and healing. Where there is a strong need to focus on the wound itself, it can sometimes be helpful to apply pressure to it, using the fingertips or fingernails but without any movement. That way, there is a strong sensation and engagement with the focal point of the wound, but no accompanying breaking or disruption of the surface. This again allows the wound some respite and healing time and lessens the impact of the scratching or picking. Washing hands and cleaning fingernails before and after scratching and picking are an important hygiene measure. Aftercare treatments for scratched and picked skin can also be an important component of reducing the immediate and long-term damage from the wounds. For all injuries that involve breaking the skin, Arnold & Magill (1997) recommend an up-to-date tetanus vaccination.

High risk and never safe injuries

Some forms of self-injury are always a high risk; they can never be made safe and always require immediate medical attention. These are swallowing substances or objects, which might include medications (ie. overdosing), sharp and/or harmful objects such as batteries, and substances such as household cleaners. It is impossible to predict or limit the harm that any of these will cause once they have been swallowed. Many people who swallow substances (ie. overdose) may have done so on a number of previous occasions and have survived without experiencing lasting negative consequences (see Joseph's experience in Chapter 1). This may lead them to conclude that, if they monitor the quantity of substance that they swallow, they can also control its effects. However, this is incorrect; there is no way to predict tolerance or lethality, and each time a harmful substance is ingested, it is potentially fatal. Any previous instances where harmful substances or objects have been swallowed without long-term negative consequences are simply lucky escapes, which may or may not happen again. In addition to being potentially fatal, swallowing harmful objects and substances may also result in a range of irreversible effects, including organ failure, permanent internal damage and loss of bodily functions. Therefore medical attention must always be sought after swallowing an object or substance, as there is no means of reducing the risks.

Ingesting objects/substances is not the only particularly risky form of self-injury. Other injuries, such as cutting the wrist, neck and groin, are always high risk, because arteries and/or tendons are close to the surface in these areas. Cutting other parts of the body where there is more flesh and fewer vulnerable structures close to the surface, such as the stomach or outer thigh,

169

can significantly reduce the risk. Tying ligatures around the neck is also high risk, in that the effects of this are hard to control and it can quickly cause unconsciousness. It may also cause death or permanent damage by blocking the passage of air through the throat.

Finally, intoxication with alcohol and/or drugs always makes self-injury unsafe and unpredictable, because of the associated lack of control and awareness. Alcohol and drugs can act as disinhibitors, making it possible for people to hurt themselves much more severely than they would when sober, and thereby increasing risks of fatal and unintended damage (see McCafferty, 2012 and Chapter 1). Alcohol and drugs can also be risky in emotional terms, in that people often consume them to try to feel better, but find that they only intensify negative feelings. This was true for Amanda, who found that intoxication worsened her emotional state and the severity of her injuries: 'I would have abused drugs and alcohol, and I think, like, substances *add* to it and make it more intense and make it worse.' Alcohol and drugs can also create further complications if they are mixed with other substances that have been swallowed. Therefore, it is never safe to use intoxicants and to self-injure at the same time. Alcohol and drugs inhibit the mental clarity required to reduce risks, and often increase the emotional distress as well as the potential for causing unintended, irreversible and fatal damage.

Overall, then, some forms of self-injury are always high risk and can never be made safe. However, it is still possible to apply harm-reduction principles to these situations by ensuring the person has accurate information about all of the risks involved and knows how to seek help. A crisis card can be a useful resource for someone who has high risk injuries (see below). However, there are ways in which most injuries can be made safe through the use of a clean kit or a safe kit.

Clean kit, safe kit and alternatives to self-injury

People who self-injure in ways that cut or break the skin risk contracting a range of infections if the implement they use is not clean or if it has been used by another person. These infections can include septic reactions to dirt or rust, or blood-borne infections such as hepatitis and HIV. Therefore, it is essential that people who hurt themselves in this way always use a clean implement and do not share it with others. For people who cut with blades, a clean supply and safe disposal are essential. If people cut or break the skin with other implements such as glass, scissors or sharp objects, it is useful to sterilise the implement before and after use. This can be done with boiling water (although this will also make a metal implement very hot) or a range of easily available disinfectants. Ideally, this implement should be kept solely for this purpose and should be stored away from everyday items. For example, scissors or compasses that are used for self-injury should not, if possible, be returned to the stationery box or kitchen drawer, but should be disinfected and stored separately.

It is most effective if the implements of injury (along with any required disinfectant) are stored in the first aid kit (see above). This means that the implements of injury and the means to take care of it are always available together, making it more likely that aftercare will be used. When people store their method of injury alongside their aftercare, it is called a safe kit.

Service-providers and parents are often uncomfortable with the idea of allowing someone, especially a young person, to have a safe kit. They often feel that it is their duty to remove any possible means of injury. However, we have already seen that it is impossible to prevent someone from self-injuring, even in contexts where there are high levels of monitoring and control. Furthermore, if someone's usual or safe method of injury is removed from them, it is much more likely that they will injure themselves using an unfamiliar and unsafe object, and therefore run much higher risks. They are also much more likely to feel increasing distress and shame. Alternatively, where someone is able to keep their means of injury (and aftercare) with them, this can provide a reassuring emotional safety net, which often means they are less – not more – likely to need to use it (Pembroke, 1996). They are also less likely to experience the emotional harms caused by shame, secrecy and disapproval of self-injury. Similarly, when self-injury is forbidden, it often takes place in conditions of heightened anxiety and urgency, so the injuries are made more quickly and there is less care-taking and control. A safe kit alleviates the urgency and secrecy of self-injury, making it physically safer and emotionally less fraught.

A safe kit can be developed for most forms of injury where risk-reduction is possible (see above). As with the first aid kit, it requires specific attention to each individual's method of injury and means of reducing the risks. Also, like the first aid kit, the safe kit can provide a practical vehicle through which to engage with someone about their self-injury. Michael Moyer (2008), a school counsellor, developed a version of the safe kit in his work with young people. He encouraged the youngsters to decorate a container for their safe kit in a way that they felt represented the feelings and meanings of their self-injury. This helped the young people to externalise some aspects of their self-injury, and the decorated kit often became the basis for significant conversations about it.

Moyer also encouraged the youngsters to place objects in the container that related to their self-injury. These objects not only included the means of injury but also items that provided a broad range of support (aftercare items should also be included). Such support items could be objects of comfort, such as a photograph or (small) cuddly toy, or items that express feelings, such as a music CD, poem or picture, and writing or drawing implements. Some youngsters included the phone number of a friend or someone they could talk to in times of distress. Moyer found that the process of creating the kit was hugely beneficial to the young people in terms of understanding their self-injury and reducing risks.

This kind of safe kit uses some of the creative approaches explored in Chapter 5 and therefore engages with self-injury at both direct and symbolic levels. Any of the creative means of expression that resonate with the person can be included in the safe kit. Likewise, any strategies that someone finds useful to externalise or express their feelings can also be included. These might be pencils to snap, stress balls to manipulate or a small towel to twist.

A complete safe kit contains the implements of injury, the necessary aftercare, and items that provide support, comfort and self-expression in times of distress. In this way, the kit provides a holistic emergency service, uniquely tailored to the person who hurts themself. Furthermore, a helper who works with an individual to develop a safe kit demonstrates significant levels of acceptance, non-judgment and caring. An interaction about self-injury that embodies these qualities is in itself a significant benefit. It can challenge some of the stigma, shame and hostility people may have previously experienced about their self-injury, and instead can create a context that promotes self-worth and self-care.

Another possibility for inclusion in the safe kit are alternatives to self-injury. Alternatives to self-injury are methods that create a similar physical sensation or experience to self-injury, but without causing bodily damage. Common examples include holding ice against the skin instead of cutting or burning, and rubbing chilli powder into the skin or writing words on parts of the body instead of scratching or cutting. Some people cut an orange or the skin of a fruit, and others draw on or injure a picture of themselves. However, these alternatives may not always meet the full criteria of harm-reduction in that, while they reduce physical injury, they do not always reduce emotional harm or promote self-care. For example, writing harsh words on the body or injuring a picture can be emotionally damaging. Likewise, holding ice against the skin is less physically harmful than cutting or burning, but there is no obvious aftercare, and nor, therefore, engagement with the healing impulse in self-injury. Similarly, a focus on alternatives to self-injury can be much more about alleviating the distress of helpers, rather than meeting the needs of the person who hurts themself. Alternatives to self-injury might therefore be seen as a solution in contexts where there is no deeper engagement with self-injury and where the primary emphasis is on cessation rather than self-care. One service manager described alternatives to self-injury as 'actually *promoting* the self-harm':

> Because if you say to a person, 'Look, I don't want you to cut yourself anymore, I want you to hold this ice instead, that's going to really hurt as well,' this is about *hurting* instead of *caring*. I also thought that if you tell a person to hold ice instead it might hit the spot *that* day, but it's going to revert back to cutting at a later day.

Simply substituting other actions for self-injury is unlikely to be effective in the long term. For example, Rachel used a range of alternatives, including physical theatre and performance art, in place of her self-injury, but in the long term she found the substitution ineffective:

> I just really *needed* to do it [ie. self-injure], and my friend was like, 'Come round and I'll put needles [piercings] in your back.' And it's like, it's not going to work, it's not right. It needed to be something that had that intensity.

As a general principle, then, alternatives to self-injury should only be considered within an understanding that, in isolation from other supports, they are unlikely to be effective in the long term. Furthermore, for alternatives to be effective, they must not only reduce physical risks but also emotional harms, and they should promote self-care. Alternatives must also meaningfully connect with the functions of the self-injury. For example, if someone hurts themself in order to comfort themself, then writing on their body is not useful for them. However, if someone hurts themself in order to express the pain they feel, then writing on their flesh might be a relevant alternative – although it is not clear how aftercare might take place here. If there is no element of aftercare or comforting in an alternative to self-injury, then the person ultimately risks making themself feel worse. For example, in the case of writing on the skin, the words might entrench feelings of unloveableness or isolation, rather than releasing them. In contrast, the aftercare provided for the cuts may well provide the sensation of loving and caring that alleviates the pain.

Finally, it is important that alternatives are only considered in terms of their benefits for the person who hurts themself, and not simply to alleviate the fears of those around them. When all of these issues are considered, alternatives may provide a useful means of harm-reduction but, as with all interventions, they should not be unilaterally applied to everyone; they should instead be worked out in collaboration with each individual.

Overall, the safe kit provides a practical resource for physical and emotional harm-reduction and self-care. It ensures that physical risks from injuries are minimised by using clean and safe implements, and that aftercare is always close at hand. The acceptance of self-injury and promotion of self-care that is embodied by the kit provides a supportive context for self-injury that challenges stigma and hostility. It positions self-injury as an understandable and cared-for experience, rather than a shameful secret. In this way, self-injury becomes less desperate and anxious, and this provides further opportunities to reduce risks through slowing it down.

Slow it down

Self-injury is especially risky when it happens in panicked, rushed situations, and where emotions are intensified by fear and prohibition (see Clare's story, above). It is much safer when it occurs in a context where there is time for preparation and care-taking. A harm-reduction approach allows for clarity, time and space around the self-injury, and the safe kit can play a central role in slowing down the process and making injuries safer.

When someone is resourced with harm-reduction information and a safe kit, choice and control become possible, which creates a space for time and safety around the injuries. For example, if someone feels that they need to hurt themselves, they can choose to go to a safe and private space with their safe kit. They can then unpack the items they need for the injury and its aftercare, along with any of the supportive items or alternatives that they have in their kit. In this context, should they go ahead and hurt themself, the process is slower and less panicked and stressful. The injury is surrounded by supportive, caring materials, and is less likely to result in irreversible or unwanted damage.

Slower and safer injuries can also be achieved by combining the preparations made via the safe kit with what has been called the '15-minute rule' (LifeSIGNS, 2004). In the 15-minute rule, each of the stages of preparing to injure is accompanied by a period of waiting a few minutes – 15, if possible – before going on to the next stage. The period of waiting allows the individual to reflect on their feelings, rather than being overwhelmed by them, and to see if the feelings persist. If the feelings remain, then the next stage of the injury is approached in the same way. For example, the person will go to their safe, quiet space and see if they can wait for 15 minutes before they unpack their safe kit. If it is not possible to wait this long, or if, after 15 minutes, they still feel the same, then they go ahead and open the kit. Once they have sorted out – and cleaned, if necessary – the implement they will use, they then see if they can wait another few (or 15) minutes before they hurt themself. They might also engage with one of the alternative or expressive objects in their kit for a further 15 minutes, to see if this alleviates the need for injury. In this way, self-injury is always available as an option, but its urgency and intensity is reduced and choice and control are increased. Therefore, even if the injury does take place, it occurs in a careful and considered context, with appropriate aftercare immediately available. (A 15-minute pause should not be included between the injury and aftercare.)

The 15-minute rule can also be adapted to use with breathing patterns, rather than time periods. Breathwork can be calming and grounding and further reduce anxiety and risks (Inckle, 2010b). Thus, instead of counting minutes between each stage in the injury process, the person can take some slow, deep breaths. It may be that no more than one or two breaths are possible, but even this is enough to allow some space and control within the injury process. Breathing slowly can reduce the intensity of the injury, as it focuses attention directly on the feelings and sensations in the body, whereas stress and panic reactions tend to draw awareness away from the physical self and make deeper injuries possible. Breathing slowly up to and during the injury can also reduce some of the difficult emotions, such as fear, shock and panic. Paying attention to breathing in this way also allows for focused aftercare. Breathwork is often a key element of the mindfulness practices now widely available as drop-in, evening and online courses (see Chapter 5). These can provide valuable techniques that can be useful for slowing down self-injury.

It is important to remember that slowing down self-injury is not the same as preventing it. At each stage in the process, it is perfectly acceptable for the person to move on to the next step. The goal is not to prevent the injury but to allow some time for choice, reflection and safety. Even pausing for just one breath in the whole process is an important step in self-care. The ethos of harm-reduction means that every change that someone makes, big or small, is recognised as a courageous and valuable achievement. As Clare emphasised, harm-reduction entails:

Recognising and celebrating recovery or care-taking in whatever form that happens. It might be about somebody cutting their stomach instead of their forearm, or somebody taking care of their wounds after they've injured, or cutting themselves instead of taking a paracetamol overdose, and celebrating when somebody *has* taken that care. Not just seeing it as a huge failure that they're self-harming.

The combination of the safe kit and slowing down the process of injury by minutes or breathwork can be significant in reducing the risks of injuries and making self-injury safer. However, this will not always prevent injuries from occurring, and here, as with injuries that can never be made safe (such as swallowing harmful objects and substances), medical attention may be needed. Medical settings can often be places of emotional (and physical) harm, and it is crucial that emotional harm-reduction is prioritised just as much as reducing physical risks.

Emotional harm-reduction

It is essential to remember that, just as self-injury is always physical, emotional and contextual, harm-reduction also needs to promote physical and emotional wellbeing and safe contexts (see below). Emotional harm from self-injury may relate to the act itself, or it may result from external factors. However, much of the emotional harm that occurs when a person hurts themself is external to them and results from the ways they are treated. Service-providers consistently highlighted that harm was often caused externally, by the responses to people who hurt themselves:

By and large self-injury is badly understood, and by and large people who self-injure are not treated very well.

It still feels incredibly stigmatised... you know, there is still some *really* difficult stuff that goes on at A&E and in GP surgeries and things like that.

Where people are put in seclusion, or when they're being *watched* – you know, either they have someone with them the whole time or every 15 minutes or something like that – it's like you're keeping that person physically *safe* but, actually, you're not really paying attention to what's going on on the inside, and they might be emotionally in a *much* worse state from being treated *like that*. But because they're physically safe, on one level it looks better, but actually what it does emotionally, it often might be worse.

The emotional harm caused in these kinds of responses can cause lasting damage, often reinforcing the negative beliefs and experiences that underlie self-injury. It may also make people less likely to seek help. For Emma:

> It was when my distress was treated as abnormal that I felt like it wasn't ok to share how I felt, or that I was a freak, or that there was something incurably wrong with me.

Louise Pembroke described similarly damaging impacts from the consistently negative and hostile treatment she received in A&E:

> Going to Accident and Emergency had become a form of self-harm. The judgement of staff confirmed that I really was the lowest form of life and reinforced every negative feeling I ever had about myself. (Pembroke, 1996: 36)

A harm-reduction approach to self-injury must therefore focus on reducing both the physical risks and the emotional harms. Emotional harms can be just as damaging as physical harms, and can have similar long-term risks. It is essential, then, that helpers do not respond in ways that add to the pain and damage of self-injury at any level and put someone at deeper risk. Mark highlighted both the danger and the illogic of treating people who were already vulnerable and suffering in ways that compound their difficulties:

> People go through absolutely horrendous things in their life, very difficult times, very difficult experiences and they do what they can to cope with that. Let's not make it worse by heaping judgement and [negative] responses. I mean, you know, people say, 'Well, self-injury is *mad*,' but then, responding to somebody who is self-injuring to deal with very distressing things in a way that distresses them more is *completely insane!*

Harm-reduction requires providing a context that is physically and emotionally safe and supportive and promotes self-care (see also crisis cards and context, below). An important aspect of emotional harm-reduction can be supporting a person to integrate their experiences of self-injury in a life-enhancing way. For Elaine, this involved recognising how her self-injury had enabled her to reach her current point in life.

177

> I refuse to beat myself up for doing it – because I did it for the reasons I did it at the time *and* had I *not* done that I might not be sat here today… You do pretty much what you can with the knowledge and the strength that you have at that moment… I perhaps wish that I had been able to do something different, but I have the understanding that I *didn't, couldn't.*

Integrating the experience of self-injury in the life trajectory is particularly important in developing resilience against the emotional harms that result from the stigma and misunderstanding of self-injury in wider society. Elaine was often made to feel uncomfortable because 'people *do* look at you, and whatever situation you're in, whoever you're around… people *will* comment [on scars]… I've had people say really unpleasant things about them'. Rachel similarly described how people 'don't look at *you*, they look at the scars and it's such a hindrance. From that, you know, *you* then have to work to pull it back'.

> It's almost like someone has to completely reassess who you are as a person, they have to completely redefine you in their minds, and then *you* have to work on going, 'No I'm still here, *nothing's changed*, it's okay, you know', and you have to sort of baby people back into your space.

There is no one approach to dealing with these issues: some people choose concealment; others, especially when concealment of scars is almost impossible, adopt an affirmative approach. Elaine, whose scars were very difficult to conceal, developed a courageous strategy for managing other people's reactions:

> I would always say, 'I'm sure you've noticed' or, 'You *might* have noticed, that I have scars and I'm going to wear [garment that reveals scars] now, and I just wanted to bring it up so you don't,' you know, 'I just wanted to bring it up.' But that's all it takes to make me to feel comfortable is me saying that one sentence. I would feel *really uncomfortable* if I didn't say that sentence. But as soon as I've said it, as soon as I've stated the obvious, and that's it! *All* the worries and anxieties about it just dissolve, I just stand there in [clothes that reveal scars] because I've already said – whereas if I *didn't* say that I would be thinking 'Have they noticed?' or things like that. And most people just go, 'Yeah, cool.' And then that brings it up into conversation without anyone asking me anything about it.

It was possible for Amanda to conceal her scars, although this did involve some restrictions with what she wore. However, despite limiting her choices of clothing, she felt this was the most positive option for her:

> I always wear long sleeves now. I would just rather not have to be
> questioned for why I have scars. As far as I'm concerned, it's a healing
> journey that I've come through to not going down that route anymore and
> I don't want to have to explain myself.

Stigma and prejudice in the workplace can also be an issue, and it can be exacerbated by uncertainty about the degree of protection offered by anti-discrimination legislation. This led Emma to feel that she had to conceal her scars, particularly at work:[6]

> One thing I find difficult about my scars is that to a lot of people it is
> obvious what they are from, so if I wear short sleeves most people will
> realise that I have cut myself in the past and may make judgments/
> assumptions/comments on the basis of this. I would like to be able to wear
> short sleeves to work when it is hot – I don't feel I can do this because I
> work with vulnerable people and I could have problems at work if anyone
> found out about my self-harm.

Some user-led (LifeSIGNS, 2004; Pembroke, 1996; 2007a) and statutory services (such as the Self-Harm Service at the Royal Edinburgh Hospital) have found it useful to provide information about skin camouflage and/or demonstrations of make-up that can be used to conceal scars. The Red Cross also provides these kinds of resources. This can improve the quality of the concealment possible, increase choices around clothing, and reduce self-consciousness and difficulties presented by work and social situations.

Finally, many people also experience negative emotions around their self-injury. Therefore, while in the moment self-injury acts as an emotional salve, in the longer term the self-injury itself can also cause emotional harm (see Chapter 2). In all of these contexts, supportive work that helps to redress the negative

---

6. The 2010 Equality Act (in the UK) defines 'mental illness' – in which self-injury would be subsumed – as a disability. It is, overall, illegal to discriminate against someone on the grounds of disability unless it makes them unable to do the job – eg. a blind bus driver. However, this does not mean that discrimination does not take place and the Act is reactive rather than preventative. Furthermore, legal redress for discrimination can be a costly, time-consuming and stressful process.

associations of self-injury and relocate it in a broader holistic understanding of human embodiment and distress can be an important antidote. Indeed, the ethos of this book is to reposition self-injury as something commonplace and comprehensible, rather than shameful and strange. Similarly, peer support groups (See Chapter 5) can also be helpful in this regard.

Overall then, emotional harm can occur in a variety of ways. It may be external to the person who hurts themselves and originate from hostile attitudes and poor treatment in services, as well as stigma and prejudice in wider society. Emotional harm may also occur from the injury itself or alternatives to it (see above). In all of these instances, emotional harm can be just as detrimental to the individual's wellbeing as physical harm, and a supportive intervention must reduce the risks and impacts of these harms. This may well involve addressing the context in which the person who hurts themselves is located, and one way to do this is through the use of a crisis card.

Crisis cards

The crisis card was developed by service-users to reduce some of the emotional and psychological harm that can occur when people seek emergency medical attention for their injuries (LifeSIGNS, 2004; Pembroke, 2007a). The crisis card is particularly important when people have high-risk injuries: if, for example, they self-injure while intoxicated, or they have hurt themselves so that they have lost full consciousness or become traumatised and unable to communicate. In situations where communication is impaired, as well as when people have ongoing communication difficulties, the crisis card ensures that all the necessary information is immediately available in the treatment setting.

The crisis card should be prepared when someone is not feeling the need to hurt themself, and it should include their name, address, date of birth and the contact details of their next of kin/carer. It should also include details of any medication they are taking or treatment they are receiving, as well as any allergies they have and support services they are engaged with. The crisis card can also contain brief details of what a person might need but may be unable to communicate while in distress. Examples of useful information might be: 'I have a long history of hurting myself and am seeking help around it;' 'I can't read or write;' 'I am not able to speak right now but I can hear you;' 'Please don't leave me on my own in a cubicle if there are men nearby.'

Providing this kind of information reduces stress and confusion for both the service-user and service-provider. It alleviates some of the fear and uncertainty that service-providers often feel when faced with someone who has hurt themself (see Hadfield et al, 2009), and it supplies all the information that services need in order to provide appropriate treatment in a straightforward and efficient manner. As such, in addition to ensuring that all the information vital to the service-user's wellbeing is present, it circumvents difficult interactions and the related harms to the service-user.

It is still not uncommon for interactions with healthcare professionals to be fraught with anxiety, confusion and fear on both sides, and sometimes outright hostility on the part of the service-provider. People who have hurt themselves may be left until last to be treated; they may be stitched without anaesthetic, or punished and berated for hurting themself (Harris, 2000; Pembroke, 1996; Simpson, 2006). And, while the crisis card may not redress outright hostility, it does function very effectively when difficulties arise because the provider lacks training and awareness. The crisis card provides all the required patient details alongside any additional explanatory information, and thereby decreases the pressure on both parties. It gives voice to the service-user's needs, and affirms their right to decent treatment. From the service-provider's perspective, it reduces feelings of uncertainty, particularly around their role and responsibility in responding to the person who has hurt themself.

Some statutory services have taken the use of crisis cards a stage further. Often referred to as 'green cards', these are service-issued cards that operate as a passport to a range of on-demand services, including specialist crisis support (Wilhelm et al, 2007) and emergency hospital admission (Kapur et al, 2010; McDougall, Armstrong & Trainor, 2010). In this way, support is available at any time and, crucially, it is not dependent on the person having already hurt themself. Green cards were found to be very effective for working both with young people (McDougall, Armstrong & Trainor, 2010) and adults because they promoted 'help-seeking and offered an on-demand crisis admission' (Kapur et al, 2010: 5).[7] There is some evidence that green cards also resulted in a reduction in self-injury – although this has been challenged in subsequent studies (Kapur et al, 2010; McDougall, Armstrong & Trainor, 2010). Nonetheless, the green cards studies highlight the importance of direct, unquestioned access to emergency/crisis support services when self-injury is

---

7. In Australian hospitals, green cards were used in a slightly different way (Wilhelm et al, 2007): the green cards offered a next-day appointment, a list of emergency contacts and access to a structured, three-session support programme in the hospital. They were found to have some positive impacts in terms of encouraging help-seeking and take-up of the programme. However, the supports were largely focused on brief interventions and encouraging 'life-style changes'.

likely. That the person does not already have to have injured in order to be admitted to hospital or to access support is a powerful means of reducing harm. It also demonstrates how important it is that helpers are available prior to, as well as following, self-injury.

Overall then, crisis cards and green cards offer an effective means of accessing support if someone has, or is going to, hurt themself. The cards can mediate some of the communication problems that are commonplace in medical settings, and thereby reduce emotional harm and ensure that appropriate care takes place. Moreover, as with the safe kit, drawing up a crisis card can be a positive, productive and non-threatening way for a helper to engage with someone about their self-injury.

However, the crisis card is not the only method by which emotional harms can be reduced; there are other resources that might make the context less harmful.

Contexts, services and helpers

Chapter 4 explored how the context of a person's life – past and present – is hugely significant to their self-injury. It also highlighted how detrimental an environment can be if it mirrors negative formative experiences. In this context, service-providers need to be acutely aware of the potential harms caused by the way the service itself operates. As one of the service-providers I interviewed said:

> The agencies concerned, the hospitals, prisons or whatever, need to look at what is it that *we're doing here* that's possibly driving people to [self-injure] more and more and more. You know, sometimes people's self-harm just escalates and escalates and it's not just about the individual, it's about the context they're in. And it might be a context that they're in at home, but it might be about the context that they're in in hospital or in prison, or in care, some sort of care situation, residential situation.

Where someone is not able to remove themself from an unhealthy context, there are some practical steps that can be taken to try to reduce some of the difficulties.

Harm is often increased where there is little or no understanding of self-injury and it is viewed in negative and stigmatising ways. Difficulties in these contexts often arise because of fear and misunderstanding about self-injury, the reasons why someone hurts themself, and what constitutes an appropriate response. The immediate environment of, for example, the family home, hospital, residential setting, employment or education can have a significant impact on either promoting or reducing harm.

Education and resources about self-injury can be really beneficial, and are widely available from service-user and other organisations. LifeSIGNS[8] and the National Self-Harm Network[9] provide specific information for a range of contexts, including families, friends and schools, as well as for the person who hurts themself. Self-injury Support[10] provides both online and low-cost hard copy resources for family, friends and support workers and people who hurt themselves. It is good practice for schools, residential facilities and parent groups to ensure that they always have such resources available. Even a very basic understanding of self-injury as a coping mechanism, and of some of the primary 'dos and don'ts', can have a substantial impact in reducing the anxiety and potential harms for everyone in these contexts.

Resourcing is also key to providing service contexts that reduce rather than exacerbate the harms of self-injury. Sound knowledge and realistic expectations about self-injury are essential, and there is a range of resources and training available for organisations who work with people who self-injure.[11] When workers have little or no training about self-injury, and there is no clear policy on how to work with people who hurt themselves, it creates an anxious and potentially unsafe context for everyone.

Likewise, workers who do not have clear information, training or policy around self-injury often find it difficult and distressing to deal with, and may find it emotionally harmful. This distress can be compounded by a sense of powerlessness and helplessness to intervene effectively, especially if there are expectations that self-injury can be quickly stopped. This places further pressure on workers, positioning them as responsible for injuries and creating a context where there is little possibility of establishing positive relationships with the person who is self-injuring, or making supportive interventions. Information and training about self-injury and harm-reduction reduce the stress and difficulty experienced by workers (see Chapter 7). Clare reported from training evaluations that:

---

8. See www.lifesigns.org.uk/ (accessed 25 August, 2016).

9. See www.nshn.co.uk/downloads.html (accessed 25 August, 2016).

10. See www.selfinjurysupport.org.uk/publications-about-self-injury (accessed 25 August, 2016).

11. For example, Self-injury Support www.selfinjurysupport.org.uk/training (accessed 25 August, 2016), and Zest www.zestni.org/ (accessed 25 August, 2016) provide a wide range of training programmes.

What we hear is they feel it [harm-reduction] would actually *help* them on the emotional layers of working with self-harm. It would take away that sense of responsibility, the sense of *guilt*, the sense of *failure*, the sense of hopelessness, the frustration that they just can't *stop* the self-harm, or the frustration that the person who is self-harming just can't *stop* it.

Safe environments are also those that have realistic expectations of service-users and the ways in which staff work with them. Self-injury is a complex experience that has usually become part of someone's life over a long period of time. As such, it requires a long-term response, and expectations of quick fixes provide an unhelpful and potentially harmful environment for everyone.[12] One service-provider described how, as an organisation, they ensured their staff and volunteers had realistic understandings and expectations:

There isn't a magic thing that I [eg. the staff member] don't know about. Actually, I'm doing all right. This *is* how it is. This is a complex human thing and I'm doing my best, you know, I'm doing as well as I can with it. Rather than [them] thinking, 'Oh there is some *wonderful* method or process or something that other people might know about and I don't know about,' and that's why I'm not *succeeding*. And I suppose that comes out with the harm-minimisation as well, rather than, 'You've *got to* eliminate it,' 'cos that's so unrealistic.

In terms of realistic expectations, it is also important to understand that moving away from self-injury is not a linear process. Injuries may decrease when someone begins a therapeutic process, but can return later as the work progresses. The return of self-injury might be viewed as a failure and evidence that the work is ineffective, when in fact it can indicate the opposite – that the person is getting to the core of their issues and the injuries are reflecting this. Here, again, practising harm-reduction is essential in enabling the person to stay safe and continue the therapeutic work without a sense of fear or failure. One service-provider emphasised that 'just because someone self-injures, don't necessarily go after it. It can be what lets you know that other work that you're doing is going well'.

---

12. CBT – cognitive behavioural therapy – is currently in vogue as a treatment for a range of mental health issues, including self-injury. Notwithstanding evidence that indicates that CBT is not particularly effective for people who hurt themselves (Wilhelm et al, 2007), it remains popular with service-providers. Its popularity seems to originate from its relatively brief time frame (usually six sessions) and its unilateral primary focus on altering the service-user's thinking.

Overall then, specific knowledge, resources and realistic expectations around self-injury are essential to a context that avoids emotional harm to service-users and workers alike – and these should all be enshrined in a specific self-injury policy. There are also other aspects of the service context that are not specific to self-injury but have a huge impact on the wellbeing of both staff and service-users. These include a workplace culture that fosters self-care and support between workers, clear roles and boundaries, and a genuine commitment to equality (see Chapter 7). Likewise, contexts and helpers must actively avoid replicating social inequalities and reinforcing minority stress (see Chapter 4).

Finally, contexts are safe and supportive when they operate from a collaborative and strength-based ethos in which each individual's unique experiences and qualities are recognised and supported (see Chapter 5). This applies just as much to staff as it does to service-users; an organisation that is unsafe and unsupportive for its staff will always risk harm to its clients and workers.

• Chapter summary

Harm-reduction is a user-led intervention for self-injury that is increasingly being adopted in statutory services. Harm-reduction is based on an understanding that self-injury is a coping mechanism and, instead of attempting to prevent the coping mechanism, harm-reduction focuses on making it as safe as possible. This involves understanding and reducing the physical risks and emotional harms and promoting self-care. Harm-reduction respects and validates an individual's ability to make the best decisions for themselves in their particular circumstances. It promotes autonomy, choice and control – factors that have often been absent from service-users' lives and the services they receive. Harm-reduction works against stigma and marginalisation and provides a positive framework in which longer-term support can take place.

There is a range of possible practices within a harm-reduction approach and these are continually evolving and developing. However, before attempting any harm-reduction intervention, it is important to be clear that it:

1. reduces physical risk

2. reduces emotional harm

3. promotes self-care.

An intervention that does not meet all three of these criteria potentially causes rather than reduces harm. It is also important to remember that the risks caused by self-injury will be specific to each individual and the particular way that they hurt themself. Practices cannot be applied unilaterally to everyone who self-injures; an intervention that reduces risks for one person may increase potential harm for another. One service-provider highlighted that:

> It is personal. There might be some common things between people, but somebody who is self-injuring on one day might be completely different to somebody who is self-injuring on another day, so you can't really think, 'I *know* about this, and *this* is what needs to be done,' or 'This is what this person *ought* to be doing.' It's not like that. It's about where that person is at a certain time.

Overall, then, harm-reduction supports an individual to stay safe and to maintain choice and autonomy. It provides a context that reduces risk, stigma and anxiety, and that promotes self-care, as well as the possibility of a meaningful longer-term exploration of the issues and experiences that underlie self-injury.

Learning into practice

Definition	Self-injury is life preserving and risky
Working principles	• Knowledge not fear • Slow it down
Practice applications	• Reducing harms, promoting care • Balancing risk and trust

Definition: self-injury is life-preserving and risky

Throughout this book, I have emphasised that self-injury is a complex experience, and, while it may have broad themes in common, it may also be completely contradictory between individuals. For example, one person may self-injure to comfort themselves, while another may self-injure as a form of punishment. This is also true of the impacts of self-injury: it is a coping mechanism, a means of survival, but one that may also risk permanent or fatal harm. Understanding and responding helpfully to self-injury entails being able to tolerate contradiction, risk and uncertainty. This is nowhere more so than in the area of harm-reduction. Harm-reduction requires a simultaneous focus on both promoting the life-preserving aspects of self-injury and reducing the risks inherent to it.

Principles

1. Knowledge not fear

Many of the negative consequences of self-injury arise from approaches to it that are ill thought out, misguided or wrong. Anxiety about the meaning and purpose of self-injury and who is responsible if someone hurts themself – especially if they are a service-user or young person – often fuels fear-based responses. Any response that is fear-based is unlikely to be beneficial in the immediate or long term and will most likely produce more harm than good. Therefore, any response to self-injury, but especially harm-reduction, needs to be based on sound knowledge, and to be supported by a clear policy. Knowledge and reflection is the basis for a positive and purposeful response; fear only exacerbates harms.

2. Slow it down

In this chapter, one of the key methods for reducing risk in self-injury was through slowing it down. Here, slower equals safer, and the less panic and urgency surrounding an injury, the less harmful it is likely to be. Slow it down also applies to helpers. The most unhelpful responses to self-injury tend to be born of fear, panic and crisis reactions, where impulses to prevent and control take over. When helpers also slow down, pause, breathe and reflect on what is happening before they act, they are also going to respond in much more useful ways that do not cause emotional harm or exacerbate injuries.

Activity

- Investigate some simple breathing exercises and spend a few minutes every day just focusing on your breathing. When you have got used to the breathing exercise, try it out when you are stressed, harried or panicked, and see what the effect is.

Practice applications

1. Reducing harms, promoting care

Central to good practice in harm-reduction is supporting the person who hurts themself to reduce physical risks and emotional harms and to practise self-care. It can be helpful to break the response down into the following questions:

- What are the risks (physical and emotional)?
- What are the positives (eg. the person's strengths, resources etc)?
- How can self-care be promoted?
- What would be helpful:
    1. immediately?
    2. in the medium term?
    3. in the long term?

Exploring these questions with the person who hurts themself will enable a multi-faceted response that is uniquely tailored to their needs and situation. The harm-reduction techniques suggested in this chapter provide a starting point for ways of reducing harm and promoting care, but these are by no means exhaustive, and multiple possibilities exist. So long as the intervention reduces physical risks and emotional harms and promotes self-care, it offers an important harm-reduction practice. This will allow each person to stay safe with their self-injury, and provides a helpful context for exploring their underlying needs and long-term goals.

2. Balancing risk and trust

One of the major barriers to harm-reduction – or indeed any constructive response to self-injury – are the misperceptions and stereotypes about it and people who hurt themselves. If, for example, a helper believes that self-injury is sick and crazy and that people who hurt themselves are manipulative, deviant and attention-seeking, then they are unlikely to support someone in harm-reduction practices or, indeed, in any meaningful way. If, on the other hand, a helper understands that self-injury is a coping mechanism, that it is evidence of strength and survival, then they are much more likely to respond in a positive and supportive way. They are also much more likely to be able to understand harm-reduction and encourage its practice. Harm-reduction, therefore, is based to a large extent on trusting the person that hurts themself: trusting their will to survive and the meaning and purpose of their self-injury. This can be challenging, especially in some contexts where, by virtue of their label, service-users are deemed to be of diminished reliability and trustworthiness. For Emma, it was crucial for 'people to trust the self-harmer's ability to be ok'.

Trust is, however, a two-way relationship. Someone who hurts themself needs also to be able to genuinely trust their helper to have their best interests at heart, even if this creates challenges for the helper. People are unlikely to be open with, or to heed advice from a person who is not trustworthy, and therefore trust is a two-way feature of harm-reduction. Trust also has to remain in the context of risk. Even with harm-reduction, self-injury is never risk-free, and these risks can cause anxieties and attempts at control. Tolerating the risks of self-injury – in the knowledge of the deeper risks of prevention – can be a challenge for helpers but transformative for people who hurt themselves. Elaine articulated the dilemmas that harm-reduction poses to helpers, emphasising the challenges of balancing risk and trust:

> I think that there needs to be a lot *less reaction* to self-harm in terms of physical injury. In that just because someone's cut their arm, and yes there is that idea that they are at risk, but they don't need to be put into a psychiatric hospital because of self-harming, that's a reaction to the *injury*. That's a big area of confusion: I can appreciate the issues that

people have around is it really ok to send someone out with 15 stitches in their arm when they'll be back in again next week? And *are we* at risk? Are we a risk to ourselves? Is that a risk to yourself? Is that a risk? And it's like *yes, technically* I can see that it would be, *but I don't* believe it's right to put people in psychiatric units because of self-harming. I think that actually does more damage than good. And 'stopping' people self-harming isn't going to stop them doing it... It's a reaction to the injury, and it would be better dealt with if people reacted [differently]. I can *understand* because one of the most fundamental, basic human things is to react to an injury, and it's kind of *wrong* in the context of self-harm. That's why it's very difficult at the minute for it to be dealt with effectively, because people react to the injury.

Balancing risk and trust is not easy and, as Elaine points out, it is counter-intuitive in many contexts. However, for a safe response to self-injury, one in which physical risks and emotional harm are reduced and where self-care is promoted, balancing risk and trust is essential.

Activity

- Think about one or two of the ways that you know people use to hurt themselves. This might be from your own work or experiences or from the stories in this book.
- Make a list of all the risks – immediate and long-term – for each type of injury, and then reflect on some of the ways that these risks could be reduced.
- What other information or resources would be helpful in reducing these risks?

7

Policy:
making best-practice happen

Policy is rarely a word that inspires, excites and motivates. Indeed, it is usually envisaged as the opposite – as endless reams of tedious paperwork that either has little relationship with reality or that imposes absurd constraints and protocols on basic day-to-day activities – 'health and safety gone mad'. There is, however, no reason for policy to be obscure and obstructive. In fact, good policy is precisely the opposite: it is what enables best practice to happen.

Policy has been defined as 'a definite course or method of action', or as what 'determines present and future decisions' (Goldman & Schmalz, 2010: 9). For this reason, a specific self-injury policy is essential for organisations who work with people who hurt themselves. A self-injury policy sets out, in plain language/s, the roles, responsibilities, practices and protocols within that organisation. It removes the fears, uncertainties and misperceptions surrounding self-injury that can lead to confusion and counterproductive practices.

This chapter on policy is intended to be especially valuable for people who work in any type of organisation, as well as for people who hurt themselves who engage with services. The policy development framework set out in this chapter can demystify organisational practices and, more importantly, provide a resource for engaging with services around reconsidering policy and practice. For those who are not within a service context, understanding policy – and the possibilities for developments of it – can also be useful in terms of making sense of particular myths and protocols that are commonplace with regard to self-injury, and challenging them when they are encountered.[1]

This chapter provides a rationale and practical guidance for developing a self-injury policy. The policy approach adopted here is straightforward, accessible and practical. It includes all of the key constituents for an effective self-injury policy. Contrary to common perception (and practice), a comprehensive policy need be no more than two or three pages long, and it can be easy to read, understand and implement. However, before outlining the essential features of a self-injury policy, it is important to ensure that there is an appropriate context for its development.

The context for a good self-injury policy

A good self-injury policy is developed in collaboration between workers, service-users and management. It is based on a range of evidence and has a clear focus and purpose. Policy does not exist in a vacuum, and it both reflects and reinforces the culture and values of an organisation. The wider context of an organisation, its ethos and resources, will have a significant impact on the development and efficacy of a self-injury policy. In *Good Practice Guidelines for Working with People who Self-Injure*, Hilary Lindsay (1999) emphasises that any service that works with people who hurt themselves must have core conditions in place in order to enable good practice to happen. These are:

- rights and equality
- clear work practices
- empowering practices
- flexibility
- boundaries
- training and support for staff.

Rights and equality are fundamental to all stages of the policy process – including policy development. This means that service-users and workers from

---

1. It is also worth noting that different contexts have their own specific advantages and disadvantages in responding helpfully to someone who hurts themself. For example, a service context is going to be framed, and often limited, by policy and legal obligations that are not present in social and familial support networks. Thus, 'non-professional' support is much more flexible. However, social and familial supports are bound by much deeper and much more complex emotional bonds than service-provider relationships, and can be much more blurred and confusing in terms of boundaries and obligations. Therefore, each context brings with it a specific set of enablers and constraints, and policy analysis can be a means of exploring and clarifying those issues in either context.

all levels of the organisation should be involved in the policy-development process, otherwise 'equality' is nothing more than empty rhetoric. Equality is vital, both as a principle and in terms of tangible, practical benefits.

Recent years have seen increasing recognition across statutory and voluntary services that 'experts by experience' (eg. service-users) are essential to developing and delivering meaningful services, and service-user consultation is increasingly mandated in statutory services (Thomas & Hollinrake, 2014).[2] The award-winning Self-Harm Service and the Personality Disorder Project at the Royal Edinburgh Hospital were both developed in partnership with service-users and are now user-led and user-directed services. Likewise, the young people's self-harm service at 42nd Street in Manchester was developed from a user-led model, with service-providers adopting facilitator roles and functioning as conduits for the service provision (Green, 2007). Across the voluntary sector, service-providers also recognise that expertise emerges from service-user experiences: 'I honestly believe that I'm an expert now on suicide and self-harm only because I've been taught by the very best, and that's the people who have been through it.'

Overall then, good policy – and practice – emerges from collaborations between those who use services and those who provide them. But policy also needs to be based on evidence about what is effective for service-users. In recent years, the mandate of 'evidence-based practice' has moved from medical practice into the health and social care arena (Glasby, 2011a; Warner & Spandler, 2012). However, what constitutes 'evidence' is not a straightforward case of objective facts, but is bound up in power and inequality. There is a significant hierarchy of evidence in which some forms of evidence, such as medical research, are valued much more than other types of data, such as service-user experiences. However, the value of the evidence often has little to do with its applicability to a particular setting (Glasby, 2011b). For example, in medical settings, findings from randomised control trials are considered evidence *par excellence*. And while there may be some value in the outcomes from laboratory-initiated randomised control trials, these are less effective when intervening in subjective human emotions, perceptions and experiences in the context of people's daily lives. Furthermore, outside the laboratory, what counts as evidence is unequally defined: for example, medical *opinion* constitutes evidence or findings, while service-user *experience* is not considered to be valid data (Falkner & Thomas, 2002).

---

2. Although service-user consultation is increasingly mandated in policy and service development, 'consultation' can often be tokenistic and can reinforce power hierarchies and inequalities, rather than overcome them. Real power sharing requires a genuine belief in and commitment to equality (see Thomas & Hollinrake, 2014).

This skewing of 'evidence' away from service-user experiences potentially undermines the moves towards service-user inclusion and consultation – there is little purpose in consulting groups of people if their experiences are only going to be overridden by evidence claims. This anomaly has led researchers and practitioners to develop new frameworks for 'evidence'. These frameworks not only draw on and value service-user experiences on a par with other forms of data, but also incorporate the knowledge and experience of practitioners (Glasby, 2011b; Thomas & Hollinrake, 2014; Warner & Spandler, 2011). These kinds of data have been reframed as 'practice-based evidence' (Warner & Spandler, 2011), 'knowledge-based policy and practice' (Glasby, 2011b) and 'user-led research' (Faulkner & Thomas, 2002).

Therefore, a robust and meaningful policy needs to draw on a wide knowledge base. This might include some published research, but it *must* incorporate evidence from those who use and work within services – even if at times this seems counter to published wisdom. The development of harm-reduction policies and practices was for many years explicitly counter to 'expert' knowledge and 'evidence', and yet they are now being integrated into precisely the contexts that formerly rejected them (see Chapter 6). As such, a diversity of evidence is important, not only for ensuring that the policy is directly relevant to the needs of service-users, but also because it reinforces rights and equality (Thomas & Hollinrake, 2014).

In addition to equality and inclusivity in the policy development process, and a clear understanding of what kind of evidence is necessary and appropriate, there are other factors that are important to the policy development context. According to Arnold and Magill (2007), drafting a good self-injury policy requires appropriate allocations of time and space for the work to be done (including reading, discussing, reflecting and drafting); clarity about the service role and response in regard to self-injury – along with any changes that might be desirable – and relevant documents. Important documents for a self-injury policy include job descriptions (eg. roles and boundaries for workers), and confidentiality and health and safety policies (for dealing with the legal and practical issues around self-injury). The self-injury policy guidelines published by The Basement Project (Arnold & McGill, 2007) and Self-injury Support (Lindsay, 1999) are also extremely useful documents for developing a self-injury policy.

Finally, there are two important caveats with regard to a self-injury (or any) policy. The first is that the policy must have a clear purpose that directly relates to the day-to-day role and activities of the organisation. As one service-provider described it, the purpose of a policy is to make clear '*why* are you doing anything at any given place and time'. Policy should provide a straightforward and comprehensible rationale for any procedure that takes place; it should not obscure or obfuscate actions, and nor should it provide cover for dubious protocols.

The second caveat is that policy should never be proceduralistic, whereby stipulated practices are followed regardless of their impact or appropriateness for an individual. Proceduralism dehumanises the interactions between service-users and service-providers and may even put lives at risk. This is illustrated by two accounts, the first from a service manager who recounted a client's experience:

> … she had attempted to take her own life, she took an overdose. She had been attending one of the [mental health] centres and she had taken *everything* [ie. all the medication] that she had. She had stored it up a little bit, and had taken everything she had. She survived, thanks be to God, but she was sent back to the centre... referred back to the psychiatrist in her health centre, and he wrote out another prescription for her. And she was just *bewildered* and mystified by this. She had tried to take her life *with* medication, and here they were giving her *more medication* to maybe do the same thing.

Joseph, who sometimes hurt himself by taking overdoses of medication, also reported proceduralistic responses: 'My experience from going for help – that they would just give you tablets and send you off'. Therefore, while all policy must have a clear purpose in regard to why practices are implemented, this is not the same as a proceduralistic approach, which involves simply following a rigid set of practices, regardless of an individual's needs or the implications of those actions.

Ideals for best practice

Before moving on to the policy document itself, it is also important to consider what service-users and service-providers identify as key features of an ideal self-injury service, as this also provides further useful evidence for developing a self-injury policy.

Across different sectors, throughout service-user and professional perspectives, and from the UK and Ireland, remarkably similar themes emerge in regard to best practice. These include direct access to free services, services that operate in a non-clinical or homely environment, and services that have a range of support options available. One service-provider emphasised that these features are important not only in terms of meeting service-user needs but also in reducing the stigma around self-injury:

> I would like to see much better access to non-stigmatising support. For
> example, counsellors available in GP surgeries, or counsellors where you
> don't even have to go to the GP; support that you could get without having
> to be referred to a psychiatrist or to be labelled as mentally ill; where you
> could have easy access; somewhere to go; individual *and* group support;
> somewhere to go when *you* feel you need it.

Emma also highlighted the need for direct access, without referral, for both
face-to-face and telephone support:

> It would be flexible and available at short notice, [so] you would be able to
> self-refer without going through doctors etc, and you would also be able
> to get telephone support from the counsellors when you are in your own
> home, so you could choose what support felt most appropriate at different
> times, and you could build some trust over time if you wanted.

The availability of telephone support was frequently highlighted as crucial
by service-users and service-providers. Telephone support is particularly
important during evenings and weekends when people might be struggling to
cope and feeling isolated. But, paradoxically, this is the time when most services
are not available, or are certainly not available on an on-demand basis. One
service-provider explained that:

> I would like there to be much more helpline services available. I mean
> there *is* the Samaritans but they're not always very good around self-
> harm, although I think they have been trying to improve. You know, we
> can't cope with all the calls that *we get*, and we don't even advertise as a
> helpline, but people *really need* somewhere to phone, men and women and
> children, to talk about self-harm and related issues.

Another service developed a helpline service to be available specifically during
under-resourced times:

> I think the times that we run the helpline are times when it just can be
> worse for people and there aren't other services around. The times we run
> the crisis line are when traditionally you are meant to be out enjoying
> yourself, so if you're not, then it can kind of be even worse. So we just have
> quite *limited* times [when the helpline is available] but they are [important].

In addition to on-demand access, the physical environment for the service was also highlighted as significant. In the same way that direct access and self-referral circumvent some of the difficult and potentially stigmatising aspects of clinical environments, then so too should the physical environment that the service operates within. One service manager described how a non-clinical, homely setting was integral to the ethos of their service:

> We wanted a non-clinical setting. I mean if any of us are in trouble or in crisis, we don't need to go and see a person in a white coat, what we need to see is a *friend* or someone who is really going to be understanding and compassionate to us. So that's why it's a non-clinical setting because it's like coming home, to someone's home.

Emma outlined her ideal service at length, emphasising the importance of a homely environment.

> It's hard to describe what my utopia of a safe place would be like, but I think it would look just like a normal home, with a living-room, kitchen, bathroom and bedroom. There would be counsellors available to talk to if you wanted and when you chose but there would also be no pressure to talk. There would be a room you could go to scream and bash cushions if you wanted and you could choose if/when you slept in the house.
>
> In the living room there would be games to play/art and craft stuff so that you could be doing stuff and then talk in bits and pieces if you wanted because this is much less pressured and can give you something to do with your hands/an excuse to change the subject when you don't want to talk about something anymore. Art stuff would also provide another useful way to express things that are hard to say.

Finally, the need for the service to be free of charge was also emphasised by service-users and service-providers. Emma highlighted that cost has a significant impact on access and therefore an ideal service 'would also be free – including transport to and from'. This was reinforced by a service manager who emphasised that 'the fact that we're free is actually *vital*'.

> We are free because you don't need another anxiety on top of what you're going through, and if you were coming to us two or three times a week you're talking about up to €200 a week and *nobody* can afford *that!* So

we're taking away the worry. I also think that it *should* be a free service. When someone is in crisis to put a monetary sort of hint over it is distasteful, I think, to be perfectly honest.

Therefore, as much as possible when developing a policy, services should explore the possibilities of being free, available on a self-referral basis, and flexible enough to respond to service-users' different needs at different times and to work in non-clinical settings. Of course, not all of these may be possible for each service; issues such as cost and referral process may be determined by external structures. Nonetheless, these ideals or aspirations remain important touchstones for developing user-centred, purposeful and effective services for people who hurt themselves.

Writing a self-injury policy

Having explored the background and context for developing a self-injury policy, the remainder of this chapter will now focus on the key components required for an effective policy. It is based on the template below, which can be used as the basis for a self-injury policy in any service.

The policy template is designed to execute the key functions of a self-injury policy. The first function is to clearly state the key features of the service: the organisation's philosophy and purpose; who the service operates for (the client group); how clients are served; how self-injury is understood/defined within the organisation, and the organisation's procedures around self-injury.

The second function is that a self-injury policy should also cover a range of existing legal and policy issues, including health and safety, confidentiality and complaints procedures; workers' rights and responsibilities; how other services and service-users are engaged; the resources available, and how the policy is implemented, monitored and reviewed.

Throughout the chapter, I draw on examples from a range of self-injury services and service-user experiences to provide practical illustrations of key components.

At the end of this chapter, there are some examples of policies that illustrate good practice. There are two examples of confidentiality and complaints policies from 42nd Street and Self-injury Support, which are discussed individually below. There is also one example of a self-injury policy that was drafted based on this template. The self-injury policy was designed by the Tus Nua project in Dublin, which is run by Depaul,[3] and provides a supported residential service for

---

3. More information about Depaul is available at https://ie.depaulcharity.org/ (accessed 5 September, 2016).

women leaving prison. This policy, which was developed in 2011, illustrates how the general themes from the template have been applied to the specific service context in a way that combines some of the key principles of responding helpfully to self-injury, such as respect and non-judgment, with clear, practical protocols.

Self-Injury Policy Template

1. The philosophy and purpose of the organisation (2–3 sentences).

2. Client group and access: how and for whom does the service operate (2–3 sentences).

3. How are clients served: aims/ethos in practice (2–3 sentences).

---

4. **Definition: how self-injury is understood** (3–4 sentences).

5. **The procedure for:** (one paragraph/bullet points each)
   a) a service-user with a history of self-injury
   b) a service-user who has just self-injured
   c) a service-user who is about to self-injure
   d) ongoing support of service-users around self-injury.

---

6. Legal and policy issues (cross-referenced with statutory requirements and relevant policies, one short paragraph per policy area):
   a) confidentiality (breadth and limitations)
   b) health and safety issues and policy (staff role and procedures)
   c) complaints (procedures and protocols).

7. Workers' rights and responsibilities: (cross-referenced with job descriptions, one short paragraph).

8. Resources (a list of available resources for service-users, staff, family/ carers, other organisations).

9. Implementation (statement of how and when policy will be adopted (or piloted) and designated staff responsible, 2–3 sentences).

10. Monitoring and review (2–3 sentences each for formal and informal review).

1. Organisational philosophy and purpose

This statement should identify the overall ethos of the service or organisation. It should appear on all documentation and information about the service, and it should be brief and clear. The philosophy statement is important in highlighting the kinds of beliefs, ethics and principles that underpin the policy and practice, and it indicates what clients and staff can expect from the service. 42ⁿᵈ Street, the Manchester-based young people's service, defines its ethos and purpose as: 'To support young people under stress to achieve their full potential.'[4] This provides a brief, clear indication of who the service operates for and its aims and ethos – eg. that all young people have potential, which can be achieved with support and regardless of their current difficulties. The national Self-harm Service at SLaM has a lengthier philosophy that states:

> We recognise that everyone is unique and foster an environment where
> each person's safety needs are met. Our staff encourage growth, learning
> and change, and support everyone in taking responsibility for their actions.
> We believe everyone should act as advocates to others and attempt to do no
> harm (SLaM, 2010: 5).

Two further paragraphs indicate that the service 'focus[es] on health rather than illness' and 'that residents retain as much responsibility as possible across different aspects of their lives'.

In most instances, the organisation will already have a philosophy statement that can be transferred to the self-injury policy. However, if the self-injury service is new, or is a discreet unit within a wider organisation such as the NHS, then a specific philosophy should be drafted (see SLaM statement above). Brevity is useful, and two or three sentences are adequate for this purpose. The drafting process can begin by identifying key words and principles for the service/organisation and then working them into a defining statement. Allowing time for debate, refining and editing the statement is important, to ensure that the philosophy and purpose is fully representative of the service and all those involved in it.

2. Client group and access: who the service operates for

All documents should include a brief description of who the service operates for: ie. their specific client group and how the service can be accessed. For

---

4. http://42ndstreet.org.uk/about-us/ (accessed 5 September, 2016).

example, 42nd Street works with young people aged 11–25. Young people can self-refer, or be referred by an adult, such as a teacher or social worker, via the telephone or a downloadable referral form.[5] TESS, the Text and Email Support Service run by Self-injury Support, defines its client group as 'girls and young women up to 24 years in the UK affected by self-harm'.[6] It also sets out the days (Sunday to Friday) and times (7–9pm) that the service is available, and the email and text contact details. SLaM offers inpatient and outpatient services and defines its client group as those for whom 'self-harm is the primary clinical problem' (2010: 6), who are over 18 and in receipt of support from a local community health team. Referral is only via medical services – GP, psychiatrist or community mental health team.

These statements should appear together on the policy document, in simple and unambiguous language, so that it is clear who can make use of the service and how they get in contact with it. It should also highlight the kind of support available: eg. information, emotional support, physical care etc. As with the organisational philosophy and purpose, this statement should only take two or three sentences. It should also be clear and straightforward to draft, since the client group, contact hours and nature of the service are unlikely to be in question.

3. How clients are served: aims/ethos in practice

This section is important because it shows how the ethos is put into practice in terms of describing both what is offered to service-users and the context that support is provided within. This statement might include the aims of the organisation. 42nd Street describes its aims as to: 'engage with young people under stress; provide interventions that promote resilience and recovery; enable young people to take part in opportunities for personal development; improve awareness of the mental health needs of children and young people among other professionals and the wider public.'[7] These aims are realised through counselling/therapy and one-to-one support (keyworking). Zest, the community based self-injury and suicide service in Northern Ireland,[8] also uses its aims and objectives to describe how clients are served. The service aim is 'to provide a place of genuine acceptance, active safety and living hope to those who don't feel

---

5. http://42ndstreet.org.uk/individual-support/ (accessed 5 September, 2016).

6. www.selfinjurysupport.org.uk/tess-text-and-email-support-service (accessed 5 September, 2016).

7. http://42ndstreet.org.uk/about-us/ (accessed 5 September, 2016).

8. www.ZestNI.org (accessed 5 September, 2016).

accepted, who don't feel safe and are losing hope', along with a list of objectives such as 'practising these values in our own lives' and 'promoting the protection of young people and vulnerable adults from harm' (Zest, undated). It also includes a specific list of services available, which include one-to-one counselling, family support, telephone support, complementary therapies, information and bereavement support. These statements are, however, quite lengthy and general, and an abbreviated summary is preferable for a policy document.

4. Definition: how self-injury is understood

It is essential that every policy document for self-injury clearly sets out how self-injury is defined and understood within that service. As with the other policy statements, this provides a clear, unambiguous outline of how the person will be understood and treated. It is possible to define self-injury clearly and effectively in a few short sentences. For example, TESS defines self-injury as:

> Self-injury happens when someone causes deliberate injury or pain to their own body. It might take the form of cutting, burning, bruising, or pulling hair, but there are many other forms. Self-harm is often a sign that someone is hurting emotionally in some way, and self-injury is a common method of coping with emotional pain and distress.[9]

Zest define self-injury as 'carrying out physical injury or drug overdoses regularly or at times of great stress and anxiety', followed by a list of 16 possible methods, including 'swallowing poisonous substances', 'scratching', 'disfiguration of the body' and 'cutting'. Each chapter of this book has concluded with a definitional statement about self-injury and these can be worked into an effective policy definition, such as:

> Self-injury is when someone intentionally causes direct pain or damage to their own body but without intending to die. It is a coping mechanism, with a range of functions such as release, control, self-punishment, comfort and expression. It may take a variety of forms, including self-hitting, swallowing objects or substances, scratching, burning and cutting. Self-injury indicates that a person is in distress and that they should be treated with sensitivity and care.

---

9. www.selfinjurysupport.org.uk/files/docs/What%20is%20self%20injury%202014.pdf (accessed 5 September, 2016).

Some policies and policy templates include a list 'risk factors' for self-injury, which consist of a set of mental illnesses with which self-injury is associated – such as depression and anxiety (LifeSIGNS, 2008) – or personal characteristics, such as poor problem-solving skills and impulsivity.[10] However, this is both unnecessary and problematic. It can be stigmatising, and can also reinforce the perception that self-injury is somehow related to a personal flaw or dysfunction, rather than a coping mechanism that is a response to a very real issue or problem.

5. Procedures for self-injury

This is the most important part of a self-injury policy, and it is therefore likely to be more substantial than the other sections. It should be written with awareness of the resources available within the service (such as *The Hurt Yourself Less Workbook* (Dace et al, 1998) or *The Rainbow Journal* (Lucas, 2003)), as well as external supports. It should also be stipulated that, while the policy will be followed in terms of the type and frequency of support *offered*, it is flexible and does not mandate service-user take-up. A good policy will not force 'support' on someone who is not able to engage with it, and nor will it punish them for not doing so.

It is essential that the wording in this section of the policy is clear and directive. Ambiguous or general words such as 'ensure' should be avoided, as they fail to clearly indicate the actions to be taken (DeMarco & Tufts, 2014). For example, 'ensure that any sharp equipment used for self-injury has been safely disposed of following an injury' is much less clear than 'check and confirm with the service-user that any sharp equipment used for self-injury has been safely disposed of in the sharps bin or cleaned and returned to the safe kit following an injury'.

5a) For a history of self-injury

A service-user may disclose that they have a history of self-injury in a variety of ways, or it may be revealed indirectly via case notes or a referral. Whether or not the self-injury is ongoing, the policy should direct how it will be followed up. It should stipulate that self-injury will be discussed in the context of self-care, including aftercare and harm-reduction, and that support needs around underlying issues, as well as those that are specific to self-injury, are explored and addressed. This should include working out an individual plan with the

---

10. www.rcpsych.ac.uk/pdf/Knightsmith%20Jodi%20-%20Self-Harm%20Policy.pdf (accessed 5 September, 2016).

person for what would be helpful if they feel they are going to hurt themselves again, as well as long-term support (see section (d), below). The policy should make clear that the service has an obligation to directly address self-injury and stipulate a time period within which it must be followed-up.

5b) If someone has just self-injured

This section covers the physical, emotional and social issues that follow self-injury. For the physical aspects, this section (and section (c), below) should be linked to the health and safety policy on dealing with injuries, blood and sharp or dangerous implements, alongside responsibility for care of injuries, and when medical attention is required. It should also be linked to the job descriptions of staff in terms of their responsibilities for providing physical/ medical care. The policy should direct how injuries will be treated and implements made safe (eg. disposed of in a sharps container or cleaned and returned to a safe kit). It should stipulate in which situations medical attention will be called, and if a member of staff will accompany the service-user to A&E – remembering that medical attention is always required for ingestion of substances or objects.

The emotional and social aspects of self-injury should also be covered in this section of the policy, including the kind of emotional support that will be provided to someone after they have self-injured, and stipulating the frequency of follow-up. This should initially be daily and then negotiated with the service-user. It should also include access to self-injury-specific resources and other external forms of support. In an organisation where other service-users maybe present (such as residential or inpatient settings), those who might have witnessed the event or its aftermath, or who are concerned about the individual, should also be provided with support within a stipulated time period. Likewise, debriefing and support for the staff involved should be mandatory before the end of their shift – debriefing can be provided in a variety of ways, such as by a line manager, peer debriefing, during supervision, or via telephone support. Finally, the policy should stipulate the type of records of the incident that are required, as well as possible obligations in regard to other policies – such as confidentiality or incident reporting (Arnold & McGill, 2007).

5c) If someone is about to self-injure

This is probably the most difficult aspect of a self-injury policy in terms of balancing the need for a clear organisational protocol with the specific needs of each individual. This area also tends to produce the most anxieties in services, despite it being rare that the actual act of self-injury is apparent to others (Lindsay, 1999). If someone is already known to have a history of, or ongoing, self-injury, then an individual plan should be available – see section (d) below. This plan should be easily accessible to relevant staff and used in collaboration with the service-user.

The policy should make clear that service-users will not be physically restrained and nor will attempts be made to physically prevent their self-injury. However, if a service-user has identified alternatives to self-injury or other forms of expression that are useful for them, then these will be explored. As with section (b), the health and safety policy is also relevant here in terms of dealing with injuries on the premises.

Staff and other service-users who were engaging with the individual up to and/or during their self-injury should have the opportunity to debrief as soon as possible afterwards, and no later than the same day.

5d) Ongoing support for people who hurt themselves

The policy should set out the type and frequency of the support provided to individuals who hurt themselves within the organisation, including emotional, practical and social supports. The policy should mandate that every service-user who hurts themself will be provided with the opportunity to develop an individual support plan around their self-injury. This process should begin as soon as their self-injury is identified, but it is unlikely to be quickly completed. The plan will be an evolving document as the person explores their self-injury and the range of interventions possible for expressing their feelings and experiences. It should include a list of immediate supports required if a person feels they are going to hurt themself, or if they have just self-injured, as well as long-term support. The plan should include self-care, aftercare and harm-reduction appropriate to that individual, including the development of a safe kit. The role of the workers in relation to harm-reduction and developing a safe kit may vary from being able to give one-to-one direct, practical support and advice to only being able to provide links to information and resources. The plan might also include services and resources outside the organisation that the service-user can draw on. The plan should correspond with the stipulated follow-up contacts and resources set out in section (a). Finally, the service-user and the organisation should both have a copy of the plan, and the organisation's copy should be easily accessible to appropriate, designated staff.

6. Legal and policy issues

There is a range of legal obligations that a self-injury policy intersects with. The most important of these is confidentiality and mandatory reporting, especially in regard to young people and vulnerable or dependent adults. Legal requirements in this area are subject to quite frequent revision, and they also vary regionally. For example, limitations on confidentiality and obligations to report when a child or vulnerable adult is at risk vary across England, Ireland, Scotland, Wales and Northern Ireland. There is also some variation depending on the type of service and the specific client group (eg. young people, residential, penal) and the type of contact (eg. face-to-face or computer mediated). It is therefore essential to consult accurate and up-to-date information on legal obligations when writing a self-injury policy.

6a) Confidentiality

Confidentiality is one of the legal/policy areas that can prove most challenging for a self-injury policy. In most confidentiality policies, self-injury is presented in terms of serious risk – especially for young people – and this risk is seen to justify breaching confidentiality. It is therefore useful to reassess the organisation's confidentiality policy in regard to risk in general, and young people in particular, in order to create a fully integrated self-injury policy.

- Risk

Most confidentiality policies stipulate that client-provider interactions and records remain confidential unless the service-user is 'at risk of causing harm to themselves or others'. This standard protocol is problematic because it does not distinguish between self-injury and suicide. Therefore, even though self-injury is a coping mechanism and a means by which people keep themselves safe, it is conflated with elevated risk, suicide and harm to others, which must be reported. It is therefore advisable that confidentiality policies are reworded to be more specific and less problematic in regard to self-injury: eg. 'Confidentiality will be maintained unless there is risk of harm to others or life-threatening risk to the self.' This ensures that suicide-prevention and child protection policies can be maintained without any ambiguity or unnecessary breaches of confidentiality regarding self-injury.

- Young people and confidentiality

Issues around maintaining confidentiality become even more complex where young people are involved. Confidentiality policies tend to not only stipulate that confidentiality will be breached when there is a 'risk of harm to the self', but also that parents must be informed if there is any 'risk' to their child. However, the definitions of 'harm' and 'risk' are often interpreted in ways that seem to be aimed at protecting the organisation, rather than a fully considered analysis of what is actually in the best interest of the young person. As one service provider explained:

> People working with children are more anxious because of the responsibility thing for children and young people, particularly those under 16, people tend to be very anxious about.

However, young people often avoid disclosure to their parents, for a variety of reasons, including a desire to protect the parents, communication difficulties, or risks of further harm to themselves. Joseph was clear that, 'when I started cutting myself I knew *not* to say anything to my parents because I knew they wouldn't understand'. Reporting to parents might be a concern for the young person not only because of the distress that their self-injury will cause them; in some cases, it is because parents (guardian/s or carer/s) are the problem. To protect children and young people in this situation, Childline provides young people with detailed information about how to 'cover your tracks' by deleting their internet history, hiding the Childline webpage and using private browsing.[11]

A report by the Newham Asian Women's Project (1998) found that young women from Asian backgrounds often experienced particular difficulties in accessing appropriate, confidential support. Primary care providers, such as GPs, frequently violated young Asian women's confidentiality in ways that would be almost unheard of for white patients. This occurred when GPs from the same community felt duty-bound to disclose the content of the consultation to the young woman's parents or, conversely, when white GPs, through misplaced ideas about cultural appropriateness, believed that different norms and boundaries of patient confidentiality applied to young women from Asian communities.

Breaches of confidentiality to parents can have significant impacts on the wellbeing of young people and their ability to access the kind of support that they need. For example, as a young teenager Emma was referred to a

---

11. www.childline.org.uk/info-advice/bullying-abuse-safety/online-mobile-safety/cover-tracks/ (accessed 5 September, 2016).

professional who 'broke my confidentiality to tell my parents that I was suicidal'. This not only destroyed any possibility of effective support from this person, because Emma 'didn't trust her'; it also impacted on the support she received as an older teenager.

> I didn't talk to her about my experiences of abuse or going into anything in much depth with her partly because I didn't feel ready and partly because I figured that once I was over 18 I would have more of a right to confidentiality.

Overall then, standard confidentiality policies may prevent young people from being able to access the kind of support they need. This not only impacts on their immediate and long-term wellbeing but also has implications for their sense of self-determination and control – which can be significant features of self-injury (see Chapter 2). One service-provider reported that 'one of the things that gets repeated from young people is they just don't want it taken it out of their hands'.

These problems with confidentiality policies have led organisations such as ChildLine[12] to develop an approach that maintains young people's confidentiality to much higher levels than are possible within, for example, a school environment – but, nonetheless, retain some limitations in regard to suicidality and abuse if a child's name and whereabouts are known. Similarly, it has been found that 'absolute confidentiality' that ensures 'clear and demonstrable service criteria [...] basic service rights [...] and explicit measures of confidentiality' is essential for providing effective services for young women from BME communities (Newham Asian Women's Project, 1998: 35). However, the level of confidentiality available is ultimately going to depend on the type of service: face-to-face services will never be able to offer the same degree of confidentiality as those that are mediated by technology. For example, services that operate telephone, text and email services can ensure confidentiality through software that encrypts the caller's identification. This means that, if a caller does reveal an 'at risk' situation, the caller is able to discuss it without unwanted action being imposed on them, as one service-provider explained:

> [The helpline is] a confidential space for people to talk out whatever they *want*. If they are going to want to say or report something it *can* be a first

---

12. www.childline.org.uk/Pages/Home.aspx (accessed 5 September 2016).

step, sort of *airing* something. There are enough other places where you can go if you *do* want something taken on legally, but not so much if you want something confidential.

This kind of approach is crucial for enabling service-users, and especially young people, to explore their experiences and make sense of them in their own time and under their own control. This does not abdicate services from the responsibility of being able to provide correct information and advice in regard to legal processes, but it does avoid it being forced on the young people, as the same service-provider explained:

> *If* people want to disclose information, if they want to take those steps, then we need to know what to advise them. So we have *that* responsibility, to respond to on that level, but we don't actually want to do it on a mandatory basis.

Another way in which services attempt to work with a client-centred approach towards confidentiality is to provide clear information about the situations in which confidentiality will be breached, and what kinds of disclosure of information will trigger this process. TESS, for example, uses encryption software to erase all contact details. However, the confidentiality policy reminds service-users that if they disclose identifying information alongside a 'risk' situation, then this will result in a mandatory follow-up (see the policy reproduced at the end of this chapter). Similarly, 42nd Street also highlights the conditions under which confidentiality can and cannot be maintained, leaving young people with enough information to make a fully informed choice about what they choose to reveal and the consequences of doing so (reprinted at the end of this chapter). Likewise, an Irish service that provides face-to-face support for children who hurt themselves clearly sets out the boundaries and limits of confidentiality to young people and their adult carers when they first engage with the service:

> The parents or the guardians are brought in right from the beginning and we explain what we're going to do. They will be told that most of the conversation with the child *will be* confidential for the child's sake, *but* if there is anything that we feel, you know if there is any neglect discovered or anything else going on that we will report [to statutory services], we *have* to... The other thing is that we insist on telling the parents how the

child is doing, *not* to repeat what the child is saying, but we insist on telling them how the child is doing because who cares *more* about the child than the parents?! So it's really important that we keep them in the loop the whole time and we also offer support to them.[13]

As a mother herself, Emma felt from a parent's perspective it was important that children's rights and confidentiality are respected, so long as the services they were provided with were credible and accountable:

As a parent I would be ok with my child having confidential counselling but I think I would want to know that the child really had some understanding of the counselling process and that the counsellor was a good one – I'd want there to be a way to check that vulnerable children weren't being further damaged by the professionals.

Overall then, confidentiality policies and obligations to report certain 'risk' factors can present significant challenges for an effective self-injury policy. However, some careful consideration of the issues and the wording of a confidentiality policy can ensure that legal obligations are adhered to while confidential support with clear boundaries is provided to people who hurt themselves.

6b) Health and safety

As noted above, the health and safety policy is going to be particularly relevant for a self-injury policy in terms of the practical impacts of self-injury and the staff roles and responsibilities in dealing with it. This will include how to deal with injuries, spillages of blood and implements that carry risk of injury and infection – such as blood-streaked glass. Unless the self-injury policy attempts to extend the duties of staff into providing direct physical/medical care when this is outside of their usual job remit, the health and safety issues are generally less complex than the confidentiality protocols.

Health and safety issues require a clear procedure and checklist for dealing with injuries, implements and environmental impacts, alongside the necessary resources for implementing them, such as sharps bins and first aid kits. Nonetheless, developing the procedure and check list does require careful

---

13. Zest also integrate family support within their work with people who hurt themselves and this is important both as a resource (section 8) and a context intervention (Chapters 4 and 6 and Epilogue).

attention to addressing the range of possible situations and the most effective way to deal with them. Some health and safety policies also include risks to mental/emotional wellbeing, and these should link to the provisions on self-injury (see section 5, above) to ensure follow-up, debriefing and ongoing support is available for affected individuals – eg. the person who hurts themself, workers and other service-users.

6c) Complaints procedures
Complaints procedures have an essential role in maintaining equality and accountability in a service, especially in regard to appropriate treatment of people who hurt themselves. Good complaints procedures are clear and non-judgmental and are easily available to staff, service-users and visitors alike. Protocols also need to be in place for multiple possible configurations of complaints, not just those that are the easiest to anticipate, such as when a service-user makes a complaint against the organisation or a member of staff. These other situations might include a junior member of staff making a complaint about their line manager; a visitor who witnesses inappropriate staff conduct, or one service-user making a complaint against another. 42nd Street provides an example of a thorough, user-friendly and effective complaints procedure (reprinted at the end of this chapter, along with the TESS complaints policy). The self-injury policy should make direct reference to the complaints procedure and ensure that it is easy to access and implement.

7. Workers' rights and responsibilities
A service is only going to be as good for its clients as it is to its staff. It is not possible to provide a supportive, holistic, rights-based service if the organisation is authoritarian and dismissive of the needs of staff and does not value its workers. Therefore, the rights and responsibilities of staff are integral to ensuring that a self-injury policy is agreed upon, resourced and implemented effectively. Staff roles, responsibilities and boundaries must be clearly set out in the job description, and these boundaries must be respected and reiterated in the self-injury policy. Areas of particular importance in regard to self-injury include the provision of first aid and medical care, attending accident and emergency with service-users, and dealing with 'hazards' – such as blood or implements used for self-injury. In services for people with intellectual disabilities (and some mental health services), physical restraint might be part of a job description, although from a rights-based perspective this is unacceptable in a self-injury policy.

A self-injury policy should also mandate that staff who work with people who hurt themselves have comprehensive information and resources about self-injury, along with ongoing training and development, and robust support from within the organisation (Arnold & Magill, 2007; Lindsay, 1999). Support for staff should be stipulated as regular, ongoing supervision sessions, as well as the on-the-spot support provided after an incident of self-injury.

8. Resources: workers, clients, other services and service-users

There is a range of people, beyond the individual who self-injures and the immediate staff, who will also be impacted by the self-injury policy, and therefore need consideration within it. These include other service-users and other services.

Other service-users frequently know about an individual's self-injury before staff are aware of it, and they may also be actively supporting the person who hurts themself (see Jones et al, 2010). It is essential, therefore, that all service-users have some information and/or training about self-injury and understanding and responding to it. Clearly, service-users do not have the same roles and responsibilities as staff around self-injury, but the impact on them as part of the service community must be understood and appropriately resourced. The policy should set out what information, training or resources are available for service-users and how they can access it. It is particularly important that a service-user who witnesses self-injury or who was engaging with the person immediately prior to their injury receives support and debriefing (see section 5, above).

People who hurt themselves are often engaged with more than one service, and different organisations may have very different perceptions of self-injury. This can be detrimental to a service-user and can create conflict between services. The self-injury policy should stipulate that all the services who work with someone who hurts themself will be invited to meet within a specified time period to discuss how self-injury is being responded to and to agree an informed and consistent approach. It is useful to have identified resources for services (below). When either a meeting and/or agreement about a collective understanding of self-injury is not possible between services, the organisation must work with the service-user to enable them to manage the conflicting responses to their self-injury.

For a self-injury policy to be effective, it needs to be appropriately resourced. This not only includes the time and resources required to develop the policy, but also a range of resources that ensure the policy can be implemented effectively. This includes information and training for staff and service-users (above) and additional resources for others impacted on by self-injury. For example, the primary carer of a young person or the partner of a psychiatric service-user will also need resourcing around self-injury and how best they can support the person who is hurting themself. Many organisations will not be in a financial position to provide booklets and information videos themselves, but they should have a list of easily accessible, affordable, recommended resources – such as those provided by Self-injury Support,[14] LifeSIGNS[15] or The Basement Project.[16] As noted above, other organisations that have links with the service-user may also need information and resources on self-injury, and there should also be a list of recommended resources for service-providers – these are also provided by the organisations listed above.

9. Implementation

Policy is only effective when it is actively in use. Policy serves no purpose if it is filed away among reams of documents with no impact on day-to-day practice. Therefore, a crucial element of the policy is a statement that stipulates how and when the policy will be implemented (see also Monitoring and Review, below). The implementation period should allow time for training and necessary resources to be in place. It is ineffective and potentially dangerous to attempt to implement a policy without the appropriate training and resources to fulfil it. Arnold and McGill (2007) also advise that the policy should designate key individual/s within the organisation who have responsibility for its implementation, monitoring and review.

It is also possible to implement policy on a trial or pilot basis. Piloting new policy is increasingly common, in order to test the appropriateness, impact and efficacy of a new approach. Pilots can be trialled during a specific test period or in a designated test location, such as one care facility in a group owned by a chain. Ettelt et al (2015) suggest that piloting a new policy can also be used as a strategic measure: the piloting process can provide an opportunity to gather evidence to support a policy that might otherwise be contentious – such as a harm-reduction approach. As with implementation, the pilot process must be clearly set out in the policy document, along with the time period and location of the pilot, and the full knowledge and consent of all those affected. A pilot

14. www.selfinjurysupport.org.uk/publications-about-self-injury (accessed 5 September, 2016).

15. www.lifesigns.org.uk/guidance-for-others/ (accessed 5 September, 2016).

16. https://basementprojectbooks.wordpress.com/books-on-self-harm/ (accessed 5 September, 2016).

must also be linked to a clearly structured evaluation or review process, to assess its impact and efficacy. And all policy – pilot or not – should be subject to monitoring and review to ensure its continued appropriateness and to address any emerging problems, such as complaints about a particular practice.

10. Monitoring and review

All policy and practice should be evaluated on a regular basis. This will include formal evaluations of the policy, which should elicit feedback from all of those involved in the service – workers, service-users, family/carers and other organisations. There should also be ongoing, less structured forms of review, including feedback, discussions in staff and service-user meetings, and reviews of complaints. The policy document should stipulate when the evaluations will take place and how and by whom the service will be evaluated. It should also stipulate how content from reviews and complaints will be applied to the policy document and include a brief indication of the protocol for making changes to policy.

• Chapter summary

Good policy enables best practice to happen. It provides a framework for clear, reasoned and consistent responses to people who hurt themselves. The organisational context is also important in facilitating good practice; organisations cannot operate effectively for service-users if they are authoritarian and do not value and care for their staff. Policy development should be collaborative and inclusive. Developing a good self-injury policy will require time and resources. Nonetheless, the process of policy writing and the policy itself do not have to be laborious; they can be brief, accessible and highly effective.

Learning into practice

Definition	Self-injury requires a consistent and considered response
Working principles	• I say as I do • Clarity and consistency for everyone
Practice applications	• Equality and inclusion • Reflection and review

Definition: self-injury requires a consistent and considered response

Self-injury is a complex and sensitive human experience that requires a well thought out, clearly understood and considered response. People who hurt themselves need a consistent and caring response to their injuries, as well as the underlying feelings and issues that give rise to them. A self-injury policy provides the mechanism and framework for considered, consistent and helpful responses to self-injury.

Working principles

1. I say as I do

The old adage 'Do as I say, not as I do' perfectly captures everything that a self-injury policy should *not* entail. Policy is not just a list of protocols, it is also a commitment to a set of values and an ethos. These values should be visible in the actions and attitudes of all the employees. Crucially, for self-injury, this includes the promotion of self-care. Zest (undated), for example, emphasises that its ethos is based on 'practising these living values in our own lives'. In this way, service-providers embody the processes they espouse, and the ethos and values of the organisation should be central to the recruitment and training processes.

2. Clarity and consistency for everyone

The aim of a self-injury policy is to create an environment where there is a clear and consistent understanding of, and response to, self-injury. Without clarity and consistency, environments become confused and unhealthy – often mirroring the formative experiences of service-users and creating conflict and burnout for staff. Clarity and consistency of ethos and practice do not just apply to service-users. Staff at all levels of an organisation should be treated likewise. As one service-provider pointed out, 'How you treat staff reflects how you feel about service-users.' Clarity and consistency also alleviate confusion about boundaries and responsibilities that are at the root of many negative responses to self-injury.

Activity

- Have you experienced a context or organisation where you felt there was good clear policy guidance that was fully implemented and embodied in staff attitudes and behaviour?
  - If so, what were the specific strengths that you noticed?
  - How might you bring some of these strengths to developing a self-injury policy?
  - If you have never experienced a good policy context, why do you think this is, and what are the negatives you would strive to avoid in a self-injury policy?

Practice applications

1. Equality and inclusion

A genuine belief in and commitment to the equality of all people are key to the efficacy of a self-injury policy. Equality creates an environment where everyone is valued and respected, regardless of their identity or life situation. This is crucial not only in transforming many of the underlying experiences that relate to self-injury, but also in developing policy and practice. Staff and service-users from all areas of an organisation need to be involved in key decision-making, policy development and review. This does not detract from the specific roles and responsibilities that different groups and individuals have within an organisation, but it does ensure that different life or work situations are not equated with being 'better' than other people. Most importantly, equality and inclusion mean that there is a much wider pool of knowledge, experience and skills available when decisions are being made, and this is to everyone's benefit.

2. Reflection and review

Reflective practice is key to safe and effective work with people who hurt themselves, as well as the development, implementation and review of policy. Reflection entails taking a step back and viewing the issue, experience or practice with care and openness from multiple dimensions. Reflection is often positioned as a critical vantage point, but there is a difference between criticality and criticism. Criticality entails being able to view a range of perspectives and possibilities – positive, neutral and negative – and to evaluate the merits and implications of each. Criticism is a negative and often personalised challenge to a person, situation or action. Reflection is made possible by an egalitarian environment where individuals can acknowledge less than perfect actions or beliefs without feeling judged, blamed or criticised as a result. Review is the formalisation of reflection within a structured evaluation process. Collaborative reflection and review of policy and practice are crucial to ensuring that protocols are effective and purposeful – especially in light of the changing contexts in which services operate and the changing needs of service-users.

Activity

- Keep a detailed journal for a week in which you are very honest, but non-judgmental, about your actions, thinking processes, achievements, goals and motivations.
  - Set aside some time at the end of the week to read through the journal. What have you learned about yourself?

TESS confidentiality policy

What is the rule of confidentiality on TESS

At TESS everything you tell us is private and confidential. We understand that a confidential service makes it easier to talk about difficult things. We don't see your phone number or email address and we don't know who or where you are. We never trace calls or email addresses.

You don't need to tell us who and where you are and we won't ask.

However, we would need to break confidentiality if:
- we believe you are at risk of significant harm or death *and* you have told us who and where you are
- you have given us information about someone else who is at risk of harm and you have told us who and where they are

Please bear in mind that if you give us any information about where you might be – that stays on our system. That information could be linked together at a later date to find you if we were worried about your safety. As an organisation we share safeguarding concerns across our support services.

If you have told us who and where you are and you ask us to report a situation where you are at risk we can do this. However, as we are only open limited hours we recommend the agencies below who are open 24 hours a day, 7 days a week and are set up to do this.
- Childline   08001111   (Talk, webchat and email)
- The Police   999 (emergency number) or 101 (non–emergency number)

We also would have to contact the police for any threat of terrorism.

For people who work on TESS
We also have confidentiality for our workers. We don't give out our own names because we work as a team and don't always work with the same people. We also don't disclose our own experiences in a conversation because it can take the focus away from the person who has contacted us.

42nd Street confidentiality policy

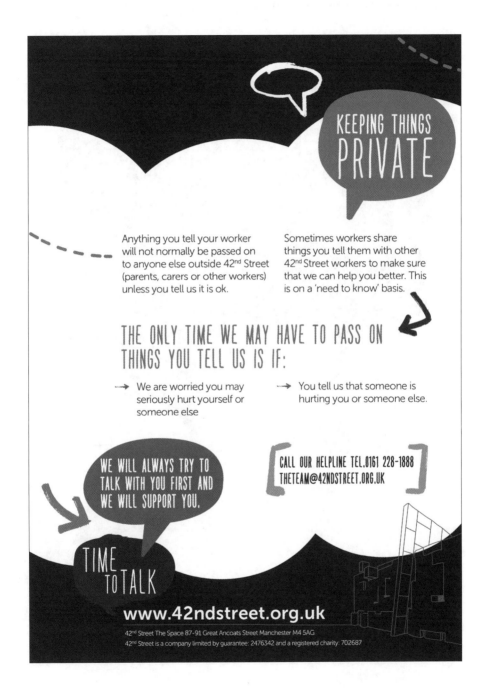

42nd Street complaints policy

IF YOU NEED HELP...
JUST ASK!

If you have a problem with our service you can talk about it with your worker and try to sort it out. If that doesn't work or you don't feel comfortable talking to your worker (or any other worker), you can talk to any manager. You can also write a letter to the Chief Executive to complain – if you want help with this then just ask!

You can also meet up with the Chief Executive and talk to them about the problem.

42ND STREET WILL...

→ Reply to let you know we've got your complaint (within 3 days)

→ A senior manager will look into your complaint

→ The Chief Executive will either write to you or meet with you to talk about the decision (within 28 days)

If we can't do this in time, we will let you know and tell you why. If you're still not happy, tell us and we will try to sort it out.

CALL OUR HELPLINE TEL.0161 228-1888
THETEAM@42NDSTREET.ORG.UK

TIME to TALK

www.42ndstreet.org.uk

42nd Street The Space 87-91 Great Ancoats Street Manchester M4 5AG
42nd Street is a company limited by guarantee: 2476342 and a registered charity: 702687

TESS complaints policy

Self Injury Support

TESS Complaint and Feedback Guidelines

Complaints and Feedback

Feedback of any kind including complaints is seen by TESS as a vital part of developing our services. It helps us to improve what we do, and enables us to reflect on how we are viewed by those outside the organisation.

To give anonymous feedback you can use our online form

If you would like to make a formal complaint you are welcome to do so through the medium that you feel comfortable using. These are our contact details:

Email – info@selfinjurysupport.org.uk

Writing – TESS c/o Self Injury Support, Po BOX 3240, Bristol, BS2 2EF

Telephone - 0117 927 9600

We will respond to your complaint within five working days of receiving it. The process may happen in more than one stage to include a conversation to hear your experience and then a further conversation to respond to what you have told us.

Depaul self-injury protocol

TUS NUA

Self-Injury Protocol

Definition:
Self-injury (also referred to as self-harm) involves the deliberate *non-suicidal* injuring of one's body. There are many forms of self-injury. The most common form is cutting but it also covers a wide range of behaviours, including, but not limited to, burning, scratching, banging or hitting body parts, interfering with wound healing, hair pulling and the ingestion of toxic substances or objects.

Why would one self-injure?
Some of the reasons put forward include:

- To block out painful feeling. It's mainly about trying to cope with great pain. A person may have suffered neglect or abuse. Like taking risks or gambling, it may provide danger and distraction.

- To release unbearable tension. This may be caused by anxiety, grief or anger. It puts their pain 'outside', where it feels easier to cope with.

- It relieves feelings of guilt or shame.

- As a 'cry for help', a way of showing that one has suffered and is in pain and that someone should take notice of their distress.

- It's a way of feeling 'real' and alive, or having control over something in one's life.

Please note:

- Self-injury is a way of carrying on with life, not of dying. Injuries are seldom life-threatening.

- Someone who self-injures is directing her hurt and anger at herself, not at others.

- Self-injury is a sign of distress, not necessarily mental illness; a sign of someone trying to cope with her life as best she can. They may not have had the opportunity to learn positive ways to deal with feelings and emotions.

General principles to apply when supporting someone who has self-injured:

- Always treat the serviced user with respect, compassion and a non-judgemental attitude.
- Take full account of the likely distress associated with self-injury.
- Ensure privacy for the service user and confidentiality of information disclosed.
- Record ALL information in relation to the circumstances of the service user's self-injury and follow up in appropriate documentation – casenotes, incident report etc (nature of injury, risk assessment, information provided by staff, all efforts to encourage the service user to seek medical help, alternatives considered, service user's decision, any other actions taken).
- All necessary information as to the service user's care should be shared among the team.
- Ensure all incidents of self-injury are followed up on with the service user. They will need time to reflect and consider their actions.

Please remember that our primary aim is to support a service user in emotional distress, offering advice and information available to us on treatment. **We should not take responsibility to prevent or restrict a person from self-injuring.**

When a service user presents with a self-injury:

- Make an assessment of the extent of the injury, if possible. If the service user has cut their arms, check if the cuts are superficial (surface level), or more serious (deeper) cuts.
- Encourage the service user to tend to the would themselves. Offer treatment for the injury if necessary. If the cuts are superficial, first aid may be able to be applied on site. Basic first aid can be applied by trained staff. If staff are tending to the wound, ensure that full personal protective equipment is used. If the wounds are more serious, advise the service user that they will need to be seen by a healthcare professional (GP, A&E).
- Involve the service user in treatment decisions. Give the service user the options available. If you are unsure of the options available, consult with LMT/On Call. It may be necessary to ring the emergency services for support and advice (999). Ensure you have as much detail as possible from the service user as to the nature of the injury and what was used to inflict the injury eg. a razor.
- Make an initial assessment of risk of further self-injury. Consider the following:
    - The service user's state of mind – signs of depression, hopelessness, suicidal intent

- All of the social, psychological and motivational factors specific to the act of self-harm
- History of self-injury
- Ask the service user to explain in their own words why they have self-injured and explain their feelings.

- Discuss with the service user the option of removing the items used to cause injury from them. These can include razors, utility knives, scissors, needles, broken glass. Some people burn themselves with cigarettes or lighters. They may refuse this. If they do refuse, and are staying in the project, ensure they are linked in with regularly for the next 24 hours (if item poses a health and safety risk to others, then it must be handed over).
- If one self-injures, as well as treatment for the physical injury, they need to be referred to mental health professionals and this should be sought at the earliest opportunity (the GP, A&E etc will normally make the referral). A service user should always be offered to seek immediate support eg. A&E.

If the service user refuses to accept needed medical support (serious injury) and wants to stay in the project:

- Advise the service user of the consequences of not receiving treatment eg. infection or wound, serious loss of blood. Please note, if a person has swallowed a toxic substance, they need to go to hospital straight away.
- Such a refusal would raise concerns for this service user's state of mind and would suggest increased risk of further self-injury. Explain our concerns to the service user and your duty of care.
- Seek support from LMT/On Call.
- Ring emergency services for advice.

Ongoing strategies for working with a resident who self-injures:

- Complete a risk assessment.
- Complete a risk management plan and crisis management plan as appropriate.
- Refer the service user to support services – see below.
- Explore new coping mechanisms in keyworking: positive coping skills can be learned at any point in life. People who self-injure can learn to use new and healthier coping mechanisms. This may include exercising, painting, writing, yoga or dancing. A process that involves self-expression is often helpful. Whatever works as an alternative method of coping with the feelings of anxiety or stress or 'numbness' is often a food start towards recovery.

- Educate about safe methods of cutting to reduce infection and long-term effects of self-injury.

- Devise Harm Reduction strategies for the person who is self-injuring. This should be done in conjunction with your lie manager. Examples of harm reduction strategies include use of ice cubes on the arm, using a rubber band around the arm and snapping it, using a red marker on the arm.

Important: After dealing with someone who has self-injured, please ensure that you allow yourself time to debrief to another staff member, LMT or On Call and seek supports that you need.

Some helpful organisations and websites:

Pieta House
Old Luca Road
Lucan
Co. Dublin
Tel: (01) 601 00 00
Email: mary@pieta.ie
www.pieta.ie

Offers free, specialist therapeutic support for those who self-injure or who are at risk of suicide.

Irish Association for Counselling and Psychotherapy
211 Dublin Road
Bray Co.
Wicklow
Tel: 01 2723427
Fax: 01 2869933
www.irish-counselling.ie

Provides a list of fully accredited, qualified and registered therapists in Ireland. It is a good idea to check with individual therapists if, and how, they work with people who experience self-injury as practice varies widely.

The Samaritans
Ph: 1850 60 90 90

Provides confidential, non-judgemental support, 24 hours a day for people who are experiencing feelings of distress, despair, including those which could lead to suicide.

DEPAUL IRELAND – Central Office, 18 Nicholas Street, Dublin 8, Ireland.
Telephone: +353 1 4537111. Fax: +353 1 4537551. Email: depaul@depaulireland.org

Company Registration No. 357 828
Charity registration No. CHY 14753

8

Epilogue
Going the distance:
a case study of Zest (Northern Ireland)

The closing section of this book comprises a brief case study of Zest, the Derry/Londonderry community support service for self-injury and suicide.[1] I have chosen to finish with a case study of Zest because they exemplify many of the themes and issues addressed in this book and provide testament to the fact that these practices and principles can be incorporated into 'real-life' service delivery and integrated with statutory services. Furthermore, Zest's approach is outstandingly successful in terms of client evaluations and feedback, as well as statutory measures of service efficacy – ie. a reduction in rates of self-injury and suicide attempts.[2]

This case study highlights that responses to self-injury that are based on a holistic, social-contextual and embodied understanding of an individual's distress and self-injury are not only viable and effective but are already practised to great effect. This is not to suggest that there are not challenges to be faced in this kind of work, particularly in terms of funding, wider health policy decision-making and constraints, and the complex social inequalities in the Northern Irish context. However, Zest has remained true to its underpinning ethos, and continues to be valued and respected by its service-users and other statutory and voluntary providers – see for example, the special feature on Zest in the *Truth Hurts* report (Mental Health Foundation, 2006).

---

1. See http://www.zestni.org/ (accessed 5 September, 2016).

2. In 2012 I was commissioned to conduct an evaluation of SHINE, the Self-Harm Interagency Network, a self-injury and suicide support service run by Zest. This was paid for by Public Health Northern Ireland, and this is where the data for this case study are drawn from.

Origins and ethos

Zest was initially set up as a charity in 1996 to provide support to young people who were moving from residential care to independent living. The service was run as a collaboration between the social services Leaving Care and After Care teams, who provided three social workers (covering three half-days per week), and community volunteers. The service was established because the young client group was particularly vulnerable and presented with high rates of self-injury and suicidal ideation. Two years after Zest was formed, budget cuts meant that all social service support was withdrawn. At this point Zest began to operate as an independent charity, supporting people at risk of self-injury and suicide across the local community. Its ethos was to provide a community-based, specialist service that people could access either directly themselves or by being referred by their GP or healthcare professional, ensuring that needs could be met as and when they arose.

Today Zest employs four full-time staff, two part-time staff and 12 sessional counsellors. Zest is currently funded by the Northern Irish Public Health Agency to deliver its support programme in both the Western Health and Social Care Trust and the Northern Health and Social Care Trust. People are referred to Zest by the community mental health teams after an episode of self-injury and/or attempted suicide. Zest's other main source of income is from delivering training to statutory and community services throughout Northern Ireland in understanding and working with self-injury.

Zest was founded on a person-centred ethos, where each person is valued and respected and their distress is viewed in a holistic and non-judgmental framework. This is encapsulated in Zest's principle, 'It is ok to be me,' which translates across all its working practices and embodies the principles of acceptance and equality. This ethos is perhaps best exemplified in its 'no-reject' policy. This policy means that anyone who is hurting themself or feeling suicidal can attend Zest, regardless of their identity, life situation or other issues. As such, Zest provides support to clients who are often excluded by other services on the grounds of their alcohol/substance misuse, psychiatric diagnosis or long-term history of self-injury. Zest also maintains an open-door aftercare policy, whereby any ex-client who experiences a 'relapse' or feels at risk can return for top-up support.

The genuineness of the support and care provided by Zest is something that resonates deeply with service-users and is much appreciated by them. A service evaluation (Inckle, 2012) found that 99 per cent of Zest's clients were either satisfied or very satisfied with the support they received, and experienced significant benefits in their mental health and quality of life as a result. Service-users often included personal testimonies in their evaluations, and the caring, kindness and acceptance demonstrated by Zest staff were consistent themes – illustrated in the following three clients' reports.

> You've helped me to understand why I was hurting myself and have taught me new ways to cope. You will never know how much this means to me and especially my children. They have their mammy back.

> Thank you so much for listening to me and for the support you gave me. I really valued all your wisdom, understanding and kindness... I know it's your job but you do it so well. Thanks for listening and the time and effort you took. You were a very nice person to talk to and understanding.

> Having someone who listened and obviously cared helped me so much. I never felt judged once even when I was angry and fighting everyone... I now have my life back and I will never forget you for that.

Service and outcomes

Zest is not just noteworthy in regard to its service ethos but also in terms of the range of support it offers to clients. This includes at least six, and up to 12 individual counselling sessions. These sessions are flexible and tailored, in collaboration with the individual, to address their specific needs and concerns. In some cases, this might involve a support session taking place outside of the Zest premises in order to fulfil a particular goal. These sessions might also include education about the risks associated with self-injury, or problem-solving-based work around a key issue for the client. Zest's community-based ethos means that it is well integrated within a range of local support systems and organisations, and is able to direct clients to specific issue-based services, such as LGBT or housing support and advice, when necessary. All Zest's clients present with more than one issue at the time of referral, and therefore being embedded into this diverse network of specialist support is essential in ensuring that all presenting problems can be tackled. Zest also provides two sessions of complementary therapy, such as reflexology, aromatherapy and Indian head massage, in order to provide an opportunity for clients to explore a range of support and care.

Zest is also committed to providing family support as part of its model of care, and this is currently being maintained by Zest, despite receiving no funding to do so. Family support has proven to be particularly effective in supporting the client, addressing unmet needs of family members and developing community-based strengths and understanding around self-injury. Four to six sessions of family support are provided to a family member, friend or partner identified by the service-user as their key support person. These sessions will help the family member to develop a deeper understanding of self-injury and how to support the person who is hurting themself. The session will also explore the concerns of the family member, enabling their own needs to be met. The provision of services to significant others is essential for developing supportive contexts around self-injury, both in the immediate environment and in the community at large. It is also deeply appreciated by family members, as reported here:

> I was so worried about him, I didn't realise how my fears were adding to his difficulties... It was great to have somewhere to go to talk about how difficult it was for me too, sometimes it's just the person with the problem that gets the help. The help I got was priceless.

This multifaceted and holistic approach to self-injury has been found to be effective in statutory health measures. For example, rates of mental distress and incidence of self-injury and attempted suicide are all significantly reduced by the Zest approach. Furthermore, the individually-tailored, person-centred and holistic interventions used are also incredibly cost effective. The cost of a person attending the full Zest programme can be a little as one-tenth of the cost of the same person attending psychiatric services for a similar period of time (Inckle, 2012).

Since 2009, Zest has been integrated into the referral pathway of statutory mental health and primary care services. This began with the Self-Harm Interagency Network – or SHINE – whereby those who attended A&E or community mental health services following an incident of self-injury or attempted suicide were directly referred to Zest and guaranteed follow-up contact within 24 hours. This project ran for six years, and Zest's work was much appreciated by staff in the referring services, particularly because it ensured that specialist help was immediately available and because it reduced pressure on the referring service:

People who have self-harmed need a point of contact, someone to talk to about the crisis or how to deal with self-harm in the long term. Otherwise they would be in the mental health service, but they don't really need tier three service, they might be in crisis but it's not necessarily a tier three mental health problem. One of the positives and unique features [of Zest] is knowing that they are followed up immediately and then you'll get feedback about how the patient is doing from the service.

The SHINE project was closed in 2015 and was replaced by SHIP – the Self-Harm Intervention Programme. This programme was put out to tender across the Northern Irish health and social care trust regions, with each organisation entitled to provide services in only two regions. Zest successfully competed for and was awarded the tenders for the delivery of services in the Western and the Northern Health and Social Care Trusts. The SHIP contract was initially for a two-year period, with a possible further three years of funding, depending on an annual review of service provision. This means that, although Zest remains firmly established as a key provider at the time of writing, their future financial position is still precarious.

In 2016 Zest celebrated its 20th birthday, which was marked in December of that year at their annual Zestfest fundraising festival. In 2016, Zest also began running a new specialist training programme for clergy of the four main Northern Irish churches. This project, called Flourish, is funded by the Northern Irish Public Health Authority, and involves training around understanding suicide, supporting those at risk and providing support and pastoral care for families bereaved by suicide, as well as self-care for the clergy themselves. Following the success of this innovative project, the training was rolled out to clergy and staff from all churches across Northern Ireland.

Therefore, despite precarious funding and constantly changing health service structures, Zest continues its work to support clients in the local community as well as to develop and provide specialist training and consultancy across Northern Ireland.

Appendix
Learning resources

SELF-INJURY QUIZ

Section 1: True or false?

		T	F
1.	Cutting is the most common form of self-injury.	☐	☐
2.	Self-injury is an indication that a person is suicidal.	☐	☐
3.	People who self-injure may find it hard to verbalise or articulate their feelings.	☐	☐
4.	People who self-injure are likely to be violent towards others.	☐	☐
5.	Binge drinking and anorexia are forms of self-injury.	☐	☐
6.	Self-injury is completely different to normal day-to-day behaviour.	☐	☐
7.	More females than males self-injure.	☐	☐
8.	Adults and older people do not self-injure.	☐	☐
9.	Child protection legislation has clear guidelines around self-injury.	☐	☐
10.	Self-injury is attention-seeking behaviour and if you ignore it they will stop.	☐	☐
11.	The best way to deal with someone who self-injures is to try and prevent it.	☐	☐
12.	The 2004 and 2011 NICE guidelines for self-injury recommend a harm-reduction approach.	☐	☐

Section 2: Circle which of the following are true

2a) People self-injure:

To feel better   To manipulate other people   To comfort themselves

To punish themselves   To be a part of a group   To feel alive and real

To stop feelings   To block memories and thoughts

To express their experiences   To escape from reality   To express difficulties

To try and change something   To relieve emotional pain   To stay alive

2b) Any other reasons why someone might self-injure?

....
....
....
....
....

2c) People who self-injure are likely to have experienced:

Abuse   A sick or addicted parent   Neglect

Parental separation   Death of a parent   Traumatic experiences

Social marginalisation   Bullying   Invalidation of feelings/experiences

Hospitalisation   Intellectual/communication difficulties   Homelessness

2d) Any other experiences that might be connected with self-injury?

....
....
....
....
....

Section 3: Feelings checklist

Which of the following best describes how you feel about helping someone who self-injures right now? (There are no right or wrong answers, this checklist is to assist reflective practice.)

I feel knowledgeable about self-injury.   Agree / don't know / disagree

I feel confident helping someone who self-injures.   Agree / don't know / disagree

I feel clear about the best way to support someone
who self-injures.   Agree / don't know / disagree

I feel anxious about helping someone who self-
injures.   Agree / don't know / disagree

I feel accountable for someone else's self-injury.   Agree / don't know / disagree

My other feelings about self-injury are:

. . . .
. . . .
. . . .
. . . .
. . . .
. . . .
. . . .
. . . .
. . . .

SHORT SELF-INJURY THINKING EXERCISES

These questions can be explored individually or in small discussion groups. The exercises are intended to highlight the problems with conventional approaches to self-injury and to help develop critical and creative thinking about self-injury.

1. Coping mechanisms

Make a list of all the coping strategies you can identify that people regularly use (eg. going shopping, drinking alcohol, talking to a friend). Spend some time working through this until you have quite a long list. Next, divide the list of coping mechanisms into two categories: healthy and unhealthy. Examine both lists and identify which of the coping mechanisms you think are the most common. Reflect on whether it is likely or possible that anyone uses only healthy coping mechanisms and then consider why self-injury is so stigmatised.

2. Listening or labelling?

Make a list of all the possible mental illnesses (eg. anxiety disorder, borderline personality disorder (BPD)) or personality traits (eg. attention-seeking, impulsive) that someone who self-injures might be labelled with. When you have completed the list, reflect on the impact these labels have and how you would feel about engaging with someone who has one or more of these identifiers.

Next, write a list of all the possible feelings that a person might have related to their self-injury (eg. lonely, ashamed). Read through the list and notice how you feel about responding to someone who might be feeling one or more of these emotions. Finally, reflect on how the different perspectives – labels or feelings – impacted on you and the kind of response they are likely to engender in you.

This exercise is designed to highlight the negative impacts of most labels that are applied to people who hurt themselves and the ways in which they create barriers to communication and understanding. In contrast, focusing on feelings tends to create a much more empathic and helpful response. This exercise also highlights how it is much more helpful to think about what someone is feeling rather than to focus on what they have done.

3. Who is self-injury a problem for and why?

To answer this question, write down all the people who might be impacted by someone's self-injury, starting with the person who hurts themself. Affected people might include: teacher, social worker, nurse, GP, friend, partner, child and so on. Then write down all the ways in which self-injury is a problem for each of these people. Next, take a look at how the problems for the affected people contrast with the ways in which self-injury is a problem for the person who hurts themself. Examine the contrasting needs of the different people involved, and then consider whose needs will be met by two or three different types of intervention, such as prevention, alternatives to self-injury or harm-reduction. Finally, consider which intervention you would choose if you were prioritising the needs of the person who hurts themself.

This activity is designed to highlight, first, that the problems for the person who self-injures are very different to the problems for those around them, and, second, that it is usually everybody else's problems that are prioritised in conventional responses to self-injury.

SELF-INJURY POLICY TEMPLATE

1. The philosophy and purpose of the organisation (2–3 sentences).

2. Client group and access: how and for whom does the service operate (2–3 sentences).

3. How are clients served: aims/ethos in practice (2–3 sentences).

4. **Definition: How self-injury is understood** (3–4 sentences).

5. **The procedure for:** (one paragraph/bullet points each)
   a) a service-user with a history of self-injury
   b) a service-user who has just self-injured
   c) a service-user who is about to self-injure
   d) ongoing support of service-users around self-injury.

6. Legal and policy issues (cross-referenced with statutory requirements and relevant policies, one short paragraph per policy area):
   a) confidentiality (breadth and limitations)
   b) health and safety issues and policy (staff role and procedures)
   c) complaints (procedures and protocols).

7. Workers' rights and responsibilities: (cross-referenced with job descriptions, one short paragraph).

8. Resources (a list of available resources for service-users, staff, family/carers, other organisations).

9. Implementation (statement of how and when policy will be adopted (or piloted) and designated staff responsible, 2–3 sentences).

10. Monitoring and review (2–3 sentences each for formal and informal review).

Bibliography

Affi M (2007). Gender differences in mental health. *Singapore Medical Journal 48*(5): 385–391.

Adams J, Rodham K, Gavin J (2005). Investigating the 'Self' in deliberate self-harm. *Qualitative Health Research 15*(10): 1293–1309.

Alexander N, Clare L (2004). You still feel different: the experience and meaning of women's self-injury in the context of lesbian and bi-sexual identity. *Journal of Applied and Community Social Psychology 14*: 70–84.

All Ireland Traveller Health Study Team (2010). *Our Geels: all Ireland Traveller health study.* Dublin: UCD.

Arnold L (1995). *Women and Self-injury: a survey of 76 women.* Bristol: Bristol Crisis Service for Women.

Arnold L, Magill A (2007). *Getting it Right: a guide to creating a self-harm policy.* Abergavenny: The Basement Project.

Arnold L, Magill A (1997). *What's the Harm? A book for young people who self-harm of self-injure.* Bristol: The Basement Project.

Babiker G, Arnold L (1997). *The Language of Injury.* Leicester: BPS Publications.

Baer RA (ed) (2006). *Mindfulness-based Treatment Approaches: a clinician's guide to evidence-based approaches.* Amsterdam: Elsevier Academic Press.

Baladerian NJ (1991). Sexual abuse of people with developmental disabilities. *Disability and Sexuality 9*(4): 323–335.

Balsam KF, Beauchaine TP, Mickey RM, Rothblum ED (2005). Mental health of lesbian, gay, bisexual and heterosexual siblings: effects of gender, sexual orientation and family. *Journal of Abnormal Psychology 114*(3): 471–476.

Bass E, Davis L (2002). *The Courage to Heal: a guide for women survivors of child sexual abuse (2nd ed).* London: Vermillion.

Beale D, Hoel H (2011). Workplace bullying and the employment relationship: exploring questions of prevention, control and context. *Work, Employment & Society 25*(2): 5–18.

Beckett S (2010). Azima ila Hayati – an invitation into my life: narrative conversations about sexual identity. In: Moon L (ed). *Counselling Ideologies: queer challenges to heteronormativity.* Farnham: Ashgate (pp201–208).

Benson S (2000). Inscriptions of the self: reflections on tattooing and piercing in contemporary Euro-America. In: Caplan J (ed). *Written on the Body: the tattoo in European and American history.* London: Reaktion Books (pp234–254).

Bhui K, Stansfield S, McKenzie K, Karlson S, Nazroo J, Weich S (2005). Racial/ethnic discrimination and common mental disorders among workers: findings from the EMPIRIC study of ethnic minority groups in the United Kingdom. *American Journal of Public Health 95*(3): 496–501.

Birch S, Cole S, Hunt K, Edwards B, Reaney E (2011). Self-harm and the positive risk taking approach: can being able to think about the possibility of harm reduce the frequency of actual harm? *Journal of Mental Health 20*(3): 293–303.

Blyth C (2010). Commercial gay space and the regulation of disabled bodies. In: Sparkes AC (ed). *The Auto/Biography Yearbook 2009: British Psychological Association*. Nottingham: Russell Press (pp71–88).

Bordo S (1993). *Unbearable Weight: feminism, western culture and the body*. Oakland, CA: California University Press.

Bowen S, Chalwa N, Marlatt GA (2011). *Mindfulness-Based Relapse Prevention for Addictive Behaviours: a clinician's guide*. New York: Guilford Press.

Boyce M (2012). 'It's a Safe Space': the unique role of self-injury self-help groups. Unpublished conference paper. Everybody Hurts Sometimes... one-day conference on self-injury. Dublin: Trinity College Dublin, 2 March.

Bradshaw J (1988a). *Healing the Shame that Binds You*. Florida: Health Communications.

Bradshaw J (1988b). *Bradshaw on the Family: a revolutionary way of self-discovery*. Florida: Health Communications.

Brain R (1979). *The Decorated Body*. London: Hutchinson & Co.

Brettell CB, Sargent CF (2004). *Gender in Cross Cultural Perspective*. New Jersey: Prentice Hall.

Breggin P (1991). *Toxic Psychiatry*. New York: St Martin's Press.

Brumbaugh AG (1993). Acupuncture: new perspective in chemical dependency treatment. *Journal of Substance Abuse Treatment 10*(1): 35–43.

Bufton S (2004). Social class. In: Taylor G, Spencer S. *Social Identities: multidisciplinary approaches*. London/New York: Routledge (pp14–34).

Butler C, das Nair R, Thomas S (2010). The colour of queer. In: Moon L (ed). *Counselling Ideologies: queer challenges to heteronormativity*. Farnham/Burlington, VT: Ashgate (pp105–122).

Cadman L, Hoy J (2009). *Cutting the Risk: self-harm minimisation in perspective. Teaching and learning guidelines*. London: The National Self-harm Minimisation Group/Mind.

Cameron R (2007). Calming down: self-injury as stress control. In: Spandler H, Warner S (eds). *Beyond Fear and Control: working with young people who self-harm*. Ross-on-Wye: PCCS Books (pp79–90).

Carless D, Douglas K (2009). Opening doors: poetic representation of the sport experiences of men with severe mental health difficulties. *Qualitative Inquiry 15*(10): 1547–1551.

Chandler A (2013). Inviting pain? Pain, dualism and embodiment in narratives of self-injury. *Sociology of Health & Illness 35*(5): 716–730.

Chandler A (2012). Self-injury as embodied emotion work: managing rationality, emotions and bodies. *Sociology 46*(3): 442–457.

Chandler A, Myers F, Platt S (2011). The construction of self-injury in the clinical literature: a sociological exploration. *Suicide and Life-Threatening Behaviour 41*(1): 98–109.

Chernoff N, Widdicombe S (2015). 'I was bored so...': motivational accounts of participation in an online EMO group. *Journal of Youth Studies 18*(3): 305–321.

Chödrön P (2001). *Start Where You Are: a guide to compassionate living*. Boston: Shambala.

Clarke L, Whittaker M (1998). Self-mutilation: culture, contexts and nursing. *Journal of Clinical Nursing 7*: 129–137.

Clark V, Peel E (2007). *Out in Psychology: lesbian, gay, bisexual and trans perspectives*. Chichester: Wiley.

Cochran SD (2001). Emerging issues in research on lesbians' and gay men's mental health: does sexual orientation really matter? *American Psychologist, November*: 932–947.

Cohen S (1972). *Folk Devils and Moral Panics*. London: MacGibbon & Keel.

Conner KR, Bagge CL, Goldston DB, Ilgen MA (2014). Alcohol and suicidal behaviour: what is known and what can be done. *American Journal of Preventative Medicine 47*(3): s204–208.

Cooper J, Murphy E, Webb R, Hawton K, Bergen H, Waters K, Navneet K (2010). Ethnic differences in self-harm: rates, characteristics and service provision: three-city cohort study. *British Journal of Psychiatry 197*: 212–218.

Corcoran J, Mewse A, Babiker G (2007). The role of women's self-injury support-groups: a grounded theory. *Journal of Community and Applied Social Psychology 17*: 35–52.

Cresswell M, Karimova Z (2010). Self-harm and medicine's moral code: a historical perspective, 1950–2000. *Ethical Human Psychology and Psychiatry 12*(2): 158–175.

Crouch W, Wright J (2004). Deliberate self-harm at an adolescent unit: a qualitative investigation. *Clinical Child Psychology and Psychiatry 9*(2): 185–204.

Crowe M, Bunclark J (2000). Repeated self-injury and its management. *International Review of Psychiatry 12*: 48–53.

Csordas TJ (2002). *Body/Meaning/Healing*. Basingstoke/New York: Palgrave Macmillan.

Dace E, Faulkner A, Frost A, Parker A, Pembroke L, Smith A (1998). *The Hurt Yourself Less Workbook*. London: National Self-Harm Network.

Davis K (2003). *Dubious Equalities and Embodied Differences: cultural studies on cosmetic surgery*. Lanham, MD: Rowman & Littlefield.

Davidson D (2017). *The Tattoo Project: commemorative tattoos, visual culture and the digital archive*. Toronto: Canadian Scholars Press.

D'Eath M, Walls M (2010). *Quality of Life of Young People with Intellectual Disability in Ireland*. Dublin: National Disability Authority.

Deliberto TL, Nock, MK (2008). An exploratory study of correlates, onset and offset of non-suicidal self-injury. *Archives of Suicide Research 12*(3): 219–231.

DeMarco R, Tufts KA (2014). The mechanisms of writing a policy brief. *Nursing Outlook 62*(3): 219–224.

Dennis M, Wakefield P, Molloy C, Andrews H, Friedman T (2005). Self-harm in older people with depression: comparison of social factors, life events and symptoms. *British Journal of Psychiatry 186*: 538–39.

Dickinson T (2015). *Curing Queers: mental nurses and their patients*. Manchester: Manchester University Press.

DiStefano AS (2008). Suicidality and self-harm among sexual minorities in Japan. *Qualitative Health Research 18*(10): 1429–1441.

Equality & Human Rights Commission (EHRC) (2011). *Hidden in Plain Sight*. London: EHRC.

Ettelt S, Mays N, Allen P (2015). The multiple purposes of policy piloting and their consequences: three examples from national health and social care policy in England. *Journal of Social Policy 44*(2): 319–337.

Evans T, Wallace P (2008). A prison within a prison? The masculinity narratives of male prisoners. *Men and Masculinities 10*(4): 484–507.

Faulkner A, Thomas P (2002). User-led research & evidence-based medicine. *British Journal of Psychiatry 180*: 1–3.

Favazza AR (1996). *Bodies Under Siege: self-mutilation and body modification in culture and psychiatry (2nd ed)*. Baltimore, MD: John Hopkins University Press.

Fein O (1995). The influence of social class on health status. *Journal of General Internal Medicine*

10(10): 577–586.

Fortune S, Sinclair J, Hawton K (2005). *Adolescents' Views on Prevention of Self-Harm, Barriers to Help-Seeking for Self-Harm and How Quality of Life Might Be Improved.* Oxford: Centre for Suicide Research, University of Oxford.

Frimberger K (2013). 'Playful' research: exploring intercultural experience through arts-based methods. [Blog.] Glasgow Refugee, Asylum and Migration Network (GRAMNET), 24 July. http://gramnet.wordpress.com/tag/estrangement/ (accessed 21 September 2016).

Frost L (2000). *Young Women and the Body: a feminist sociology.* Basingstoke: Palgrave Macmillan.

Gale CR, Dennison EM, Cooper C, Sayer AA (2011). Neighbourhood environment and positive mental health in older people: the Hertfordshire cohort study. *Health Place 17*(4): 867–874.

Gallup R (2002). Failure of the capacity for self-soothing in women who have a history of abuse and self-harm. *Journal of the American Psychiatric Nurses Association 8*(1): 20–26.

Gannon B, Nolan B (2003). *Disability and Labour Market Participation.* Dublin: ESRI.

Gathercole P (1988). Contexts of Maori Moko. In: Rubin A (ed). *Marks of Civilisation: artistic transformations of the human body.* Los Angeles: University of California Press (pp171–8).

Gavriel Ansara Y (2010). Beyond cisgenderism: counselling people with non-assigned gender identities. In: Moon L (ed). *Counselling Ideologies: queer challenges to heteronormativity.* Farnham/Burlington, VT: Ashgate (pp168–200).

Germer CK, Siegel RD, Fulton PR (2005). *Mindfulness and Psychotherapy.* New York: Guilford Press.

Glasby J (2011a). Introduction. In: Glasby J (ed). *Evidence, Policy and Practice: critical perspectives in health and social care.* Bristol: Policy Press (pp1–10).

Glasby J (2011b). From evidence-based to knowledge-based policy and practice. In: Glasby J (ed). *Evidence, Policy and Practice: critical perspectives in health and social care.* Bristol: Policy Press (pp99–118).

Glassman LH, Weierich MR, Hooley JM, Deliberto TL, Nock MK (2007). Child mal-treatment, non-suicidal self-injury, and the mediating role of self-criticism. *Behaviour Research & Therapy 45*: 2483–2490.

Goldman K, Schmalz K (2010). Be it resolved: writing resolutions to influence health policy. *Health Promotion Practice 11*(1): 9–12.

Gollust SE, Eisenberg D, Golberstein E (2008). Prevalence and correlates of self-injury among university students. *Journal of American College Health 56*(5): 491–498.

Gowan T, Whetstone S, Andic T (2012). Addiction, agency and the politics of self-control: doing harm-reduction in a heroin-users' group. *Social Science and Medicine 74*(9): 1251–1260.

Grant A, Biley F, Walker H (2011). *Our Encounters with Madness.* Ross-on-Wye: PCCS Books.

Gratz KL, Conrad SD, Roemer L (2002). Risk factors for deliberate self-harm among college students. *American Journal of Orthopsychiatry 72*(1): 128–140

Green K (2007). Finding your own voice: social action group work with young people. In: Spandler H, Warner S (eds). *Beyond Fear and Control: working with young people who self-harm.* Ross-on-Wye: PCCS Books (pp51–64).

Greenson J, Brantley J (2009). Mindfulness and anxiety disorders: developing a wise relationship with the inner experience of fear. In: Didonna F (ed). *The Clinical Handbook of Mindfulness.* New York: Springer (pp171–188).

Groves A (2004). Blood on the walls: self-mutilation in prisons. *The Australian and New Zealand Journal of Criminology 37*(1): 49–64.

Gutridge K (2010). Safer self-injury or assisted self-harm? *Theoretical Medical Bioethics 31*: 79–92.

Hackett E (1973). *Blood: the paramount humour.* London: Jonathan Cape.

Hadfield J, Brown D, Pembroke L, Hayward M (2009). An analysis of accident and emergency doctors response to treating people who self-harm. *Qualitative Health Research 19*(6): 755–765.

Hamer M (2006). *The Barefoot Helper: creativity and mindfulness in social work and the caring professions.* Dorset: Russell House Publishing.

Harkin G (2000). *Carousel Emotions.* Derry/Londonderry: Zest.

Harris J (2000). Self-Harm: cutting the bad out of me. *Qualitative Health Research 10*(2): 164–173.

Hasking P, Momeni R, Swannell S, Chia S (2008). The nature and extent of non-suicidal self-injury in a non-clinical sample of young adults. *Archives of Suicide Research 12*(3): 208–218.

Haw C, Hawton K, Casey D, Bale E, Shepherd H (2005). Alcohol dependence, excessive drinking and deliberate self-harm: trends and patterns in Oxford, 1982–2002. *Social Psychiatry Psychiatric Epidemiology 40*(12): 964–971.

Hawton K (2011). Psychiatric assessment and the management of deliberate self-poisoning patients. *Medicine 40*(2): 71–73.

Hayes SC, Follette VM, Linehan MM (2004). *Mindfulness and Acceptance: expanding the cognitive-behavioural tradition.* New York: Guilford Press

Healy C, Bennachie C, Marshall R (2012). Harm-reduction and sex workers: a New Zealand response: taking harm out of the law. In: Riley D, Pates R (eds). *Harm Reduction in Substance Use and High-Risk Behaviour.* Chichester: Wiley-Blackwell (pp252–262).

Help the Aged (2004). *Hidden Voices: older people's experience of abuse.* London: Help the Aged.

Heslop P, Macaulay F (2009). *Hidden Pain? Self-injury and people with learning disabilities.* Bristol: Bristol Crisis Service for Women.

Hodgson S (2004). Cutting through the silence: a sociological construction of self-injury. *Sociological Inquiry 7*(2): 162–179.

Holley C, Horton R, Cartmail L, Bradley E (2012). Self-injury and harm-minimisation on acute wards. *Nursing Standard 26*(38): 51–56.

Horne O, Csipke E (2009). From feeling too little and too much, to feeling more and less? A nonparadoxical theory of the functions of self-Harm. *Qualitative Health Research 19*(5): 655–667.

Hunter D (2007). *The Art of Facilitation: the essentials for leading great meetings and creating group synergy.* Auckland/London: Random House.

Hurry J (2000). Deliberate self-harm in children and adolescents. *International Review of Psychiatry 12*(1): 31–36.

Illich I (1976). *Limits to Medicine: medical nemesis – the expropriation of health.* London: Marion Boyars.

Inciardi JA, Harrison LD (2000). Introduction: the concept of harm reduction. In: Inciardi JA, Harrison LD (eds). *Harm Reduction: National & International Perspectives.* Thousand Oaks: Sage (ppvii–xix).

Inckle K (2014). Strong and silent: men, masculinity and self-injury. *Men & Masculinity 17*(1): 3–21.

Inckle K (2012). *An Evaluation of SHINE – the Self-Harm Interagency Network.* Derry/Londonderry: Northern Ireland Public Health Authority.

Inckle K (2011a). The first cut is the deepest: exploring a harm-reduction approach to self-injury. *Social Work in Mental Health 9*(5): 364–378.

Inckle K (2011b). Scarred for life: women's creative self-journeys through stigmatised embodiment. *Somatechnics 1*(2):314–333.

Inckle K (2010a) At the cutting edge: creative and holistic responses to self-injury. *Creative Nursing 16*(4): 160–165.

Inckle K (2010b). *Flesh Wounds? New ways of understanding self-injury.* Ross-on-Wye: PCCS Books.

Inckle K (2007). *Writing on the Body? Thinking through gendered embodiment and marked flesh.* Newcastle-upon-Tyne: Cambridge Scholars Publishing.

Jeffery D, Warm A (2002). A study of service providers' understanding of self-harm. *Journal of Mental Health 11*(3): 295–303.

Jones J, Nolan P, Bowers L, Simpson A, Whittington R, Hackney D, Bhui K (2010). Psychiatric wards: places of safety? *Journal of Psychiatric Nursing 17*(2): 124–130.

Jones V, Davies R, Jenkins R (2004). Self-harm by people with learning disabilities: something to be expected or investigated? *Disability and Society 19*(5): 487–500.

Jutengren G, Kerr M, Stattin H (2011). Adolescents' deliberate self-harm, interpersonal stress and the moderating effects of self-regulation: a two-wave longitudinal analysis. *Journal of School Psychology 49*(2): 249–264.

Kaplan GA (1996). People and places: contrasting perspectives on the association between social class and health. *International Journal of Health Services 26*(3): 507–519.

Kapur N, Cooper J, Bennewith O, Gunnell D, Hawton K (2010). Postcards, green cards and telephone calls: therapeutic contact with individuals following self-harm. *British Journal of Psychiatry 197*(1): 5–7.

Karlson S, Nazroo JY (2002). The relation between racial discrimination, social class and health among ethnic minority groups. *American Journal of Public Health 92*(4): 424–631.

Kelly L, Regan L (2001). *Rape: the forgotten issue.* London: Child and Woman Abuse Studies Unit.

Kennedy M (1996). Sexual abuse and disabled children. In: Morris J (ed). *Encounters with Strangers: feminism and disability.* London: Women's Press (pp116–134).

Kessler RC, Mickelson KD, Williams DR (1999). The prevalence, distribution and mental health correlates of perceived discrimination in the United States. *Journal of Health and Social Behaviour 40*(3): 208–230.

King M, McKeown E (2003). *Mental health and social wellbeing of gay men, lesbians and bisexuals in England and Wales.* London: Mind.

Kirk E (2007). Edges and ledges: young people and informal support. In: Spandler H, Warner S (eds). *Beyond Fear and Control: working with young people who self-harm.* Ross-on-Wye: PCCS Books (pp37–50).

Kissane S, Guerin S (2010). *Meeting the Challenge of Challenging Behaviour.* Dublin: National Disability Authority.

Klesse C (2010). I did it my way: relationship issues for bisexual people. In: Moon L (ed). *Counselling Ideologies: queer challenges to heteronormativity.* Farnham/Burlington, VT: Ashgate (pp123–142).

Leese M, Thornicroft G, Shaw J, Thomas S, Mohan R, Harty MA, Dolan M (2006). Ethnic differences among patients in high-security psychiatric hospitals in England. *British Journal of Psychiatry 188*(4): 380–385.

Levine P (1997). *Waking the Tiger: healing trauma.* Berkley: North Atlantic Books.

Lewis SP, Heath NL, St Denis JM, Noble R (2011). The scope of nonsuicidal self-injury on YouTube. *Pediatrics 127*(3): e552–e557.

Liebling H, Chipchase H, Velangi R (1997). Why do women harm themselves? – surviving special hospitals. *Feminism & Psychology 7*(3): 427–437.

LifeSIGNS (2004). *The LifeSIGNS Self-Injury Awareness Booklet: information for people who self-injure/self-harm, their friends, family teachers and healthcare professionals.* Birmingham: LifeSIGNS Self-Injury Guidance and Network Support.

LifeSIGNS (2008). *Creating a School Self-Injury Policy V2.* Birmingham: LifeSIGNS.

Lindsay H (1999). *Good Practice Guidelines for Working with People who Self-Injure.* Bristol: Bristol Crisis Service for Women.

Long M, Jenkins M (2010). Counsellors' perspectives on self-harm and the role of the therapeutic relationship for working with clients who self-harm. *Counselling & Psychotherapy Research* 10(3): 192–200.

Lord EA (2008). The challenges of mentally ill women in prisons. *Criminal Justice & Behaviour* 35(8): 928–942.

Lucas C (2003). *The Rainbow Journal.* Ross-on-Wye: PCCS Books.

Lupton D (2003). *Medicine as Culture.* London: Sage.

Mallot JE (2006). Body politics and the body politic. *Interventions* 8(2): 165–177.

Martins V (2007). 'To that piece of each of us that refuses to be silent': Working with self-harm and black identity. In: Spandler H, Warner S (eds). *Beyond Fear and Control: working with young people who self-harm.* Ross-on-Wye: PCCS Books (pp121–134).

Mayock P, Bryan A, Carr N, Kitching K (2009). *Supporting LGBT Lives: a study of the mental health and well-being of lesbian, gay, bisexual, and transgendered people.* Dublin: Gay and Lesbian Equality Network.

McAllister M (2003). Multiple meanings of self-harm: a critical review. *International Journal of Mental Health Nursing* 12(3): 177–185.

McCafferty C (2012). 'It's Just a Wee Drink': the counsellor's experience of the impact of alcohol abuse on counselling self-harming clients. Unpublished conference paper. Everybody Hurts Sometimes… one-day conference on self-injury. Dublin: Trinity College Dublin, 2 March.

McCarthy M (1996). Sexual experiences and sexual abuse of women with learning disabilities. In: Hester M, Kelly L, Radford J (eds). *Women, Violence and Male Power.* Milton Keynes: Open University Press (pp119–129).

McDougall T, Armstrong M, Trainor G (2010). *Helping Children and Young People who Self-Harm: an introduction to suicide and self-harming behaviours for health professionals.* London: Routledge.

McNeill A (2004). Harm reduction. *British Medical Journal* 328(7444): 885–886.

McNeil J, Baily L, Ellis S, Morton J, Regan M (2012). *Trans Mental Health Study 2012.* Edinburgh: Scottish Transgender Alliance.

McNiff S (2004). *Art Heals: how creativity cures the soul.* Boston/London: Shambhala.

McQueen C (2007). Weaving different practices: working with children and young people who self-harm in prison. In: Spandler H, Warner S (eds). *Beyond Fear and Control: working with young people who self-harm.* Ross-on-Wye: PCCS Books (pp149–161).

McRuer R (2006). *Crip Theory: cultural signs of queerness and disability.* New York: New York University Press.

Menninger KA (1936). *Man Against Himself.* New York: Harcourt, Brace and Wood.

Mental Health Foundation (2006). *Truth Hurts: report of the National Inquiry into Self-harm Among Young People.* London: Mental Health Foundation.

Meyer IH (2003). Prejudice, social stress and mental health in lesbian, gay and bisexual populations: conceptual issues and research evidence. *Psychological Bulletin* 129(5): 674–697.

Miller D (1994). *Women Who Hurt Themselves.* New York: Basic Books.

Mills CW (1959 [2000]). *The Sociological Imagination.* Oxford: Oxford University Press.

More K, Whittle S (eds) (1999). *Reclaiming Genders: transsexual grammars at the fin de siecle.* London/New York: Cassell Press.

Morey C, Corcoran P, Arensman E, Perry IJ (2008). The prevalence of self-reported deliberate self-harm in Irish adolescents. *BMC Public Health* 8(79): 1–7.

Morris J (2004). *One Town for My Body, Another for My Mind.* York: Joseph Rowntree Foundation.

Morris J (1996). *Encounters with Strangers: feminism and disability.* London: The Women's Press.

Morton A (1998). *Diana: her true story – in her own words.* New York: Simon & Schuster.

Moyer M (2008). Working with self-injurious adolescents using the safe kit. *Journal of Creativity in Mental Health* 3(1): 60–68.

Moyer M, Marbach C (2008). Self-injurious behaviours on the net: a survey of resources for school counsellors. *ASCA Professional School Counselling* 11(2): 277–284.

Moyer M, Nelson K (2007). Investigating and understanding self-mutilation: the student voice. *Professional School Counselling* 11(1): 42–48.

Mudiwa L (2009). Challenging ethnic minority health inequalities in Ireland. *Irish Medical News* (April).

Murray CD, Fox J (2006). Do internet self-harm groups alleviate or exacerbate self-harming behaviour? *Australian e-Journal for the Advancement of Mental Health* 5(3): 1–9.

Murray CD, Warm A, Fox J (2005). An internet survey of adolescent self-injurers. *Australian e-Journal for the Advancement of Mental Health* 4(1): 1–9.

National Institute for Health and Clinical Excellence (NICE) (2004). *Self-harm: the short-term physical and psychological management and secondary prevention of self-harm in primary and secondary care.* London: NICE.

National Institute for Health and Clinical Excellence (NICE) (2011) *Self-harm: longer-term management.* London: NICE.

National Self-Harm Network (NSHN) (2000). *Cutting the Risk: self-harm, self-care and risk reduction.* London: NSHN.

National Suicide Research Foundation (2010). *National Registry of Deliberate Self-Harm 2009.* Cork: National Suicide Research Foundation.

National Suicide Research Foundation (2008). *National Registry of Deliberate Self-Harm, Ireland. Annual Report 2006–2007.* Cork: National Suicide Research Foundation.

Newham Asian Women's Project (NAWP) (1998). *Growing Up Young, Asian and Female in Britain: a report on self-harm and suicide.* London: Newham Asian Women's Project/Newham Innercity MultiFund.

Orbach S (1986). *Hunger Strike.* London: Faber.

Parker K (2000). Living with our scars. In: National Self-Harm Network. *Cutting the Risk: self-harm, self-care and risk reduction.* Nottingham: National Self-Harm Network (pp47–60).

Pattison EM, Kahan J (1983). The deliberate self-harm syndrome. *The American Journal of Psychiatry* 140: 867–872.

Pembroke LR (2007a). Harm-minimisation: limiting the damage of self-injury. In: Spandler H, Warner S (eds). *Beyond Fear and Control: working with young people who self-harm.* Ross-on-Wye: PCCS Books (pp163–172).

Pembroke LR (2007b). *Dedication to the Seven: hearing voices in dance (2nd edition).* London: Mind.

Pembroke LR (1996). *Self-harm: perspectives from personal experience (2nd edition).* London: Survivors Speak Out.

Pengelly N, Ford B, Blenkiron P, Reilly S (2008). Harm minimisation after repeated self-harm: development of a trust handbook. *Psychiatric Bulletin* 32(2): 60–63.

Phelan A (2013). *International Perspectives on Elder Abuse.* Abingdon/New York: Routledge.

Pitonyak D (2005). Ten things you can do to support a person with difficult behaviours. [Online.] www.dimagine.com/10things.pdf (accessed 15 September 2016).

Pollard N (2012). *The Pollard Review: report.* London: BBC Trust.

Pompili M, Mancinelli I, Girardi P, Ruberto A, Tatarelli R (2004). Suicide in anorexia nervosa: a meta-analysis. *Journal of Eating Disorders* 36(1): 99–103.

Riley D, O'Hare P (2000). Harm reduction: history, definition, practice. In: Inciardi JA, Harrison LD (eds). *Harm Reduction: national and international perspectives*. Thousand Oaks, CA: Sage (pp1–26).

Riley D, Pates R (2012). Introduction. In: Riley D, Pates R (eds). *Harm Reduction in Substance Use and High-Risk Behaviour*. Chichester: Wiley-Blackwell (pp1–3).

Riley D, Pates R, Monaghan G, O'Hare P (2012). A brief history of harm–reduction. In: Riley D, Pates R (eds). *Harm Reduction in Substance Use and High-Risk Behaviour*. Chichester: Wiley-Blackwell (pp5–16).

Ring E (2012a). Medics' sex abuse may top church scandals. *Irish Examiner*, 7 March.

Ring E (2012b). Self-harming put the world on hold for me, says teen. *Irish Examiner*, 3 March.

Rogers A, Pilgrim D (2003). *Mental Health and Inequality*. Basingstoke: Palgrave Macmillan.

Rosenfield S, Vertefuille J, McAlpine DD (2000). Gender stratification and mental health: an exploration of dimensions of the self. *Social Psychology Quarterly 63*(3): 208–223.

Rossow I, Ystgaard M, Hawton K, Madge N, Van Heering K, deWilds E, DeLeo D, Fekete S, Morey C (2007). Cross-national comparisons of the association between alcohol consumption and deliberate self-harm. *Suicide and Life-Threatening Behaviour 37*(6): 605–615.

Rubin A (ed) (1988). *Marks of Civilisation: artistic transformations of the human body*. Los Angeles, CA: University of California Press.

Ryan S (2009). *The Final Report of the Commission to Inquire into Institutional Child Sexual Abuse*. Dublin: The Stationery Office.

Sadler C (2002). Self-harm: look beyond the scars. *Nursing Standard 17*(12): 16–18.

Samaritans (2003). *Youth and Self-Harm: a report*. Surrey: Samaritans.

Sandahl C (2003). Queering the crip or cripping the queer? Intersections of queer and crip identities in solo autobiographical performance. *GLQ: Journal of Lesbian and Gay Studies 9*(1–2): 25–56.

Schrader AM (2000). Branding the other/tattooing the self: bodily inscription among convicts in Russia and the Soviet Union. In: Caplan J (ed). *Written on the Body: the tattoo in European and American History*. London: Reaktion Books (pp174–192).

Sedgwick P (1982). *Psycho Politics*. London: Pluto Press.

Seng JS, Lopez WD, Sperlich M, Hamama L, Reed Meldrum CD (2012). Marginalised identities, discrimination burden and mental health: empirical exploration of an interpersonal-level approach to modeling intersectionality. *Social Science & Medicine 75*: 2437–2445.

Shakespeare T, Gillespie-Sells K, Davis D (1996). *The Sexual Politics of Disability: untold desires*. London/New York: Cassell Press.

Shaw C, Hogg C (2004). Shouting at the spaceman – a conversation about self-harm. In: Duffy D, Ryan T. *New Approaches to Preventing Suicide: a manual for practitioners*. London/Philadelphia: Jessica Kingsley Publishers (pp167–177).

Shaw C, Shaw T (2009). harm-ed: Dublin presentation. Unpublished conference paper. There's No Shame in Self-Injury. Trinity College Dublin, 2 March.

Shaw C, Shaw T (2007). A dialogue of hope and survival. In: Spandler H, Warner S (eds). *Beyond Fear and Control: working with young people who self-harm*. Ross-on-Wye: PCCS Books (pp25–36).

Shefer G, Rose D, Nellums L, Thornicroft N, Henderson C, Evans-Lacko S (2013). 'Our community is the worst': the influence of cultural beliefs on stigma, relationships with family and help-seeking in three ethnic communities in London. *International Journal of Social Psychiatry 59*(6):535–544.

Siddiqui H, Patel M (2010). *Safe and Sane: a model of intervention on domestic violence and mental health, suicide and self-harm amongst black and minority ethnic women*. London: Southall Black Sisters Trust.

Simpson A (2006). Can mainstream health services provide meaningful care for people who self-harm? A critical reflection. *Journal of Psychiatric and Mental Health Nursing 13*(4): 429–436.

Smith B, Sparkes A (2005). Men, sport, spinal cord injury and narratives of hope. *Social Science & Medicine 61*(5): 1095–1105.

Smith G, Cox D, Saradjian J (1998). *Women and Self-Harm*. London: Women's Press.

South London and Maudsley NHS Foundation Trust (SLaM) (2010). *Self-Harm Service*. London: SLaM.

Spandler H (1996). *Who's Hurting Who? Young people, self-harm, and suicide*. Manchester: 42nd Street.

Spandler H, Warner S (2007). Introduction. In: Spandler H, Warner S (eds). *Beyond Fear and Control: working with young people who self-harm*. Ross-on-Wye: PCCS Books (ppix–xxii).

Stancliff S, Phillips BW, Maghsoudi N, Joseph H (2015). Harm reduction: front line public health. *Journal of Addictive Diseases 34*(2–3): 206–219.

Starr D (2000). *Blood: an epic history of medicine and commerce*. London: Warner Books.

Storey P, Hurry J, Jowitt S, Owens D, House A (2005). Supporting young people who repeatedly self-harm. *The Journal of the Royal Society for the Promotion of Health 125*(2): 71–75.

Strong M (2000). *A Bright Red Scream: self-mutilation and the language of pain*. London: Virago.

Sutherland JI (1997). Body of radiant knots. In: Friedman L, Moon S (eds). *Being Bodies: Buddhist women write on the paradox of embodiment*. Boston/London: Shambala (pp3–9).

Swannell S, Martin G, Scott J, Gibbons M, Gifford S (2008). Motivations for self-injury in adolescent inpatient population: development of a self-report measure. *Australasian Psychiatry 16*(2): 98–103.

Sylla M, Harawa N, Grinstead Reznick O (2010). The first condom machine in a US jail: the challenge of harm-reduction in a law and order environment. *American Journal of Public Health 100*(6): 982–985.

Synott A (1993). *The Body Social: self, society and symbolism*. London: Routledge.

Taylor TL, Hawton K, Fortune S, Kapur N (2009). Attitudes towards clinical services among people who self-harm: a systematic review. *The British Journal of Psychiatry 194*(2): 104–110.

Thomas W, Hollinrake S (2014). Policy-makers, researchers & service-users – resolving the tensions of working together. *Innovation: The European Journal of Social Science Research 27*(1): 31–45.

Thompson T, van de Klee D, Lamont-Robinson C, Duffin W (2011). Out of our heads! Four perspectives on the curation of an on-line exhibition of medically themed artwork by UK medical undergraduates. *Medical Education Online 15*: 5395.

Thompson T, Lamont-Robinson C, Younie, L (2010). 'Compulsory creativity': rationales, recipes, and results in the placement of mandatory creative endeavour in a medical undergraduate curriculum. *Medical Education Online 15*: 5394.

Timimi S (2008). Child psychiatry and its relationship with the pharmaceutical industry: theoretical and practical issues. *Advances in Psychiatric Treatment 14*: 3–9.

Tyler KA, Whitbeck LB, Hoyt DR, Johnson KD (2003). Self-mutilation and homeless youth: the role of family abuse, street experiences and mental disorders. *Journal of Research on Adolescence 13*(4): 457–474.

UNICEF Ireland (2011). *Changing the Future. Experiencing adolescence in Ireland: mental health*. Dublin: UNICEF Ireland.

Ussher J (1991). *Women's Madness: misogyny or mental illness?* Amherst, MA: University of Massachusetts Press.

van Son R (2000). Putting women in the picture. In: Byrne A, Lentin R (eds). *(Re)Searching Women: feminist research methods in the social sciences in Ireland*. Dublin: Institute of Public Administration (pp214–236).

Vickers AJ, Cronin AM, Maschino AC, Lewith G, MacPherson H, Foster NE, Sherman KJ, Witt CM, Linde K (2012). Acupuncture for chronic pain: individual patient data meta-analysis. *Archive of Internal Medicine 172*(19): 1444–1453.

Vohra-Gupta S, Russell A, Lo E (2007). Meditation: the adoption of Eastern thought to Western social practices. *Journal of Religion and Spirituality in Social Work 26*(2): 49–62.

Vuylsteke B, Das A, Dallabetta G, Laga M (2009). Preventing HIV among sex workers. In: Mayer KH, Pizer HF (eds). *HIV Prevention: a comprehensive approach*. Amsterdam: Elsevier (pp376–406).

Walker A, Parmer P (1993). *Warrior Marks: female genital mutilation and the sexual binding of women*. London: Jonathan Cape

Walker A (1992). *Possessing the Secret of Joy*. New York/London: Pocket Star Books.

Walby S, Myhill A (2001). New survey methodologies in researching violence against women. *British Journal of Criminology 41*(3): 502–522.

Warm A, Murray C, Fox J (2003). Why do people self-harm?' *Psychology, Health and Medicine 8*(1): 71–79.

Warm A, Murray C, Fox J (2002). Who helps? Supporting people who self-harm. *Journal of Mental Health 11*(2): 121–130.

Warner S, Spandler H (2012). New strategies for practice-based evidence: a focus on self-harm. *Qualitative Research in Psychology 9*(1): 13–26.

Watts A (2005). *Self-harm and Suicide Among Black and Minority Ethnic Women: a conference report*. Glasgow: Glasgow Violence Against Women Partnership.

Wendell S (1996). Towards a feminist theory of disability. In: Davis LJ (ed). *The Disability Studies Reader*. London/New York: Routledge (pp260–279).

White A (2006). Men and mental wellbeing – encouraging gender sensitivity. *Mental Health Review 11*(4): 3–6.

Wilhelm K, Finch A, Kotze B, Arnold K, McDonald G, Sternhell P, Hudson B (2007). The green card clinic: overview of a brief patient-centred intervention following deliberate self-harm. *Australasian Psychiatry 15*(1): 35–41.

Wilkerson A (2002). Disability, sex radicalism, and political agency. *NSWA Journal 14*(3): 33–57.

Williams DR, Neighbours HW, Jackson JS (2003). Race/ethnic discrimination and health: findings from community studies. *American Journal of Public Health 93*: 200–208.

Williams F, Hasking P (2010). Emotion regulation, coping and alcohol use as moderators in the relationship between non-suicidal self-injury and psychological distress. *Prevention Science: the Official Journal of the Society for Prevention Research 11*(1): 33–34.

Williams R (2009). Masculinities and vulnerability: the solitary discourses and practices of African-Caribbean and white working-class fathers. *Men and Masculinities 11*(4): 441–461.

Women's Health Council (WHC) (2007). *Violence Against Women and Health*. Dublin: WHC.

World Health Organization (WHO) (2008). *Closing the Gap in a Generation: health equity through action on the social determinants of health*. Geneva: WHO.

Zest (undated). *Self-Harm and Suicide Support*. Information leaflet. Derry/ Londonderry: Zest.

SUBJECT INDEX

251

NAME INDEX

J

Jackson JS 97, 107, 111, 112
Jenkins M 11, 22, 122, 123, 124, 127
Jeffery D 123, 129, 148
Jones J 146, 212
Jones V 82, 101, 103
Jenkins R 82, 101, 103
Jutengren G 68, 74, 75, 77, 80, 88

K

Kahan J 22
Karimova Z 13, 86
Kerr M 68, 74, 75, 77, 80, 88
Kaplan GA 107
Kapur N 181
Karlson S 111, 112, 113, 115
Kelly L 69
Kennedy M 82, 83, 104, 105
Kessler RC 97, 107
King M 88, 90
Kirk E 80
Kissane S 102
Klesse C 97, 98

L

Lamont-Robinson C 127
Leese M 111
Levine P 85
Liebling H 28, 82, 159
Lindsay H 192, 194, 205, 212
Linehan MM 135
Lo E 136
Long M 11, 22, 122, 123, 124, 127
Lord EA 11, 28, 40, 159, 160
Lucas C 203
Lupton D 57

M

Macaulay F 12, 13, 24, 28, 46, 55, 79, 87, 89, 90, 102, 102, 104, 122, 124, 133, 159
Magill A 158, 168, 169, 194, 212
Mallot JE 54, 58, 126
Marbach C 148
Marlatt GA 136

Marshall R 157
Martins V 90, 113, 114
Mayock P 88, 90, 97, 98, 99, 100
Mays N 213
McAllister M 69, 74, 76, 122
McAlpine DD 99, 104
McCafferty C 170
McCarthy M 102, 104
McDougall T 181
McKeown E 88, 90
McNeill A 156
McNeil J 25
McNiff S 130, 138, 150, 152, 153
McQueen C 79, 88
McRuer R 82
Menninger KA 8
Mewse A 141, 146
Meyer IH 97
Mickelson KD 97, 107
Miller D 16, 19, 20, 21, 71
Mills CW 42
More K 25
Morey C 12
Morris J 58, 103, 105,
Morton A 110
Moyer M 12, 25, 80, 124, 148, 171, 172
Mudiwa L 113
Murray CD 11, 16, 69, 71, 123, 146, 148, 162
Myers F 11
Myhill A 68

N

Nazroo JY 111, 112, 113, 115
Neighbours HW 97, 107, 111, 112
Nelson K 25, 80, 124
Nock, MK 17
Nolan B 103

O

O'Hare P 156, 157
Orbach S 52, 53

P

Parker K 45